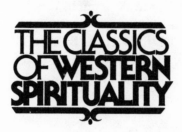

THE CLASSICS
OF WESTERN
SPIRITUALITY

THE CLASSICS OF WESTERN SPIRITUALITY
A Library of the Great Spiritual Masters

Quaker Spirituality
Selected Writings

EDITED AND INTRODUCED BY
DOUGLAS V. STEERE

PREFACE BY
ELIZABETH GRAY VINING

PAULIST PRESS
NEW YORK • RAMSEY • TORONTO

Cover Art:

Bust of George Fox, bronze, Alfred Turner. Courtesy of the Library of the Religious Society of Friends, London.

Acknowledgments
The Publisher gratefully acknowledges the use of material from the following books:
The Journal of George Fox, *edited by John L. Nicholls. Used by permission of The Library Committee of the Religious Society of Friends in Great Britain.*
The Journal and Major Essays of John Woolman, *edited by Phillips P. Moulton. Copyright © 1971 by Oxford University Press, Inc. Reprinted by permission.*
Finding the Trail of Life *by Rufus M. Jones. Copyright 1926 by Macmillan Publishing Co., Inc., renewed 1954 by Mary Hoxie Jones. Reprinted with permission of Macmillan Publishing Co., Inc.*
The Luminous Trail *by Rufus M. Jones. Copyright 1947 by Macmillan Publishing Co., Inc., renewed 1975 by Mary Hoxie Jones. Reprinted with permission of Macmillan Publishing Co., Inc.*
A Testament of Devotion *by Thomas R. Kelly. Copyright © 1941 by Harper & Row, Publishers, Inc., renewed © 1969 by Lois Lael Kelly Stabler. Reprinted by permission of Harper & Row Publishers, Inc.*
The Eternal Promise *by Thomas Kelly, edited by Richard M. Kelly. Copyright © 1966 by Richard M. Kelly. Reprinted by permission of Harper & Row, Publishers, Inc.*

Library of Congress
Catalog Card Number: 83-63537

ISBN: 0-8091-2510-2 (paper)
       0-8091-0335-4 (cloth)

Published by Paulist Press
545 Island Road, Ramsey, N.J. 07446

Printed and bound in the United States of America

CONTENTS

PREFACE   ix
FOREWORD   xi

INTRODUCTION   1

Abridgment of
THE JOURNAL OF GEORGE FOX   57

A Selection of Passages from
THE EPISTLES OF GEORGE FOX   127

Selections from
THE LETTERS OF ISAAC PENINGTON   137

Abridgment of
THE JOURNAL OF JOHN WOOLMAN   159

Selections from
QUAKER STRONGHOLDS *by* Caroline Stephen   239

Selections from
THE WRITINGS OF RUFUS M. JONES   259

Selections from
THE WRITINGS OF THOMAS R. KELLY   287

BIBLIOGRAPHY   317
INDEXES   321

Editor of this Volume

DOUGLAS V. STEERE was a Rhodes scholar at Oriel College, Oxford University. He received his Doctorate in Philosophy at Harvard University with a thesis entitled "Critical Realism in the Religious Philosophy of Baron Friedrich von Hügel." Dr. Steere has taught philosophy at Haverford College for thirty-six years and is the T. Wistar Brown Professor Emeritus of Philosophy.

Professor Steere joined the Religious Society of Friends as a convinced member in 1932 and has been intimately connected with the life of the Quakers both in the United States and abroad for almost half a century. For fifteen years he was on the Board of Managers of the American Friends Service Committee (AFSC) and has been on missions for AFSC in Europe, Africa, the Middle East, and Asia. Dr. Steere was the Clerk of the Worship and Ministry Meeting of Philadelphia Yearly Meeting from 1944–1947. One of the founders of Pendle Hill (a Quaker center for religious and social studies), he was the chairman of the board for sixteen years. He also served as the Quaker Observer for three sessions of Vatican Council II and at the Anglican Lambeth Conference in London in 1968.

Dr. Steere has also been the chairman of the Friends World Committee (1964–1970), president of the American Theological Society (1945–1946), and Harry Emerson Fosdick Guest Professor at Union Theological Seminary (1961–1962). In 1967 he drew together a colloquium of Zen masters and Christian spiritual leaders in Japan and a similar group of Hindus and Christians in India. His books include an early translation from the Danish of Sören Kierkegaard's *Purity of Heart; Prayer and Worship; On Beginning from Within; Doors into Life; Time to Spare; Friends Work in Africa* (with Dorothy Steere); *On Listening to Another* (British title: *Where Words Come From*); *Work and Contemplation; Dimensions of Prayer; Spiritual Counsels and Letters of Baron Friedrich von Hügel;* and *God's Irregular: Arthur Shearly Cripps.*

Author of the Preface

ELIZABETH GRAY VINING is a graduate of Germantown Friends School, Bryn Mawr College, and Drexel Institute School of Library Science. She is a member of the Philadelphia Yearly Meeting and of its Committee on Worship and Ministry. For many years she has been a trustee of Bryn Mawr College and a member of the Pendle Hill Board. Chairman of the Women's Committee of the Japan International Christian University Foundation, she was from 1946 to 1950 tutor to the Crown Prince of Japan. She is the author of twenty-five books, including: *The World in Tune; Friend of Life: The Biography of Rufus M. Jones; Windows for the Crown Prince; Quiet Pilgrimage;* and *Being Seventy: The Measure of a Year.*

PREFACE

QUAKERISM—as Douglas V. Steere so clearly explains in the Introduction to this volume—is a multifaceted faith and requires for its presentation the writings of more than one of its interpreters over the three hundred years of its existence. Depending on the direct leadings of the Spirit, as well as on the Bible and the writings of articulate Quakers, the faith of the Society of Friends is not static but moves with the development of scientific and psychological as well as religious thought and inspiration. It has accumulated a body of writings of contemporary, historical, and orthodox interest. To present Quakerism in a single volume it is necessary to include the insights of more than one generation of Friends.

In relation to their short history—three hundred years—and their small numbers, Friends have produced an extraordinary amount of religious and spiritual writings, many of which—including, for example, John Woolman's *Journal*, Thomas Kelly's *Testament of Devotion*, Rufus Jones's many devotional books, and Douglas Steere's own books on prayer—have moved out of the sectarian orbit into the realm of religious classics, valued by many who have no further interest in Quakerism itself.

No other modern Friend is so well qualified as Douglas Steere to make this selection or to write the Introduction that opens up Quaker thought and practice and explains its varying elements, its ways of worship and action. Out of a formidable mass of material he has gathered a selection that is illuminating, interesting, and inspiring. His own years of studying and interpreting Quakerism, of teaching philosophy in Haverford College as successor to Rufus Jones; his numerous books, which include *On Beginning from Within, On Being Present Where You Are*, and *Work and Contemplation;* his innovative

ix

PREFACE

energy in drawing together religious leaders in colloquia that included Catholics, Buddhists, Hindus, Protestants, and Quakers; his wide experience in conducting retreats, all make him uniquely well qualified to gather together in one volume a number of Quaker writers whose work reveals the breadth as well as the depth, the variety and the underlying unity of these three hundred years of Quaker expression and dedication.

No living Friends are included in this anthology, which begins with George Fox, the founder, and ends with Thomas Kelly. Fortunately Douglas Steere himself, by his interesting and lively, as well as scholarly, Introduction and his informative paragraphs about the writers included is assured of his rightful place among the interpreters of Quakerism past and present.

FOREWORD

IN MANY of the volumes of this series on Western spirituality, a single classic has been chosen and if it has not been written in English it has been freshly translated with interpretative notes. In this single volume on Quaker spirituality it seemed best to select half a dozen sources from the three centuries of Quaker witness in order to share the changes, the variety, and yet the deep underlying togetherness that is embedded in the spirituality of the Quakers.

The journals of George Fox and of John Woolman have been drawn at greater length than the other selections included here. This has been done because they are critically important windows both to the heart of Quaker spirituality and to the scene in the seventeenth and eighteenth centuries into which this spirituality came.

Isaac Penington's seventeenth-century letters, many of which were written from prison, are essentially letters of spiritual direction. In the late nineteenth century, Caroline Stephen, coming into the Society of Friends in middle life, brought a fresh and not uncritical eye to the spiritual climate that drew her to the Quakers. Rufus Jones grew up in a deeply rooted Quaker family in rural Maine and became the most impressive Quaker leader of the first half of our own century. Thomas Kelly burst into full spiritual strength between 1937 and his early death in 1941. Both of these men are our own contemporaries and speak freshly to our time.

The ever repeated miracle of the corporate meeting for worship on the basis of silence and obedience, which keeps reappearing in most of these selections, is a means of nuturing the interior life that should not be considered a monopoly of the Quakers. It belongs to the treasury of Christian spirituality where all may have access to its

FOREWORD

use. The witness in these selections to the Quaker faith in the personal and corporate guidance of the Holy Spirit is another accented treasure, and the accompanying fearless carrying out of "concerns" is a further aspect of Quaker spirituality, which these selections portray. Closely linked to them are the Quaker testimonies of simplicity, integrity, and opposition to violence as well as their long and continuing concern for the humane treatment of prisoners, the mentally disturbed, and those of other races. The vast simplification of the existing ecclesiastical structures that is mirrored in the plainness practiced in Quaker worship turns out to be a hidden query to their fellow Christians that is seldom absent from any of these selections.

We live in a rare moment of openness in our varied religious traditions and this very venture of collecting for our use this feast of Western spiritual classics is one of the rich gifts of our time.

I have been greatly helped, guided, and encouraged in this whole undertaking by Richard Payne and Caroline Whiting. Professor Edwin Bronner of Haverford College has given me immense help out of his vast treasury of knowledge of Quaker history and has rescued me at several critical points. In Britain I have been able to consult with Edward Milligan, Maurice Creasy, Hugh Doncaster, Roger Wilson, and Elfrida Vipont Foulds, and in the United States with Edwin Bronner, Hugh Barbour, and Canby Jones about the selections they thought should be included. Canby Jones has shared his favorite Epistles of George Fox with me. Mildred Hargreaves has typed the selections in her usual matchless way and Dorothy Steere has helped me at every point of the way and has edited and typed my own Introduction to the selections. My thanks to them all is a frail exchange for their caring kindness.

INTRODUCTION

I was touched when the Paulist Press suggested to me that in this fascinating series of specimens of Western spirituality they were drawn to invite the preparation of a volume on the spirituality of the Quakers. I doubt if they realized just how individualist Quakers are and how unlikely it would be that any one of us could satisfy our fellow religionists in what we might present under that intriguing title of "Quaker Spirituality".

When President Chaim Weizmann of the new state of Israel came to the United States very soon after his inauguration in order to thank Harry Truman for his almost instant recognition of the new state, it is reported that he found President Truman very depressed. He kept repeating to him that no matter what he did, some section of the American people were always criticizing him. President Weizmann finally is reported to have said to him, "President Truman, do you think that you are criticized? You ought to be in Israel. You, sir, here in the United States are the President of two hundred million American Citizens, but in Israel I am the President of a million presidents!" Quakers and Jews have much common ground in their individualism.

Bearing in mind this rugged individualism in the Quaker spirit, I would like from the outset to identify the point of vantage from which I have chosen the Quaker authors and the selections from their writings for inclusion in this volume. I am not a birthright Quaker but became a Friend "by convincement" some fifty years ago. I came, at that time, into the classical, unprogrammed, nonpastoral, silent-meeting-for-worship type of Quakerism that marked the first two centuries of its life. It is still this form that is practiced in Britain, Ireland, Australia, New Zealand, Southern Africa, Europe, and in a good deal of the Atlantic region of the United States as well as in a number of college and university communities in the United States and Canada. It is this form of Quaker spirituality that this collection of selections will seek to present and to interpret.

It is important to note, however, that since just after the

3

middle of the nineteenth century, the unique pattern of worship and ministry that will be described in these selections has been altered by a large group of American Quakers. The changes have included the appointment of paid pastors and the conducting of the season of worship in a way that, apart from a brief period of silence and the absence of the sacraments, would differ very little from that of any plain and simple Protestant service. The same Wesleyan evangelical wind that drew these American Friends to make these changes also encouraged a missionary outreach that established groups in Kenya, Burundi, Cuba, Mexico, Guatemala, Bolivia, Peru, Taiwan, China, India, Palestine, and Alaska. This revised form of ministry and worship has also been shared with these missionary congregations. The Quaker heritage of the experiential response to the interior Guide and the Quaker testimonies on war and social concern have continued, however, and the Friends World Committee for Consultation has done much to keep Friends of all species in touch with each other.

Altogether there are only about two hundred thousand Quakers in the world today, with three-fifths of them living in America. I used to tell my Roman Catholic friends at Vatican Council II that, numerically at least, the Quakers did not constitute any very serious threat to their company of well over half a billion souls! One old Quaker is said to have asked another, "Friend, does thee think there will be any other than Quakers in heaven?" To which his fellow-Quaker replied, "Well, if there aren't, it would hardly pay to keep the place open."

One more thing I should add: that in making these selections from this company of Quakers who have lived in and by the more ancient and classical form of Quaker practice, I have not drawn on the writings of any who are presently living.

THE very term "spirituality" is a little awesome to Quakers. Gerald Heard, who was a distinguished religious thinker in the middle years of this century, once wrote a little book entitled *Training for the Life of the Spirit.* An old Quaker who had read the book, when asked his opinion of its worth, replied that it seemed to him too much like "straining for the life of the spirit." When it comes to the technique of prayer, Augustine's word always returns in which he says, "We come to God by love and not by navigation," and Madame

INTRODUCTION

de Chantal when asked for a method of prayer replied that the best method is to have none! Quakers find it hard not to look with suspicion on talk about the interior life and about the practices that nurture it.

However understandable this shyness may be with its attempt to avoid the pharisaical display of their alleged virtue, which in our generation they know to be greatly exaggerated, the plain fact is that they do possess a spirituality of their own. They do possess testimonies that they seek to embody; they do have a deep faith in divine guidance and in the concerns that often spring from it; they do have practices that enhance discernment; they do have a unique form of corporate worship on the basis of silence and obedience; they do have a special form of vocal ministry and a unique way of conducting their meeting for business and of arriving at decisions—to mention only a few of the more important aspects of their spirituality that I hope may be shareable.

One of the first things that the Quakers would accent is that revelation is still going on. In the autumn of 1963 at an early meeting of the second session of Vatican Council II, Cardinal Suenens of Belgium rose to criticize what he insisted was a serious omission in the draft of the schema before the council that dealt with the nature of the Church. In the entire schema, Cardinal Suenens complained, he found no mention of the charisms (the gifts, the holy nudges) that often come in the course of the services of the Church, not only to bishops or to priests, but to lay members of the congregation. He declared that no schema on the Church could ever be complete that did not freely acknowledge these charisms as an integral part of the very Church itself. Cardinal Suenens urged the commission to correct this grievous omission.

Soon afterward, Cardinal Ruffini, of Palmero, Sicily, rose to speak. He deplored the suggestion that Cardinal Suenens had made and said that he fervently hoped that the commission would reject it. He went on to say that at one time he had himself been a professor of the New Testament and he knew full well that in the book of Acts there were instances of charisms, gifts of guidance, being given by the Holy Spirit and obeyed by their receivers, who were often of modest station. He quickly added, however, that this was in the Apostolic period! Now, he warned, the Canon of Scripture is closed and the Apostolic Age is over. Now the Holy Spirit speaks through the Magisterium of the Church! He concluded by saying that if the commission were to revise the schema to encourage the acknowledgment of charisms that might come to the laity, the Church would eventually be drowned in a tidal wave of subjectivity!

Happily, in my judgment at least, the commission accepted the suggestion of Cardinal Suenens. But Cardinal Ruffini with his usual clarity had raised a most searching question. Is the Apostolic Age really over? Does the Holy Spirit still speak to ordinary people? Is the guidance of the Holy Spirit still operative? Is all revelation concluded? It is at this point that an account of Quaker spirituality and its presuppositions might comfortably begin.

The Religious Society of Friends was first drawn together in the middle of the seventeenth century in Britain at the period when the sharp Civil War had resulted in a victory for the parliamentary forces under Cromwell. It was a time of immense spiritual and political ferment, and if modern democracy can be said to have had a moment when its true spiritual roots were most visible, this 1650 period in Britain might well be chosen. Perhaps this can best be illustrated by the fierce debates that took place within the ranks of Cromwell's army over the rights of the "commonest he" in the realm. These rights were grounded in the fact that every man was regarded as a possible vehicle of the Holy Spirit, of the voice of the living God speaking to the time, and a favorite text of the Bible was the one that refers to the soul of man as "the candlestick of the Lord." Both the spiritual and political implications of such a time may be seen most clearly in noting the way in which Oliver Cromwell, the supreme general of the Commonwealth army, gave instructions to his own aides that they must never deny access to any common soldier who wished to see him, for Cromwell feared that God might be speaking to him through that ordinary man and that if he did not listen to him the Lord might cast him off.

While the revolutionary political implications of this spiritual view of man and of man's freedom to worship God in any pattern he was inwardly drawn to follow were already implicitly there in 1650, it was four hard decades before they were seriously implemented in both the religious and political fields, and by this time the Quakers were estimated in Britain and the colonies to number at least 75,000.

It was in this climate and precisely at this seething mid-point of seventeenth-century Britain that George Fox drew this Quaker movement together. The saint or the prophet who so often is responsible for such a movement is never completely detached from his time, for he seems to have been sent to speak to it. But he cannot speak to it unless he is himself inwardly identified with it and has a message for it, a message that speaks out of a ground that in the sting of its rebuke as well as in the appeal of its vision is seen as coming from something universal that is beyond the contemporary situation and yet is intensely relevant to it.

George Fox was such a man. A leather worker and a shepherd with little formal education, this man of the people, after long and fruitless searching in the formal religion of his time, had a series of profound mystical experiences that refocused his life and gave him his sense of mission. His own discovery of the living Christ within and his repeated experience of the inward tendering of the Holy Spirit which are movingly recorded in his *Journal* brought him into a whole new relationship with his fellow creatures and with creation.

After these years of searching, during which one professional clergyman after another had failed him and even the dissenting groups whom he sought out could not meet his needs, George Fox had a great opening that came to him from within. An old Philadelphia friend of mine, Dr. William Sullivan, once asked, "Have you ever had a moment of awe and glory that has cloven your life asunder and put it together again forever different than it was before?" Fox's *Journal* describes this opening of his as precisely such an experience: "When all my hopes in them and in all men were gone so that I had nothing outwardly to help me, nor could tell me what to do, then, Oh then, I heard a voice which said 'There is one, even Christ Jesus, that can speak to thy condition' and when I heard it my heart did leap with joy. Then the Lord did let me see why there was none upon the earth that could speak to my condition ... that Jesus Christ might have the preeminence, who enlightens and gives grace and faith, and power. Thus when God doth work who shall prevent it? *And this I knew experimentally.*"[1] This last line is an important one for understanding the spirituality of the Quakers. Fox continued in this *Journal:* "Now I was brought up in spirit through the flaming sword into the paradise of God. All things were new and all the creation gave another smell under me than before, beyond what words can utter."[2]

---

1. George Fox, *Journal*, ed. J. Nickalls (Cambridge: Cambridge University Press, 1952), p. 11.
2. Ibid., p. 27.

INTRODUCTION

His conversion was continuous and his *Journal* in 1647 is sprinkled with flashes of fresh insight: "I saw that there was an ocean of darkness and death, but an infinite ocean of light and love which flowed over the ocean of darkness. And in that also I saw the infinite love of God and I had great openings!"[3] "I was taken up in the love of God so that I could not but admire the greatness of his love." He was shown that "all was done by Christ."[4]

Fox had in the first years of his ministry spent a time in prison and had kindled a small but devoted following, but it was in the North in 1652 that Quakerism surged forward to become a really significant movement.

It would not be accurate to say in an unqualified way that George Fox "founded" the Quaker movement. He was in its beginnings the gatherer of a large number of able "seekers," who were especially strong in the less-developed part of England. These seekers were not easy with the religious institutions of that period and many had already withdrawn from them completely and had come to meet together often in silent worship. They longed for a fresh, authentic, vastly simplified and dynamic Christian movement into which they could pour their lives. After paying due notice to the important role that these seekers played in furnishing so many leaders of the early Quaker movement, there can, however, be no denying the words of Geoffrey Nuttall when he says of Fox that "nothing can rob him of the glory of having founded Quakerism, and of having done it alone by the sheer force of his personality and of faith in his mission."[5]

In his journeys over Britain, Fox preached and described the transforming mercies of the interior Christ in the hearts of men and women and bid them to listen within for the "Christ who has come to teach his people himself" and having listened and found, to obey him. He encouraged them as a corporate group to sit together in the silence, to open themselves to the gathering power of the spirit of Christ, to experience the power of the inward quickening that had marked the primitive Christian community, and to experience it as a reality that was not alone historic but was an event that could take place here and now among ordinary men and women in mid-seventeenth-century Britain. It could give them power to carry out this

---

3. Ibid., p. 19.
4. Ibid., p. 14.
5. Ibid., p. xxv.

INTRODUCTION

revolution of fellowship and love with which first-century Christianity was charged.

There was no formal membership in the first years of the Quaker movement. The spirituality of those who cared to meet together was to participate inwardly as well as outwardly in the corporate meetings for worship and to live out in daily life what was laid on them in the silence, to follow the testimonies and to be willing to suffer the persecutions that almost instantly rose against them.

Francis Howgill, one of the earliest companions of Fox, has left us a classic statement of the way George Fox was received when, with this loose fellowship of radical Christians still in embryo, he moved through the North of England and by his kindling messages spoke to the hearts of those scattered bands of seekers in the Westmoreland and Lancaster regions:

> We were reckoned, in the north part of England, even as the outcasts of Israel, and as men destitute of the great knowledge which some seemed to enjoy; yet there was more sincerity and true love amongst us and desire after the living powerful presence of God than was among many in that day who ran into heaps and forms that left the cross behind them. God out of his everlasting love did appear unto us, according to the desire of our hearts, who longed after him; when we had turned aside from hireling-shepherds' tents, we found him whom our souls loved; and God, out of his great love and great mercy, sent one unto us, a man of God, one of ten thousand, to instruct us in the way of God more perfectly; which testimony reached unto all our consciences and entered into the inmost part of our hearts, which drove us to a narrow search, and to a diligent inquisition concerning our state, through the Light of Christ Jesus. The Lord of Heaven and earth we found to be near at hand, and, as we waited upon him in pure silence, our minds out of all things, his heavenly presence appeared in our assemblies, when there was no language, tongue nor speech from any creature.
>
> The Kingdom of Heaven did gather us and catch us all, as in a net, and his heavenly power at one time drew many hundreds to land. We came to know a place to stand in and what to wait in; and the Lord appeared daily to us, to our astonishment, amazement, and great admiration, insomuch

that we often said one unto another with great joy of heart: "What, is the Kingdom of God come to be with men? And will he take up his tabernacle among the sons of men, as he did of old?"[6]

It was in this season that Fox, in 1652, climbed Pendle Hill in Lancashire. There he had a vision of a great people waiting to be gathered. Now with many able seekers and with others, both young men and young women, prepared to put their lives at the disposal of this utterly plain and simple Christian fellowship, George Fox at last felt the throb of an unstoppable spiritual movement.

It was on this same visit to the North in June 1652 that George Fox first met Margaret Fell, the wife of a deeply respected judge, Thomas Fell, at Swarthmoor Hall, their ample home near Ulverston, in Lancashire. She attended several of George Fox's meetings in the neighboring village of Ulverston and in the course of his powerful ministry she was pierced by his question, "You will say, Christ saith this and the Apostles say this, but what canst *thou* say? Art *thou* a child of Light and hast thou walked in the Light, and what thou speakest, is it inwardly from God?" For twenty years she had been a seeker and in these meetings she was found. Her husband, Thomas Fell, never joined the Friends, but he warmly approved of them and shielded them where he could from the regional persecutions that swiftly began.

Judge Fell gave his ready permission to Margaret Fell in opening their home to this movement. Margaret Fell, whom Geoffrey Nuttall in his introduction to George Fox's *Journal* calls "the fervent and lion-hearted woman" (whom some years after Judge Fell's death Fox was to marry), swiftly became the spiritual mother of the early Friends' fellowship and Swarthmoor Hall became its informal capital.

Out of the depths of this new fellowship there emerged from the thousands of largely ordinary country people a number of inward callings, "concerns," to leave their farms and shops for longer or shorter journeys. Traveling in pairs, they felt called to share these

---

6. Francis Howgill, "Testimony Concerning Edward Burroughs," in *Works of Edward Burroughs* (London: William Warwick, 1662). Pages unnumbered but found on fourth page of the Testimony.

fresh discoveries of inward renewal that had come to them. Today we call this first group of emissaries "The Valiant Sixty." Their journeys took them all over Britain including Scotland, Wales, and Ireland and as far afield as Constantinople, Rome, Malta, and the Barbary Coast. Later others went to the continent, especially to the Netherlands and to the Palatinate and the northwestern parts of Germany as well as to Barbados and Jamaica in the Caribbean and even to the wildernesses of the American continent that were opening to colonists in that period.

Margaret Fell raised the ample Kendal Fund to give help where needed for this travel and for the support of families of Friends who had been imprisoned in the early persecutions that had begun to swell even in the Commonwealth period.

Certainly in the beginning there is much evidence that Fox meant for the movement to be no more than a radical goad and a stripping and simplifying as well as a quickening and interiorizing of the Christian spiritual life of Britain. He had discovered the Seed of God, the living Christ, the fire of the Holy Spirit within, and it had come to him not by the liturgy, or the faithful reading of the Bible (which he knew almost by heart), or by sermons, or by singing and reading aloud set prayers in handsome stone churches. He seemed to have meant at the outset to turn his fellow-countrymen to the Christ within their own hearts and not to be bent on founding some new sect.

Isaac Penington, who came into the Quaker movement at the close of the Commonwealth period, witnesses with great clarity that he had no sense of leaving the Christian life behind but that he came into Quakerism to have it intensified: to have an *experience of* rather than a mere *knowledge about* the transforming power of Christ within. Penington writes, "We, who are reproachfully by many called Quakers, are (for the most part) a people who have much and long sought after the Lord, and after an experimental knowledge of these truths which are testified of and related in the Holy Scriptures.... We sought not after a new Christ, or a new Spirit, or new doctrines concerning Christ or his Spirit: but to know Christ so as to receive life from him; and to live in him in the life and spirit received from him; this has been the single aim and desire of our souls."[7]

---

7. Isaac Penington, *Works of Isaac Penington*, vol. 4 Sherwood, N.Y.: David Heston, 1863), p. 419.

INTRODUCTION

For though the Lord had reached the pure Seed of life in men, and had quickened my soul thereby; yet I knew not how to turn to the Seed, and abide in the Seed, and to hold my knowledge and life there; but was still striving to live and know (and comprehend and practice) in a part above the Seed; and there the enemy was still too hard for me, and did often deprive me of the benefit of the right use of what the Lord had wrought in me and freely bestowed upon me.[8]

Truly Friends I have not lost anything that I ever had, or acknowledged of God in the days of my former profession, by believing in the Light which God hath now revealed in me, but have it still with me, and in greater clearness and plainness and fuller demonstration than I then had it; but that of the flesh which mixed with it, and hindered it from being rightly serviceable to the Lord and fully comfortable to me, that the Lord hath been removing by his searching light, and by the demonstration of his Spirit and power.[9]

In an age of the rediscovery of the infinite worth of the "commonest he," George Fox and his followers invited men and women of all conditions into the freedom of a new corporate fellowship. There, without the authority of an infallible Church or an infallible Bible or the ever-present authority of a paid clergy, those in this fellowship might gather together in meetings on the basis of silence and obedience in order to assist each other in coming into the presence of Christ within, and where they might come to "know each other in that which is eternal."

In the churches of Fox's day in Britain, it was at least legally permissible at the end of a service for an attender to give some short message or ask a question of the clergyman. The young Fox, clad in his leather breeches, as he moved from town to town, is reported in his *Journal* to have been frequently inwardly drawn to brave the hostility of what he called a "steeplehouse" and to take on the clergyman, with often devastating consequences both to the clergyman's authority and to Fox's bodily welfare. After these verbal encounters, almost inevita-

---

8. Ibid., p. 63
9. Ibid., p. 421.

12

bly the furious church wardens, assisted by many in the congregation, all but tore Fox limb from limb as they ousted him from the church and often beat him or put him in the stocks or drove him out of the town's boundary, threatening to kill him if he returned.

The book of Acts in the New Testament describes frequent occasions where early apostles, who were burning with their passionate desire to share their experience of Christ's immediate presence in the Holy Spirit, were seized, beaten, and imprisoned by both religious and civil authorities, who felt threatened by their growing strength. Fox and his Valiant Sixty, in all of the fervor of their sharing of their inner discovery, stirred up a similar reaction. Neither the Old Testament prophets nor the New Testament apostles seem to have been deterred in the least by this kind of reception, and Fox was no exception. For all of his "bad manners" and the official Church's hostility, which these visits may have provoked, the plausibility of Fox's message and that of his companions touched many parishioners at the very quick, and swelled the ranks of the early Quaker movement.

This persecution, which first brought hundreds and later thousands of Quakers into sizable terms in the stinking jails of that period and often included "praemuniring"—which involved government seizure of their land, their livestock, their houses, and even the very contents of their houses, compelled the Friends to set up some structures in order to support the sufferings of their own members. In this way what had begun as a movement of Christian quickening that was meant to be widely shared was, within a decade, forced into becoming a separate group of its own. The Meeting for Sufferings, which still meets each month in London and considers the urgent physical and social needs of sufferers all over the world, began at this time as a means of looking after the sufferers within the Society of Friends itself.

From the very outset, the Quaker movement was made up of laymen and had no place in its ranks for salaried, academically trained clergymen, which it designated "a hireling ministry." Men and women shared in full equality all of the rights and privileges of the group. The form of the Quaker worship was so simple that it could take place anywhere: in private homes, in a kitchen, in a barn, or later in an unadorned building, which may be the best way to describe a Quaker meetinghouse. The group sat together waiting on God to gather them inwardly, and all shared in the responsibility for helping the meeting to become a vessel of the Holy Spirit. Out of this gathered silence some vocal ministry often emerged, as now this one and now that one felt pressed to articulate what the corporate silence had brought in the way of a message or a concern.

Here was a religious democracy in which there was a realization in the group that the Spirit might use anyone as its vehicle to speak words of truth to his or her fellows. God's messages were not limited to those who might have been trained at "Oxford or Cambridge." Out of this expectation on the part of the group there grew what would genereally be conceded to be the most democratic vehicle of Christian worship that has ever been fashioned in the Christian era for channeling the spiritual life of a worshiping group. It has often been said that the Quakers, who were fiercely "lay" in their character, had in a sense "abolished the laity" in that with *all* members potential ministers, they were the most radical implementers of "the priesthood of all believers."

Emelia Fogelklou Norlind was a brilliant Swedish Quaker woman and scholar who died a decade ago. She confirmed what has just been described regarding the Quaker's form of corporate worship—in which all were free, if inwardly called, to share in the vocal ministry—as a genuine corporate spiritual mutation. She was sympathetic with the progress the earlier Puritan groups—the Presbyterians, the Independents, the Congregationalists, and the Baptists—in Britain had made in their attempts to defeudalize the Christian Church and to make the paid clergy more responsible to their congregations. But she still saw the professional clergy in these groups keeping their hand firmly on the ark, and in one subtle way after another resuming the authority they had nominally surrendered.

In the Quaker vehicle of permitting the "commonest he," if the Holy Spirit should use him or her as a vehicle to be God's implement of vocal communication, she saw at last a genuine trust, a spiritual acknowledgment, a culmination of all of the earlier efforts to dissolve the feudal pattern of clerical authority. She regarded the Quaker meeting for business as a further mutation in its faith in a corporate group of ordinary people being able to be trusted to reach a decision that is in "right ordering" by the use of their patient openness to the Light, with each person free to share his or her insight and with a group-appointed Clerk being a sensitive vehicle to record the "sense of the meeting."

INTRODUCTION

The meetings for worship became, in effect, laboratories of the Holy Spirit where Jesus Christ fulfilled his promise that "where two or three are gathered in my name, there am I in the midst of them." The corporate character of this exercise of waiting on God gave to it a dimension that private prayer, although encouraged and much in practice by early Friends, could nevertheless not supply. For it not only drew them into God's presence but it bound them to each other in that which is eternal. Thomas Story tells of the way this corporate waiting initially moved him.

> My concern was ... to know whether they were a people gathered under the sense of the presence of God in their meetings ... and the Lord answered my desire. I was affected and tendered with them. ... The Meeting being ended, the peace of God ... remained as a holy canopy over my mind.[10]

Robert Barclay wrote,

> When I came into the silent assemblies of God's people, I felt a secret power among them, which touched my heart; and as I gave way unto it, I found the evil weakening in me and the good raised up.[11]

And he speaks of this experience as being "the cement by which we are bound to the Lord and to each other."

The use of silence in these meetings and the experience of being "gathered" and refashioned in the midst of this exercise seemed to move the Friends into what the late seventeenth-century Anglican Thomas Traherne pleads for in his *Centuries of Meditation* where he writes,

> The fellowship of the mystery that hath been hid in God since the creation is not only the contemplation of His Love in the work of redemption, tho' that is wonderful, but the end for which we are redeemed; a communion with Him.[12]

---

10. Thomas Story, *Journal* Newcastle on Tyne: Thompson and Co., 1747), pp. 32–33.

11. Robert Barclay, *Apology*, Prop. XI, Sec. 7 (Aberdeen: John Forbes, 1678), p. 252.

12. Thomas Traherne, *Centuries of Meditation* (New York: Harpers, 1960), p. 4.

INTRODUCTION

Here Traherne is suggesting that redemption is for the sake of drawing men into communion, and that it is this dimension of communion with God that men are always stopping short of. Friends found this communion something that they came to know experimentally. It is in these timeless moments of communion "in the silent assemblies of God's people" that the mystical side of Quaker spirituality is most readily discovered.

It is well known that each of the great world religions, if searched to its core, reveals a mystical dimension. Often this dimension is accented by identifiable groups and movements that have sprung up within it: Hinduism with Vedanta, Buddhism with Zen, Islam with Sufism, Judaism with Kabbala or with Hasidism, are obvious examples. In Quakerism this mystical dimension in Christianity unfolds and assumes a corporate character. From the very beginning, it focused on the mystical witness to the active presence of the "Beyond that is within," and for Quakers this Beyond is Christ, the Seed, the Spirit, the Light, which is able to speak to the condition of one who turns to it. It finds great assistance in this turning by sharing in the corporate silence of a meeting for worship, but the sense of Presence may come anywhere at any time.

The mystical accent in Quakerism does not lessen its Christian rootage even though it does break down barriers and contains within it a strong ecumenical current. In the years immediately following the First World War, the Quakers worked in Poland distributing food and clothing. A woman worker who served a cluster of villages became ill with typhus and in twenty-four hours she was dead. In this village there was only a Roman Catholic cemetery, and by canonical law it was quite impossible to bury one not of that confession in its consecrated ground. They laid their cherished friend in a grave dug just outside the fence of the Roman Catholic cemetery and the next morning they discovered that in the night the villagers had moved the fence so that it embraced the grave. This moving outward of every type of fence so that it may embrace but not erase the unique and very special witness of the different religious groups comes close to the core of the meaning of this ecumenical current. Some years ago when I was attending Hampstead meeting for worship in London, a Quaker rose and quoted a line from John of the Cross: "The Father uttered one word and that word was his Son, and he utters it everlastingly in silence and in silence a soul has to hear it." That was all he said. I knew instantly that the walls were down and that that mystical truth which went beyond all denominational boundaries was being spoken, words that went to the heart of the Christian experience. I had a similar experience once in Tokyo when William Johnston took us to the Jesuit residence not far from Tokyo University and showed us the meditation room that was always open to students and visitors. Japan-like, it had nothing on the wall that the guests faced in their meditation but a single scroll. On it in Japanese characters was a line from Hosea 2:14 that reiterated the same promise, "I will entice you into the desert and there I will speak to you in the depths of your heart." Once more the walls were down.

The Quaker witness in this mystical company is that the living promise of transformation is still accessible, is still going on here and now, and that only as we attend to it and obey its leadings will we know what being "reached" and being "tendered" means.

Although Quakerism has never explicitly formulated the matter in any major statement with which I am familiar, many Friends feel themselves a part of something that is unwalled, that is a third force, that is neither Roman Catholic nor Protestant but a part of a Christian mystical stream that has nurtured and over and over again has renewed them all.

There have been Quaker scholars who have resisted this interpretation of the mystical character of the Quakers and have insisted that Quakerism is basically prophetic. It has always interested me that Professor Friedrich Heiler, whose famous book *Prayer* was so widely read and approved of a generation ago, made a sharp distinction there between the prophetic and the mystical, and like these Quaker scholars leaned strongly to the prophetic side. Late in his life he confessed that he could no longer support this distinction and that the mystical and the prophetic, when at their best, were parts of a common experience and a common witness. Certainly George Fox was prophetic and his witness and kindling power and his readiness to draw the social implications of his experience in the testimonies against war and for the rights of the "commonest he" make this blazingly clear. But the source of his leadings and the sustaining power of his life would seem to be squarely based in communion with the Presence within. His was an ethical mysticism, and when the Society of Friends has been truly alive, both of these prime factors have been present.

INTRODUCTION

The freshly minted phrases that appear in the early journals and writings of Friends do much to authenticate this inner experience of communion and what has taken place within it. Such words and phrases as "stand still in the Light"; "bottomed in the truth"; "centering down"; "spoke to my condition"; being "reached" or "tendered"; being "brought back to the root"; having "a stop in my mind"; avoiding "bustlings"; "outrunning the Guide"; "running before we are sent"; a committee of "clearness"; and a "weighty" Friend all have a quaint and simple freshness and aptness for expressing their spiritual experiences and for their practical dealing with practical problems.

This tendering power of the Spirit at work on the heart of a member in the meetings and in the close fellowship with one another that developed in the Quaker community was an inward baptism of the whole life of the participant, and again and again drew him or her to make the successive changes that were required. The consciousness that Christ was with them in their suffering gave them the strength to face the many persecutions of imprisonment and of confiscation of property that were the almost inevitable fate of becoming identified with this movement. During the first generation of its existence, George Fox himself suffered eight arrests and spent, in all, some six years in different English prisons. Over three hundred Friends died in these imprisonments. Knowing persecution firsthand, George Fox, the ex-shepherd, in seeking to help Friends to bear their trials, wrote in his one hundred ninety-fifth Epistle: "Fear not the losing of the fleece. It will grow again."

The pan-sacramental sense of the holiness of every life relationship is also intimately connected with this inward experience of communion. The Quakers' reluctance to acknowledge the necessity of the outward sacraments of water-baptism and of the Eucharist cannot be understood without keeping this inward experience of communion in mind. The inward baptism and the experience of participation in the ever-present life and spirit of the inward Christ to which these outward, symbolic practices of baptism and the Eucharist point are both at the very center of the Quaker experience.

In the early Friends, this same tendering experience of the Spirit and the witness to it, which the vocal ministry of the meetings for worship was continually supplying, was especially concerned to clear away the reliance on theological verbiage, most of which Fox called "notions." Fox was determined to distinguish these verbal notions from genuine experiences of the guiding Spirit. This attack on notions is clearly connected with the Quakers' reluctance to map out their Christian witness in any formal written creed that those who joined them would be compelled to accept. Friends of this period were living in a time in which Protestant quarreling over religious doctrine and creeds was one of the principal indoor and outdoor sports of the day. In their aversion to notionism Friends tended to turn from nouns to verbs. The important thing to ask of those who joined them was whether they had been reached and had felt the tendering of the indwelling Christ who could speak to their condition and whether, having felt this tendering, they had been willing to yield to it.

Albert Schweitzer had a principle of never replying to written attacks on his life or his undertakings, no matter how scurrilous they might be. The seventeenth-century Quakers never reached this high a rung on the ethical ladder and there were hundreds of fierce tracts exchanged with their adversaries during these early years that make dreary reading today. Apart from Isaac Penington, William Penn, Thomas Ellwood, and Robert Barclay, the ranks of seventeenth-century Quaker intellectuals who were equipped and concerned for this kind of exchange were remarkably thin. Quaker interest in theology itself has always been at a low ebb and has never emerged from Fox's accusation of its being a notionist concoction.

The precocious Robert Barclay, at the age of twenty-six, is generally agreed to have produced in his *Apology* the nearest the Quakers have ever come to a rigorous theological defense of their position. Many Friends find that the *Apology* reflects all too prominently the marks of Robert Barclay's early rigorous theological training at the seminary in France he attended in his youth. It is interesting to note that the admirable *Christian Faith and Practice* volume, which is the book of discipline of London Yearly Meeting, instead of being a theological exposition of a creed, has chosen to devote a sizable share of its contents to a carefully chosen anthology of Quaker accounts of their own spiritual experiences, convinced that this is the most effective means of sharing the Quaker way of life.

In the past century it was pointed out, with a large degree of agreement by Quaker scholars, how startlingly free the early Friends were in using almost interchangeable terms like the inward Christ, the Seed, the Root, the Principle, the Light of Christ, the Spirit. In the same vein, early Friends in making their experiential focus on the Christ within saw in this accent no lessening of their love for the Galilean Jesus. Nor did they see any contradiction in linking both of these modes of devotion to the eternal Christ, the Logos, on whose pattern all was created.

In his famous book *Enthusiasm*, the Roman Catholic scholar Ronald Knox, with all of his ingenious skill, puts some devastating questions that point to the inherent weakness of a whole cluster of Christian religious movements, including Quakerism, that focus on "experience." The very title of the book recalls the Anglican Bishop Butler's words spoken to John Wesley: "Enthusiasm, Sir, is a horrid thing, a very horrid thing." Speaking as an advocate of order versus freedom, Ronald Knox insists that unless this experience comes in the context of, or is instantly confronted with and meshed into traditional Christian structure, the experience will most probably effervesce into excess, into triviality, and finally into disillusionment.

The questions that he puts are searching and the early Society of Friends provides in some ways fertile ground for witnessing both to the confirmation of his darkest predictions and to the refutation of them in almost the same breath. For Quakerism had its James Nayler incident with its passionate moment of excess when James Nayler rode Christlike into Bristol on a beast and was arrested and terribly punished by the state for blasphemy. It also had its brush with Ranterism, which exalted subjectivity into a final norm and looked with an antinomian contempt on all criticism of its immorality. Fox, too, was approached by the Fifth Monarchy men and invited to join their millenarian cause. Quakerism was attacked as well by fierce and persistent persecutions and by all of the world's dispersive forces before which so much of the freshness of almost any religious movement tends to fade when the first glow of its experience has passed by. Knox's book leads to but neither raises nor answers a further question as to what else the Society of Friends had that enabled it to survive these threats that Ronald Knox so brilliantly depicts.

Although Quakerism's problems of survival and renewal were and are Himalayan, it is a fact that the Nayler incident was handled by Fox and the leaders of the group as an excess that could be understood but not approved of; the Ranters were rejected and were not permitted to make serious inroads on the sound core of the

Society; and the invitation of the Millenarian Fifth Monarchy men was declined by Fox, who told them that "Christ has already come and doth dwell in the hearts of his people." The pull of the Restoration period in seventeenth-century Britain, with all of its fierce persecution, was met by the spirit depicted in William Penn's *No Cross, No Crown*, and by the Quakers' massive refusal to yield up their right to worship as they felt called to do. It was met, too, by their refusal to soften their testimonies as well as by their stubborn refusal to leave either the world or their vocations. As far as the Quakers were concerned, something has already eluded Ronald Knox's analysis and has eluded his predictions. Only as we look more carefully at the different dimensions of Quaker practice can the secret of their survival, if there is one, be fully discovered.

It is important to note that the Quaker movement as a third force never sought to replace the infallible authority of the Church by the infallible authority of the Bible as classical Protestantism had done. Nevertheless the Bible played, and must always play, a considerable role in helping them to keep within the Christian stream and to cross their inward experience with its searching power and witness. Fox wrote in his Epistle 197 (1660), "And know the power and life of God in one another, which gave forth the Scriptures, which was, before the Scripture was." Also, "Wait all on the Lord that you may be settled and stayed in the Lord, and to grow up in the Light that gave forth the Scriptures; that there may be no stumbling about the words, which came from the Light. For no Creature can read the Scriptures to profit thereby, but who come to the light and Spirit that gave them forth" (Epistle 65, 1654).

Here Fox places the emphasis where Friends have always put it. The regular reading of the Bible, both in private and in family devotions, was standard practice for the early Friends, and many are seeking to restore this in our time. They knew well what the African meant when he witnessed, "Sir, it is not I who am reading the Bible. It is the Bible that is reading me!" And while there is no formal reading of the Bible in a corporate Quaker meeting for worship, messages in meeting were nearly always opened and centered around some moving passage from the Bible, which was quoted from memory. Fox knew the New Testament most intimately and the Logos passages in the Gospel of John, where Christ is declared to be hidden in the heart of every man and woman, confirmed and shaped the very task of the Quaker message, which was to *answer* to that of God in everyone.

The Bible may have been so very real to the early Friends because they were experiencing, day by day, a level of fellowship that the Bible describes so authentically. In the midst of the early persecutions, Friends looked after each other's families and literally carried each other. They often offered to take the place of other Friends in prison. The hospitality they showed to each other knew no bounds, nor did the tenderness with which they treated each other and watched over each other's inward growth. There was no attempt at communalization in the early Friends community, but there was this deep sense of caring for each other, which Charles Williams calls "co-inherence," that seemed to be present. This being mixed in one another's troubles and in ministering to them and to the needs of others in an ever-widening circle is a form of spiritual nurture that has been a part of Quaker spirituality from the earliest period.

A further factor in this nurture was a curious Quaker public equivalent for what our Roman Catholic friends would call examination of conscience and to which the Quakers gave the apt name "Queries." These Queries varied in different historic periods and were often revised. A social history of the Friends might well be written by studying the changes in the Queries over three centuries. Meetings were asked to read out the Queries and have their members examine their consciences in regard to such questions as the taking of oaths, which act is forbidden in the New Testament; the witness against paying tithes; participation in acts of physical violence as in war; for those in trade in the seventeenth century, the asking of a different price than they expect to get; the treatment of the American Indians; the keeping of slaves; the inhuman treatment of mental patients; the concern that Friends are to show in regard to the penal system and the treatment of other races.

From the beginning these Queries also turned inward and asked whether Friends held their meetings properly and whether they ordered their lives in simplicity and found time for spiritual reading and for private waiting on God that made them able to come with the inward openness required for the public waiting on God. They queried whether they held their lives free enough from the excessive cumber of acquisitive vocations in order to have time to give to others and for opening themselves to the Light; and whether they encouraged their children in this same openness and gave them opportunity for the kind of education that might enhance this quality of life.

These Queries were only a device for raising the questions that were being unconsciously put by the close fellowship of the early Quaker communities, which met for worship not only on First-day (Sundays) but also at midweek. Farmers were prepared to attend and to wait on the Lord in company with their fellows even when it meant leaving their hay in the field. Along with this there were the Monthly and Quarterly and Yearly Meetings in which worship and broader vocal ministry were shared and where the business affairs of the group were cared for and much contagious inward searching and discovery took place. Steady exposure to this kind of search inevitably served to stimulate and broaden the private experience of Friends.

From the very outset, this lay Society was held together, its sense of spiritual expectancy heightened, and its plateaus of experience challenged by the appearance of a stream of Quaker visitors who traveled under concern. These men and women were to make such visits only under concern and after they had received the approval of their own meetings in the form of minutes of liberation commending them to those they were to visit and testifying to their spiritual helpfulness in their home meetings. If the traveling Friend was able, he paid his own way. If his means were not sufficient for the journey or for the maintenance of his family while he was absent, the Meeting that gave the approval assumed the responsibility for this care.

Quaker marriage carried with it from the outset an openness for this kind of concern to arise and to be respected. One of the touching exchanges between a Quaker couple whose lives were anchored to this kind of commitment was that between Gulielma and William Penn in the summer of 1682 when Penn felt called to leave Britain for Pennsylvania to establish his "Holy Experiment" there. Gulielma, his beloved wife, was in delicate health and with child at the time and it seemed right for her to remain in Britain, but she felt that he should follow his leading. Her words to him carry this dual commitment to God's guidance and to each other with touching simplicity: "My dearest, don't hinder any good for me. I desire thee to go. I have cast my care upon the Lord. I shall see thee again." This kind of readiness introduced into a Quaker marriage a tone that affected its character and was not lost on the family life itself. It also witnessed to the enduring possibility of a noncelibate lay spirituality.

Quaker visitation under concern often involved crossing the ocean, but even domestic travel in the seventeenth and eighteenth centuries was marked with bodily risks. William Edmundson describes the journey of two English women Friends in seventeenth-century Ireland "all on foot in winter time, wading rivers and dirty, miry ways. Anne Gould being a tender woman was much spent and stayed at Clough."[13] John Woolman and Job Scott were not the only ones to die abroad in the course of this service. Holy obedience is frequently enough described in early Quaker journals to establish the fact that it is not only the prerogative of celibate religious orders. It may operate with power in the midst of a whole Christian family living under openness to the leading of the Holy Spirit. Friends on such religious visits were not in a hurry and stayed in a Quaker community long enough to be with each Quaker family and to have an "opportunity" with members of the family and to inquire of their spiritual condition and to counsel with them, from young to old, on the fresh things that God might be asking of them.

There was a continual stream of spiritual letters pouring out from those who were especially gifted in this area to those who wrote for counsel. The Epistles of Isaac Penington and of George Fox are notable in this regard but they were only two among many. Friends from the earliest period were encouraged to set down their spiritual experiences in journals and these were widely read among Quaker families and served as a source of spiritual stimulus. The sacrifices that are often detailed there in the carrying out of spiritual visitations, as in John Woolman's or in Job Scott's journals, could not but stir others to search their hearts to discover what God was expecting and requiring of them.

There was also the regular use of family worship with readings from Scripture or from some Quaker journal, followed by an unhurried period of silent waiting and sometimes vocal prayer. There was the private use of all kinds of spiritual literature that came from other traditions, and in this the Quakers manifested considerable ecumenical openness. Such books as Fenelon's *Letters* or the writings of

---

13. William Edmundson, *Journal* (Dublin: Samuel Fairbrother, 1715), p. 18.

INTRODUCTION

Madame Guyon, or Augustine Baker's *Holy Wisdom* of which Robert Barclay spoke in warm appreciation, or *The Imitation of Christ*, or the many translations of Jacob Boehme that circulated in Britain in the late seventeenth and early eighteenth centuries were not unknown to Friends of that period.

Obviously the family worship and the climate of the Quaker grammar schools was not without its influence on Quaker children. But the close community life of the Meeting to which children were brought and the long draughts of silence to which they were exposed might shock modern religious educators. Professor Whitehead has said that it is a testimony to the perennial persistence of religion that it has managed to survive a whole century of intensive religious education! As far as records go, there is little evidence of these Quaker children having been given other instruction than the spillover from their parents' obvious sense of concern. It is fascinating to see how many Quaker children early in their lives responded to the silence of the meeting for worship and the messages that came from it and how often the young people broke through into an active inward life. One of the painful thresholds that younger adult Friends faced was sharing vocally with the meeting some insight that had been given them in the silence by rising and saying a few words about it in public meeting. The pain in this breakthrough, the holding back, and finally the yielding and the release that seemed to come with it are frequently described in Quaker journals. There are records of older Friends' readiness to encourage signs of inward development that seemed to be coming to their young people and this encouragement was certainly a formative factor in Quaker nurture. Personal example was the greatest force of all. The readiness of the elders to risk their property and their personal freedom, or to be willing to undertake what some concern required of them in order to be faithful to their inward leadings, was without doubt the main force of contagion that spread to the children the expectancy of guidance by the Holy Spirit and the importance of yielding to it that are so central in Quaker spirituality.

Quakers have had to learn again and again that young people respond to situations where they are really needed and are actively involved in carrying out concerns. Quaker children in the first generation stepped in and carried on the meetings for worship for which their parents had been seized and imprisoned. In the generation just passing, the male leadership in the American Quaker scene has to no small part come from men who spent the long testing years of the Second World War in Quaker camps for conscientious objectors or from men and women who in the years that followed the war had taken part in situations of deep human need in relief work or in the many Quaker-sponsored work camps in different parts of the world.

The central importance of the corporate meeting for worship, on the basis of silence and obedience, to the spirituality of the Quakers has been referred to frequently, but little has been said of the actual nature of its practice. Alexander Parker, who was a close companion of George Fox, wrote a classic advice that is at the same time a most apt description of entering into this form of worship:

> The first that enters into the place of your meeting, be not careless, nor wander up and down either in body or mind, but innocently sit down in some place and turn in thy mind to the Light, and wait upon God simply, as if none were present but the Lord, and here thou art strong. When the next that come in, let them in simplicity of heart sit down and turn to the same Light, and wait in the Spirit, and so all the rest coming in the fear of the Lord sit down in pure stillness and silence of all flesh, and wait in the Light. A few that are thus gathered by the arm of the Lord into the unity of the Spirit, this is a sweet and precious meeting in which all are met with the Lord. . . . Those who are brought to a pure, still waiting on God in the Spirit are come nearer to God than words are . . . though not a word be spoken to the hearing of the ear. In such a meeting where the presence and power of God is felt, there will be an unwillingness to part asunder, being ready to say in yourselves, it is good to be here, and this is the end of all words and writings, to bring people to the eternal living word.[14]

Two persons are asked to sit at the head of meeting in order to be responsible for closing the meeting. In the earlier architecture of the meetinghouse there were two or three rows of facing benches across

---

14. Alexander Parker, *Letters of Early Friends*, ed. A. R. Barclay (London: Darton and Harvey, 1841), pp. 365–66.

INTRODUCTION

the front of the meeting and in the ancient meetinghouse that I attend those closing the meeting sit in these. In most of the more modern Quaker meetings, the facing benches have been dropped and the members often sit in a hollow square. The meetings of worship are traditionally about an hour in length, although this may vary slightly. They are closed when these designated persons, feeling that the exercise is over, shake hands and members of the meeting often shake hands with those sitting near them.

The manner of entering the silence varies widely and each person must find his own way into it. Usually it takes some time for a meeting to be inwardly gathered, and the special times of feeling the full power of a "covered" meeting may be as rare as they are wonderful. Persons come to meeting with a wide web of life's demands and conflicts. It would be a miracle if these could all be shed at the door. Some remember Christ's promise that "where two or three are gathered together in my name, there am I in the midst of them." Almost a century ago a painter, J. Doyle Penrose, made a sketch of Christ standing at the head of the meeting wrapped in the love he shared with God and with those present. Copies of it were often seen in Quaker homes and schools. Some who have learned meditation techniques for stilling the body and the mind make use of them to center themselves in readiness to sense the Presence. Some give themselves to a wave of gratitude and thankfulness that they are loved and cherished by God, knowing, as William Penn once said, that "we can fall no deeper than God's arms can reach, however deep we fall."

Some pour out their gratitude in the mood of the French poet Paul Claudel, who said that all prayer is simply "thankfulness that God is." They may even spend a few moments thinking what their lives and their future would be like if God did not exist. Some lift up their hearts in thankfulness for members of the gathered company whom they know, and hold each of them up into the Presence as they may do with absent members who are in need. Some simply let go in the silence and abandon themselves and their needs in much the same way that we might do if we were walking with a dear friend and found it unnecessary to talk but simply sensed the joy of the other's presence. Others are troubled by all kinds of distractions that intrude into this silence. Some of these distractions are physical ones: noises of all kinds in this restless world we live in, a body that they find they cannot still, or the entrance into the meeting of some latecomer. These can often be dealt with by lifting the noises into an inward

INTRODUCTION

prayer: "O God, may I enter into your Presence with all of the swift movement that is in that airplane that I hear flying overhead" or "O God, I thank you that our friend who has come late has come at all, and may he or she be especially blessed."

Others may suffer from far more difficult distractions: the internal ones that come from our own mental grappling with unsettled issues, with difficult decisions, with all kinds of irrelevant thoughts that tumble in. They learn in time how to deal with these by acknowledging them as parts of their own uncollected lives that of course float up to the surface of consciousness in such a moment of freedom and that demand their attention. The Jews have a suggestive hint about dealing with mental distractions by describing them as part of ourselves that sense a blessing is about to come and appear because they want to be sure to be hallowed by it! In either of these types of distractions, Friends learn not to try to suppress them but to acknowledge their presence and abandon themselves to being open to the inward Christ, the Guide, the Renewer, even if the distractions continue to be there throughout.

Donald Court, a much loved English Quaker doctor and professor of public medicine, speaks of the press of his demanding life and confesses that he could not face it without both daily times of stillness and the weekly corporate meeting for worship.

> These are times to reach down to a level where I can see myself and my work straight, where that strength we call love can break through my anxiety and teach me how to respond instead of to react ... how to open the road to a spirit blocked by busyness, self-importance, self-indulgence, self-pity, depression and despair.... I could not have coped perhaps even survived the last thirty-five years without the meeting for worship.[15]

It is interesting that both the Eastern Orthodox and the Quakers look on the experience of the whole worshiping community gathered in corporate prayer as the truest organ for the operation of the Holy Spirit. Isaac Penington writes of the early Quaker groups, "They are like a heap of fresh and living coals, warming one another as a great

---

15. Donald Court, *The Friend*, vol. 128 (London), pp. 1109–10.

strength, freshness, and vigor of life flows into all."[16] In the corporate worship, the inward Christ seems to gather the worshiping community and again and again to draw each person from his separate solitariness into a solidarity with all who breathe.

The individualism and pride and possessiveness that often creep into private prayer is dissolved away as we meet together in worship. The inward Christ makes the individual worshiper feel all afresh that he is just one ordinary sheep in God's vast fold, and often sweeps his heart with an overwhelming sense of creatureliness. But it does not stop there. When it continues to move in the human heart it leads on to a liberation from the sin of self-absorption into personal commitment to new levels of life. It leads to the ever-repeated personal discovery that Christ's gift is most often linked to a task that may be laid on the worshiper, a task that calls for prompt fulfillment.

When earlier reference was made to a meeting for worship on the basis of silence and obedience, the word *obedience* was not added as an ornament. Fox thought that the Spirit that moved so fiercely in his heart did not stop at giving him a bracing feeling that he was not alone. It went further and laid on him things that were to be done. Once again Isaac Penington's almost matchless word spells it out ever so clearly: "There is that near you which will guide you; Oh wait for it, and be sure ye keep to it."[17] In this phrase attention and obedience are linked. There is not only the melting down, the oneing, the centering, the personal healing, but there is nearly always the Guide's laying on us changes in priorities and things that are to be done and done promptly.

Fox meant more by *experience* than emotion. He knew that in real experience the will must be involved and he did not underestimate the stages, the plateaus, the continuous conversion that were called for to bring the will into line. A great French writer[18] minces no words when he describes the role of Christian devotional literature "as never Platonic and it addresses itself to the imagination and the intellect solely to influence the will." A Basel woman mystic and physician who lived in our time and wrote under the name of

---

16. Penington, *Works*, vol. 4, p. 55.
17. Penington, *Works*, vol. 3, p. 520.
18. Abbé Bremond.

INTRODUCTION

Adrienne von Speyr says, "It is hardly ever possible to see from the start all that God is to mean to one. . . . Once open to the light, he may ask God to claim him more essentially and more profoundly. But on one condition, that he does not refuse the first small act God demands of him."[19] The "first small act" may be a visit, or a letter, or a gift, or it may be a first alert to clear the deck of one's engagements for orders that are still sealed. The mysterious thing of it all is that in God's eyes there are no "little" things. Everything matters and everything leads to something else.

We had a very old woman in our Radnor Meeting who chose to leave immediately after the rise of the meeting and to do so without any conversation with her fellow Quakers. She felt that it was her calling to do something at once about the first small acts that had come to her during the meeting. Francis de Sales would have readily understood her curious custom as an act of devotion, for he defines the word *devotion* as "the promptitude, fervor, affection and agility that we show in the service of God."[20]

I once knew a Virginia Quaker woman, Anna May Stokeley, who told me about her Quaker mother, who had been widowed when she and her brothers and sisters were all quite young. She had single-handedly brought up the family and supported them through school and college from the peanut farm whose staffing and problems were all on her shoulders. She said that her mother had what seemed to the children a strange practice of going into the little-used "parlor" in their farmhouse for half an hour of silence at eleven o'clock each morning, and the children, when they were at home, were told that she was not to be disturbed unless there was some major need. As children, they wondered what she did there. They thought that perhaps she was communing with their dead father. Later they realized that what they all did on First-day at meeting she practiced every day of her life in opening herself and her needs to the Guide and seeking to follow the clues that were often given to her there. In the Quaker experience, silence and obedience belong together.

Vocal ministry in a meeting for worship on the basis of silence is not prearranged or programmed. All attenders are assumed to be willing

---

19. Adrienne von Speyr, *The Word*, trans. Alexander Dru (London: Collins, 1953), p. 9.
20. Francis de Sales, *Introduction to the Devout Life*, trans. Joan Ryan (New York: Harpers, 1960), p. xiv or chap. 1, pp. 4–5.

vehicles for a message. If any feel inwardly drawn to speak they are encouraged to rise and share with the meeting, using as "few words as possible and as many as are necessary." Isaac Penington balances his love of meetings for worship that are without words with those where words emerge. "Yea, the ministry of the Spirit and life is more close and immediate when without words."[21] But the prophetic note in him is given only a page away when he gentles this to a more acceptable Quaker position. "For absolutely silent meetings, wherein there is a resolution not to speak, we know not; but we wait on the Lord either to feel him in words, or in silence of spirit without words, as he pleaseth and that which we aim at, and are instructed to by the Spirit of the Lord as to silent meetings, is that the flesh in everyone be kept silent, and that there be no building up, but in the Spirit and power of the Lord."[22]

Taking seriously the New Testament injunction that all believers are priests, that is, that they are to be communicators to each other in a redemptive community, the Quaker principle is, "Let none of us assume that vocal ministry is never to be our part." But Friends feel that it is equally unfortunate if some come quite certain in advance that they *will* minister. Rather we are to come to meeting in openness.

What Quakers take for granted in such an exercise of vocal ministry in a silent meeting is that the constant love of God, focused through the burning glass of the inward Christ, is forever speaking to us; that it longs to reach us, to tender us and to guide us. It also assumes that this continuous communication is intensified in such a gathering, and the Spirit uses the vocal ministry of someone in the meeting to articulate this piercing love and to confirm and consolidate what attenders at the meeting have already been inwardly experiencing.

It is not uncommon after a Quaker has spoken in a meeting to have several persons at the close of the meeting tell him that they were so thankful that he had relieved them of the necessity of ministering, for almost the same message had come to them and while they would have spoken with other words and illustrations than the speaker had used, they knew that the message had been given and that their words were no longer needed.

---

21. Penington, *Works*, vol, 4, p. 56
22. *Ibid.*, p. 55.

INTRODUCTION

Among contemporary as well as earlier Friends, there has always been appreciation of even the briefest message, which may be only a word spoken out of someone's brokenness or out of another's joy. William Dewsbury sent a word of encouragement from his prison cell in 1660, "And thou, faithful babe, though thou utter forth a few words in the dread of the Lord, they are accepted."

It is necessary to note that the freedom of the unprogramed Quaker meeting may tempt some persons to minister too frequently. Distraught persons occasionally may use it for self-expression, or some who attend the meeting seldom may find it hard to resist what for them seems an invitation to press some personal cause, quite ignoring the inner unfolding of the meeting. It is remarkable how creatively a grounded meeting can absorb this surface speaking and gather it into the worshiping silence. Often the silence and the subsequent ministry can transform it into something unbelievably helpful. Friends seem to know when, for the sake of the meeting, some eldering may be necessary, and in those cases a quiet and loving conferring with those whose ministry is unhelpful is undertaken by a seasoned Friend.

An important matter that the Quaker journals often refer to is that to receive a message is not the same as to receive a call to give it. Two remarks of John Churchman point out the fact that these are separate and distinctive stages: "To see a thing is not a commission to do it; the time when, and judgment to know the acceptable time are the gifts of God." "I began to see that there was a difference between seeing what was to be done, and being bid to do it."[23] Until the call to give the message comes, it is well to withhold it. Seldom is an important message lost.

It has always been clear that the deepest ministry in a meeting tends to come from members who are being searched by close exposure to the Bible and whose lives of prayer and of deep human involvement during the week have prepared them to grasp the inward thrust of the meeting for worship. The early Friends were critical of the clergy who had been prepared at Oxford and Cambridge, but their protest was leveled not so much at the universities as at these clerics' habits of preaching less from their own experience of the Holy Spirit in the life of their time than from piecing together the

---

23. John Churchman, *An Account of Gospel Labors and Christian Experiences* (Philadelphia: Friends Book Store, 1882), pp. 97, 52.

experiences of others. Robert Barclay in his *Apology* longed for the time when "no man . . . bringeth forth his own conned and gathered stuff, but everyone puts that forth which the Lord puts within their hearts."[24]

In the so-called Quietist period of the Society of Friends in the eighteenth century, the concept of emptiness, of making of oneself a hollow tube for the Spirit to speak through, exercised a considerable influence on the vocal ministry in the meetings. The fear that a well-furnished mind or a well-trained intellect might distort the account that the one ministering would give of the message of the inward Guide was certainly present. Fortunately at the very height of this period there were able men and women who were hard readers all their lives and who without a university education were able, as John Woolman was, to bring together the humble openness to the Presence of the inward Christ and the practical wisdom of a piercing mind, doing it in keeping with the counsel of the Guide.

There is a nineteenth-century story that is told of a deeply troubled New York State Friend who rose in meeting deploring the digging of the Erie Canal, feeling that man was intruding on God's domain. He concluded with the assertion that "if God had wanted the Erie Canal, He would have dug it Himself." A few minutes later an old Quaker woman rose in the meeting and quoted Scripture: "And Jacob digged a well," and then sat down. A "hollow-tube" Quaker in this same period rebuked an able Friend with the words: "God hath no need of thy learning," which brought in response the suggestion that perhaps God had still less use for the critical Friend's ignorance!

Out of a growing sense of their need for the nurture of fertile as well as spiritually centered minds in the Quaker community, Friends in both Britain and America began in the eighteenth century to establish secondary schools that continue to this day. In the nineteenth century a further step was taken when in the United States colleges like Haverford, Swarthmore, Bryn Mawr, Earlham, William Penn, Whittier, Guilford, Wilmington, Pacific College (now George Fox College), and Friends University at Wichita were established and were supported. But the fearless mind that could face the swiftly changing world and speak truth to it had its detractors.

The redeeming power of the ultimate integrity of an old Friend

---

24. Barclay, *Apology*, Prop. XI, Sect. 6, p. 329.

INTRODUCTION

who, like many others in his time, feared as the plague the effects on the faith of the Quaker youth of Darwin's theory of evolution, of the Harvard geologist Agassiz's view of the earth's creation, and of the higher criticism of the Bible is well expressed in a familiar Quaker story. This old Friend rose in meeting one day and told of two young men, one who was a firm believer and the other one whose faith had been shaken by the new learning. One day these two young men went out in a boat together. A terrible storm came up and the boat tipped over and the young man who had no faith drowned! At this point the old Friend sat down promptly, his message delivered. A few minutes later his body began to tremble and finally he rose to his feet again and said, "Friends, in the interest of truth, I must confess that the other young man drowned too!"

Almost like the power of a gyroscope to right a wallowing ship in a storm, there have been Quakers in each generation who, while holding infinitely precious the mystical accent of the meeting for worship, have refused to be threatened or panicked by the intellectual currents of their generation. At the same time they were prepared to search out and challenge the human consequences of these currents and to lay bare the responsibility that they and their generation carried to guide and to direct them. Isaac Penington, to whom the inward Christ's guidance was utterly central, once wrote: "For reason is not sin, but a turning from that from which reason came is sin." Here was a profound grasp of the relation of intuition and reason which in no generation of Quakerism has ever been entirely absent.

The concern for higher education, which led to the establishing of these Quaker institutions of higher learning a century and a half ago, certainly had its limitations. It was a "guarded" education and in its early days it had no touch whatever with music or art or the drama. But as something of a compensation for this early impoverishment, which has now been largely corrected, there sprang up a passionate interest in nature, in botany, in biology, in astronomy, and in the physical sciences. It is perhaps not accidental that in terms of their numbers, the Quakers in nineteenth-century Britain are said to have had more members in the Royal Society than did any other religious group.

The leadership at the turn of the twentieth century of men like John Wilhelm Rowntree and Rufus Jones and Rendel Harris found no crushing threat in the higher criticism of the Bible and believed that the interior treasure, both spiritually and socially, that Quakerism contained needed to be freshly interpreted in modern terms. They believed, too, that if one is very firmly attached at the center one can dare to be free at the periphery, and that there was no basic contradiction between openness to gifts of the inward Presence and a vocal ministry in which all of a woman's or a man's life experience might be at the disposal of the message that rose from the inward Presence.

William C. Braithwaite, who prepared the two volumes describing the first fifty years of the Quaker movement in Britain, wisely writes:

> Mystical movements, with their emphasis on inward experience, have seldom had much institutional stabilty. It would not have been surprising if Quakerism, with leadership and organization weakened by persecution had languished and declined, but the quiet meetings, resolutely maintained up and down the land, remained centers of power, and offered an invincible resistance to the persecutors. They did not hatch sedition, as the authorities feared, but there were undeniably places where local groups were continually renewing their strength and finding themselves, in the stress of suffering, touched by the life of God. The Quaker stiffness on points of conscience, which in some ways magnified trifles and fostered extravagances, here magnificently justified itself. By holding meetings through storms of persecution with unflinching tenacity, publicly and with open doors, Friends not only secured the continuance of their own Society, but greatly contributed to the preservation of Nonconformity as a whole.[25]

He continues,

> Resistance to the forces without could only be sustained by a group witness to truth enriching together the witness of the individual units. It was equally necessary that the centrifugal tendencies which were bound to show themselves where

---

25. William C. Braithwaite, *Second Period of Quakerism*, Rowntree Series, (London: Macmillan, 1921), p. 225.

35

each unit had an individual illumination should have the strong restraint of a group witness and group illumination. Unless Friends were to be shattered into fragments, this group witness was bound to be maintained so as to control the aberrations of guidance in the individual.[26]

The Perrot and the Wilkinson-Story attempts to splinter the Quaker movement that came in the Restoration period at the very height of the persecutions and sufferings are further evidence of that necessity. "The Perrot position, as events showed, led to the denial of all human arrangements, even for meeting at stated times and places, and had it been adopted, would have meant the rapid disintegration of the movement."[27] In the Wilkinson-Story separation, apart from the personality strains involved, there were additional objections to any institutional structure and especially to any group discipline that would resist the pressures of the persecutions, by insisting on full faithfulness to the basic Quaker testimonies.

By 1667 the ever-fiercer persecution under the Restoration made it clear to Fox that God's authority for all of the duties and decisions that their perilous situation required should not be entrusted to himself or to any elite group of Quaker leaders but should be placed squarely on the vast network of local meetings. These local meetings, which gathered either once or twice a week for their worship, were invited by Fox to add to their structure a monthly meeting for business where marriages, care for those in prison and their families, and care for the aged and infirm, as well as matters of delinquency and discipline, might be resolved. A few months after coming out of a long and devastating period in prison in 1666, Fox and a few companions traveled throughout Britain for the next year encouraging the setting up of these Monthly Meetings.

Women were always free to minister in the meetings for worship, but Fox believed they would be even freer to speak on affairs of business in a meeting of their own, and both Women's and Men's Meetings were established with joint consultation where necessary. Quarterly Meetings which gathered clusters of adjacent Monthly Meetings four times each year were added to this structure, but the

---

26. Ibid., p. 228.
27. Ibid., p. 233.

final authority was placed in these local Monthly Meetings where in principle it has remained to this day.

A Yearly Meeting, which gathered Friends from all over Britain, was later added and this structure of Monthly, Quarterly, and Yearly Meetings has persisted. In a country as large as the United States there are a number of Yearly Meetings and they are geographically sprinkled over the country, but the Monthly, Quarterly, Yearly pattern is usually maintained.

The corporate meeting for worship is the ground of Quaker spirituality that undergirds nearly all that Quakers do. A Quaker marriage takes place in a called meeting for worship in which the couple being married rise and make their vows to each other, without assistance, "in the presence of God and these our friends...." Worship and ministry follow in the usual way. A Quaker memorial service is in like manner a called meeting for worship in which the departed Friend is especially remembered in the ministry and the mystery of the transformation from this life to the beyond is often confirmed. Whittier's lines express this well:

> I know not where his islands lift
> Their fronded palms in air:
> I only know I cannot drift
> Beyond his love and care.

The presuppositions of the corporate meeting for worship have, from the very beginning, profoundly affected the method of decision making in the Quaker meeting for business. In both, there is faith in the Guide. There is faith in a continuous revelation that is always open to produce fresh disclosures. And there is respect and affection for each other that cuts through all diversity and that helps to kindle a faith that, with patience and openness, the group can expect to come to clearness and to resolve the problems that come before it.

The Quaker meeting for business opens with an unhurried period of waiting silence. If the meeting is properly carried through, there emerges something of this mood of openness that the meeting for worship knows so well, an openness not to *my* wishes and *my* designs and *my* surface preferences, but rather to the deepest levels where the

Guide's bidding may have its way and where the problem may be resolved in a way quite different from what I may have expected. A Quaker advice reads,

> It is our hope that in our meetings, the will of God shall prevail rather than the desires of men. We do not set great store by rhetoric or clever argument. The mere gaining of debating points is found to be unhelpful and alien.[28]

The business meeting is presided over by a Clerk, who has been chosen by the Meeting for a term of office. His role is quite different from that of a chairman who with *Roberts Rules of Order* at his mental fingertips handles motions and amendments from the floor, calls for divisions, counts votes, and announces the result.

The Quaker Clerk is ideally chosen from the most seasoned Friends in the Meeting. He is a good listener, has a clear mind that can handle issues, has the gift of preparing a written minute that can succinctly sum up the sense of the meeting, and is one who has faith in the presuppositions that were mentioned earlier. With all of this, a good Clerk is a person who refuses to be hurried and can weary out dissension with a patience borne of the confidence that there is a way through, although the group may have to return to the issue again and again in later meetings before clearness comes and a proper decision is reached.

No votes are taken in a proper Quaker meeting for business. It is the task of the Clerk, within the plexus of this corporate exercise, either to find a resolution that is in right ordering so that the assembled Friends can largely agree with it, or to follow the Quaker rule "When in doubt, wait." A London Yearly Meeting advice reads, "The Clerks should be content to wait upon God with the meeting as long as may be necessary for the emergence of a decision which clearly commends itself to the heart and mind of the meeting as the right one."[29] Coming back for a major decision after a month's interval of waiting often assists clarity.

The Quaker meeting for business is not a process that commends

---

28. *Christian Faith and Practice in the Experience of the Society of Friends*, London Yearly Meeting, London, 1960, Item 353.
29. Ibid., Item 354.

INTRODUCTION

itself to the driven ones who demand a swift decision. There is a story of a man who had been conducting a study of the longevity of different religious denominations. He was telling his friend about visiting a Quaker cemetery recently and being appalled at finding, by the birth and death dates on the small headstones, that these Quakers seemed to live longer than those of any other denomination he had come upon. His friend replied that this would not be surprising to him if he knew anything about Quakers, for it always took them longer than anyone else to make their minds up about anything!

There are times when, at a serious juncture or time of tension in the deliberations, the Clerk or some member of the Meeting may call for a time of waiting silence. At other times I have seen a business meeting settle into silence of itself. At the close of such an interval, when the Clerk calls the meeting back to the issue, there has often been a change of climate, and the decision emerges.

I will cite two examples of the power of silence in Quaker meetings for business to illumine and even at times to change the outcome of the meeting's decision. In the summer of 1937 I was on a Quaker visitation in Nazi Germany and was invited to attend the rather large executive committee of the German Yearly Meeting. The Nazi government had just ordered conscription for all able-bodied young men with no alternative service exceptions. This executive committee was struggling to find what they should recommend to the Yearly Meeting about the advice they should give to their Quaker young men in the face of a possible death sentence if they were to refuse military service.

A former teacher in a German school who had been dismissed from his post because of his Quaker views and was now living in the Netherlands felt that the Meeting should unite in advising the young men to refuse military service, no matter what the costs. Another Quaker was a German officer in World War I who had long before resigned from the army and would never accept being recalled regardless of the penalty. His point of view was that the Quaker Yearly Meeting, made up largely of those who were over-age for the draft, should leave this decision to the conscience of each young Quaker.

At this point Alfons Paquet, one of the editors of the *Frankfurter Zeitung* and a deeply respected senior Friend, asked for a time of silence. We sat for some ten burning minutes. Then Alfons Paquet rose and spoke briefly about the "Heiterkeit der Stille" (the joyousness of silence) and a whole new climate seemed to come into the meeting. When he had finished, the Clerk turned to the next item of business. A minute or two later one of these two advocates, in an all-too-human way, began to repeat his earlier views. Somehow in the new climate his words sounded hollow and no longer relevant. Without a word from the Clerk, he stopped in the middle of a sentence and simply sat down. At the close of the meeting these two adversaries who had been so tense with each other left the room with tears in their eyes and their arms around each other. Without official Yearly Meeting recommendations the Quaker young men were left with their own consciences to determine what they were called upon to do.

Per Sundberg, a Swedish Quaker and the founder of Viggby-holm School, a coeducational boarding school near Stockholm, had made two journeys to broken and desolate Germany in 1946–1947. He had seen firsthand how many of the brave, overworked, underfed, and poorly housed new German officials, who were trying to reestablish the schools, the churches, the political structure, and the youth programs, were close to the breaking point. He had a Quaker *concern* to bring twenty of them to Sweden as guests of the Swedish Quakers for a month of rest and good food. During a week of this time, he hoped to invite their opposite numbers from the Western countries: Scandinavia, France, Switzerland, Britain, and the United States, for a week of fellowship and discussion of the years ahead. He hoped that these German guests would discover how fully they were accepted by their Western neighbors and how deeply grateful these leaders in the West were for the valiant work they were so courageously carrying on. Per Sundberg's dream was that this could be carried out in April of 1948. In November 1947, Per Sundberg died of a heart attack.

At the January 1948 business meeting of Swedish Friends, with some fifteen present, person after person rose to express their thankfulness for Sundberg's life and for this typically generous intention of his, but to agree that Quakers did not undertake projects they were too weak to carry through. The complicated problems of raising the necessary funds, of getting the American and British and French military authorities to issue exit visas to the German guests, getting rail travel and transit visas to pass through Denmark, securing entry visas and food cards from the reluctant Swedish government, and handling the housing and caring for the German guests would be just too much to manage. This small cluster of Swedish Friends was already overburdened with heavy, demanding jobs and family obligations so that regretfully they saw no other alternative than to give up the project.

At this point, the meeting fell into a deep silence, which lasted for some time. The silence was broken when Emelia Fogelklou Norlind, their prophetic and deeply revered member, rose to speak. She said that like most of those who had spoken earlier, she too felt in a worldly sense that the undertaking was impractical and beyond their strength. Then with her eyes flashing she told them that in this long silence it had come to her that they could not fail Per Sundberg's concern that he had left almost as a testament to them. She had been brought to feel that they must carry it out and that strength would be given to them to accomplish it. Others rose to express how against all their surface wisdom, they too had felt the same leading.

Before the business meeeting closed, Gunnar Sundberg, Per's oldest son, offered to care for all of the secretarial work. Herman Backman, a high official in the Cooperative Movement, offered to care for getting the military permissions to leave Germany, to handle the rail transport, and to help with securing the funds. Elsa Cedegren, King Gustaf V's niece, agreed to approach the Swedish Foreign office for the Swedish entry-visas and food cards. The surface wisdom and the surface will of the earlier part of the meeting had been lifted beyond itself in the silence of this meeting for business. The German company who came in April 1948 were superb people and their opposite numbers from the Western countries who came for the week of conference were amazingly well matched with them. In retrospect few things that Swedish Friends had undertaken brought them more joy, and the Germans who are alive today still speak of their experience with awe at its meaning in this dark moment of their lives.

Another highly important issue in arriving at a decision and one that calls for a good deal of inner discipline and seasoning on the part of the members is the matter of what constitutes unanimity. It should be obvious that all need not feel equally happy about the decision the Clerk finally, after getting the "sense of the meeting," has set down in the meeting as passed. It is important to understand how this so-called Quaker unanimity is arrived at. Something that might be called participative humility in the assembled members is certainly required in the Quaker decision-making process for it to be able to operate effectively. In this process, whose decision I have been willing to accept, I am brought to realize that the matter has been carefully and patiently considered. I have been involved throughout the process and have had a chance at different stages in it of making my point of view known to the group and of having it seriously considered and weighed. Even if the decision that the group feels drawn to accept may go against what I initially proposed, I know that my contribution has helped to sift the issue, perhaps to temper it, and in the course of the process, I may have come to see it somewhat differently. A French writer, Alfred de Vigny, once remarked, "I am not always of my own opinion," and this flash of humility is not lost on me or on the Quaker process.

If I am a seasoned Friend, I no longer oppose the decision. I give it my *nihil obstat* and I emerge from the meeting not as a member of a minority who feels outflanked and rejected but rather as one who has been through the process of the decision and is willing to abide by it even though my accent would not have put it in this form.

The practice of this kind of participative humility and its capacity to help the "sense of the meeting" to emerge has done much to hold the Society of Friends together in critical moments of its life. But there is a costly spiritual dimension to the process and when this has not been present and exercised, even such a split as the Hicksite-Orthodox division of the nineteenth century (which took a century and a quarter to heal) was able to take place.

The whole matter of concerns and of the process of discernment has been mentioned earlier, but these practices require further scrutiny to understand their central place in Quaker practice. The Book of Acts in the New Testament sparkles with vivid concerns and the following of divine guidance, no matter at what cost. Believing that we are still in the Apostolic age and that we do not work alone, Quakers have experienced in their corporate meetings for worship and in their private devotions, leadings to which they have sought to be attentive. The small inner nudges (if anything is small) may be swiftly cared for, but concerns that may involve changes of career or that involve others in their unfolding call for more deliberate care. How such guidance is to be regarded and how it is to be followed raises the whole question of discernment. In what ways may individual Friends be helped to test the authenticity of a concern and how

INTRODUCTION

may they be assisted in coming to clearness about their own gifts in connection with what this may demand of them?

Here again the strong corporate side of Quakerism, which is so little understood outside the Society of Friends itself, has been able to furnish spiritual assistance that has so often proved invaluable to the one who is seeking to follow the inward Guide.

The traditional procedure is to call together a small committee of clearness. The committee meets with the person and listens to his concern, putting searching questions as to the nature of the concern, the fitness of the person in carrying it out, and what may be the Meeting's final financial obligation, should financial assistance be needed. In putting the questions and in the worshipful silence they have together to ask for divine wisdom, new facets of the concern may come to light to help the person in the clarificiation of the guidance that has come to him. The Quaker meeting for business has also been a place where concerns can be brought, especially if the Meeting itself might be involved in sponsoring the person, as in the case of a concern to travel in the ministry and in being willing to issue a minute to commend him or her for the task.

Two examples of the unfolding of Quaker concerns may be useful in seeing how a concern is carried out. Joseph Sturge was a British Quaker who lived in Birmingham in the mid-nineteenth century. He was an owner of flour mills and highly respected in the general community. As he saw his country slipping further and further into a mood of war against Russia over the Crimea, he felt personally seized by a concern to do something to prevent this catastrophe. In December 1853, he discussed with his friends the rightness of his concern for a Quaker deputation to the czar. Eventually he laid his concern before the Meeting for Sufferings in London and after considering the matter they encouraged him to carry out his leading. In this instance, they appointed two companions, Robert Charlton and Henry Pease, to go with him. They left London in January, 1854, with no assurance that Czar Nicholas I would receive them. On the continent they traveled by rail in the dead of the winter to Koenigsburg, by carriage to Riga, and on the final stretch of four hundred miles from Riga to St. Petersburg (Leningrad), the three days and nights were spent in the same carriage, which was now strapped to a sledge and drawn by seven horses.

INTRODUCTION

On February 10, 1854, the czar received them and with Joseph Sturge as the spokesman, the czar seemed deeply moved by the visit. They met the empress directly afterward, who told them, according to the report of Sturge's companion Robert Charlton, "I have just seen the Emperor and there were tears in his eyes."[30] Soon afterward, word was received of another incendiary speech by Prime Minister Palmerston in the House of Commons that cast the die, and the war became inevitable.

Joseph Sturge returned to England in disgrace with his fellow citizens for having talked with the "wicked" czar. In that wartime atmosphere this was regarded as little short of high treason. Early in the war the British fleet, having tried unsuccessfully to damage the Russian fleet at the naval base near St. Petersburg, sent ashore raiding parties and destroyed several fishing villages along the coast of Finland. Finland, at that time, was technically a Grand Duchy of Russia, but it had suffered far more from the Russians than from what the English would ever do, and the Finnish citizenry looked with the greatest respect on Britain. This wanton destruction was fully reported in the British press and questions were asked about the callous act in the House of Commons. They were quickly silenced by queries of whether the first word to give to the British fleet in a war situation was to be one of censure, and the whole matter was dropped. It was not dropped, however, in the mind of Joseph Sturge, and he felt it laid on him to do something to right this wrong done to these Finnish fishing people.

The Crimean War over, Joseph Sturge again went to his Meeting and told them of his desire to visit these Finnish villages to see if some relief was needed there that he might help to arrange. They again appointed a companion and the two went to the Baltic coast and crossed in a vessel to Finland. In visiting these villages they found that not only were they without proper fish nets, but their crops had failed and they were without seed and other necessities. Joseph Sturge returned to Birmingham, put in five thousand pounds of his own money and raised enough from the subscriptions of others to outfit three small ships full of fishing gear and seeds and food and sent them to these villages. Sturge never returned to inspect them, but other travelers in the following years reported that the people of these villages felt that the raid must have been a mistake, for these

---

30. Richenda C. Scott, *Quakerism in Russia* (London: Michael Joseph, 1964), p. 110.

44

INTRODUCTION

British people had taken such pains to meet their needs that they felt bound to them with special ties.

How little Joseph Sturge could have foreseen, when the concern to visit the czar first came, to him, what humiliation and misunderstanding this journey to Russia was to cost him in the months and years of British patriotic fervor that the Crimean War had brought on. How little, too, could he foresee that out of that humiliation and inward chastening was to come his call to Finland to release a chain of reconciliation that has not yet spent its force. Few concerns reveal more than an inkling of all that they contain, and those who carry them out must always expect to be vulnerable. Maltie Babcock, a British religious leader of the last generation, used to say that Jesus promised those who would follow his leadings only three things: that they should be absurdly happy, entirely fearless, and always in trouble!

Emma Noble was the wife of a foreman in a locomotive works near Oxford in Britain. In the early 1920s, the unemployment and misery in the coal-mining areas of South Wales were appalling. It came to her in a Quaker meeting for worship that she should visit this area and see if there was anything that the Quakers could do in this region to lessen the pain. Her husband agreed and a small committee of clearness in the Meeting found the concern in right ordering and encouraged her to follow it. In the first valley that she visited in South Wales there seemed to be no opening for the kind of assistance that the Friends could offer. She did not feel released to return home, however, and extending her journey, she looked into the Rhondda Valley. In the course of some days there, way began to open and the real purpose of her journey began to emerge. Out of the visit a way was found to release the Nobles for what turned out to be some years in this service, and a long-time program of work unfolded that eventually involved university people, members of Parliament, a royal visit, and finally a program of legislation to help to ease the ugly situation. Her first small step, which was in part a mistaken one, led to further steps and ultimately to a deeper and deeper involvement.

These examples give at least a glimpse of the manner in which concerns arise and are carried through, with failures and unpredictable breakthroughs all mixed together. In a way the concerns that have been cited are misleading, for both were rather swiftly encouraged by the Meeting members who gathered to consider their initial

45

validity, and at least two of the three concerns eventually produced visibly favorable results. Most concerns begin not as plants in full bloom but as seeds that may need scarifying in order to grow. Not only is the seed of concern something that needs careful treatment to unfold, but the one to whom the concern has come may often enough be quite unready to carry it out until he has been changed and reshaped in ways that call for great flexibility and openness. Even the community that is to encourage and perhaps support the concern may have to go through painful change before its members are ready to unite with it. It would be hard to exaggerate the patience, the humility, the purging, and the costly transformation that may have to take place not only before clarity is reached as to the form in which the concern is meant to be realized, but equally in the person and in the community before they are suitable instruments to assist in its realization.

These leadings come to us by the route of our own psychological mechanisms and are capable, therefore, of blemish. A seasoned Friend has a certain debonair attitude about being made a fool of and has learned how to wait and see how the concern and his motives for that concern look the next day or the next week. He knows enough to allow his own private detective agency to examine all aspects of the concern. He sees how it looks after wise and trusted people whom he has consulted have given him their opinions of it. If the concern can endure this kind of scrutiny, he then may take it to a committee on clearness that he may select himself, or, if it involves the Meeting, he may ask to bring it before the monthly meeting for business. The "When in doubt, wait" motto, painful as it may seem to the person or persons involved, has so often been found to test the flexibility and really centered spirit of the bearer of the concern. If this embarrassing waiting, or the prospect of it, succeeds in dissolving away the concern, its rootlessness has been exposed and it withers away and can be buried. Albert Schweitzer once suggested that when some compassionate venture, perhaps of an innovative sort, is proposed, we must not expect people to clear stones from our path. Rather they may roll a few extra boulders onto our path just to see if we really mean it.

One cannot leave this matter of concerns and of the Quaker discernment process through which they must pass without mentioning two other matters. One is the number of amazing and almost overwhelming instances in the following out of concerns: of obstacles being dissolved away; of unheard-of support in the way of persons, of money, and of services; of beautiful and moving sorts turning up that give confirmation to the fact that we are not working alone. In the same breath comes the second matter. Quakers know all too well the danger of falling victim to the *results* disease, and of the temptation to reject leadings where the results are not assured or where they appear highly doubtful. How do those who follow the Guide take failure, take the absence of results? There is the Cross, always the Cross. If we believe there is a redemptive Presence that we have known, a Presence that is trying to break through, and if we are convinced that to carry out this concern or to refuse it or fail it has cosmic consequences, then already we know in the deepest sense that whether we win or lose in this particular chapter, the book is not yet closed, and that whatever happens we are still on the winning side. We know, too, that not *our* way but love's way will some day weary out the obstacles.

On a bulletin board in the little Quaker meetinghouse in Australia's Adelaide, I once saw a word from the British Quaker educator, the late Harold Loucks, that read, "An act of love that fails is just as much a part of the divine life as an act of love that succeeds. For love is measured by its fullness and not by its reception." Tagore in his *Fireflies* has a star say, "Let me light my lamp and never debate whether it will remove the darkness." To do what we are led to do by concern and to leave the rest with the Master Harvester seems to Quakers to be the way indicated.

It seems right to conclude this description of Quaker spirituality with a few general remarks about the unfolding of the Society of Friends in the three and a quarter centuries of its existence. The Quaker willingness to suffer the persecutions of the first forty years was never in question. In the 1670s and 1680s there was a growing group in Britain who could not but admire the courage and sincerity of the Quakers in refusing to hide their meeting places, as many of the Non-Conformist groups were doing. Often neighbors who did not share the Quakers' religious views helped them by refusing to attend the actions to dispose of their goods that had been confiscated. When the bloodless revolution of 1688 took place and the new laws under William and Mary were instituted, these persecutions largely dropped away. It has been said that never in history has such an extended period of open nonviolent resistance to the state, with such visible results, been recorded.

It is interesting, too, that the Quakers, although completely nonviolent, not only insisted from the outset on each legal right that was due to them, but had no hesitation in sending their most weighty persons to "speak truth to power" and to lay their situation before the highest authority, whether it was Oliver Cromwell or King Charles II or James II. They kept a highly accurate and updated record of the number of their people who "suffered" either imprisonment or serious seizure of property and saw that the heads of government were constantly aware of what the injustices of the legal system were doing to them. With their unflinching witness against swearing an oath either in a court of law or in any contractual situation, they were always at the mercy of the court, which could at any moment put to them an oath of loyalty to the ruling power and know that after its inevitable refusal they could, if inclined, impose almost any sentence they chose or could seize their property through the praemunire process.

In all of this process of suffering their way through to a release of these prohibitions to worship in their own way, William Penn from the time of his entry into the Quaker ranks in 1667 played no small part. The son of an admiral and one who was respected by both Charles II and James II, William Penn spent a period of imprisonment (1668–1669) on a charge of blasphemy and was arrested again in 1670 for preaching in an outdoor Quaker meeting for worship. At his trial in 1670, he succeeded in getting released by a jury verdict, which the furious judge sought to quash by imprisoning the jury without food until they altered their verdict. When the jury refused to budge, the judge had to back down and the Penn-Meade case became a landmark in British legal history, vindicating the civil rights of the common man to a fair jury trial and to the carrying out of their verdict.

William Penn, as his spiritual writings indicate, was moved in his concern for the rights of human beings not alone from political motives but from his deep inward Quaker experience of which he could have said with John Woolman that "my heart was tender and often contrite, and universal love to my fellow-creatures increased in me." Yet for him, the political structure, like the human body, was something for which he was responsible. Already in the 1670s Penn

INTRODUCTION

was deeply concerned for changes in the repressive laws that were shattering the Quakers' family and civil life and forcing their Non-Conformist neighbors to go underground, and he worked with Algernon Sydney and John Locke and others to have changes made. The time was not yet propitious and the fruits of their work were still more than a decade away. Meanwhile, in the 1670s, Penn helped to draw up a constitution for the American colony of West Jersey and to do it in such a way that full religious freedom was allowed, punishments were greatly reduced, and the full rights of a free man were secured.

With the persecutions in Britain sharper than ever, Penn in 1681 had a concern to open a way for Quakers and others to emigrate in large numbers to America and to undertake what he called a "Holy Experiment." He was able to barter a large debt that Charles II owed to the estate of his father for a great tract of land in America that was to be named Pennsylvania after his father.

Now Penn sat down to draft a constitution for this new colony that was shaped after his own heart. He insisted that in this colony men and women must be given what they had asked for and been refused in Britain. The constitution under which Penn's Holy Experiment was to be carried out guaranteed religious freedom and the colony was to be launched without a militia and with only a modest police force. The hard-pressed British Quakers were, however, urged to search their motives in making the decision to emigrate and to weigh carefully whether their place was to stand firm and continue to make their witness where they were already planted or to cut their ties and accept the challenge of carrying out their Quaker witness in a new continent and under the constitutional terms of this Holy Experiment.

William Penn's 1682 constitution was, with his consent, twice revised (1683 and 1701) but its basic principles of human rights were scrupulously retained. It was under this constitution that the Quakers governed the colony until 1756 and under which Pennsylvania by the time of the American Revolution had become one of the strongest and most prosperous of the colonies. The character of this constitution was marked throughout by a special view of man. As a Quaker, William Penn saw man not as a depraved sinner but as a child of God with the Seed of the Spirit within him to be drawn out and nurtured. This view of man might be called the "Atlantic" man and was in sharp contrast to the Massachusetts Calvinist view of the "Puritan" man. Much of the American dream that appears in the preamble and constitution of the United States, drawn up in 1787 in Penn's own capital, Philadelphia, bears a strong relationship to this Pennsylvania constitution, which came from Penn's hand and heart.

The eighteenth century found the Quakers about evenly divided in numbers between Britain and the American colonies. On both sides of the Atlantic, successive generations of Quakers tended to draw together into close-knit groups. Their form of address in using the "thee" and "thou"; their plain clothing; their refusal to remove the hat; their strictness about marrying within the Quaker community; their form of silent worship; their witness against taking any part in wars or in military defense; and, in America, their tenderness to the Indians and later their testimony against the holding of slaves all contributed to making them a "peculiar" people.

The passionate outreach that swiftly swelled their ranks in the seventeenth century had now cooled, and while there was a widespread movement of visiting in the ministry that welcomed and often drew in seeking strangers, the Quakers were largely dependent on heredity, on the allegiance of their own children, for their continuance. In a number of early American colonies like Pennsylvania, the New Jerseys, Rhode Island, and the Carolinas, the Quakers in spite of their clannishness were deeply respected and took a prominent part in early governing bodies.

There was, too, on both sides of the Atlantic in the eighteenth century, a consolidation and a turning inward that is wonderfully recorded in the many journals that this century produced. The long selections from John Woolman's *Journal* that follow in this book give a portrait of this consolidation at its very best. While this period of Quakerism is usually, with some justification, referred to as the era of Quietism, Woolman's *Journal* reveals the spiritual and social union and outreach that this century's closely focused Quaker spiritual life, for all of its limitations, was able to produce.

From the very outset, the Quaker testimony on rigorous honesty, integrity, and simplicity had a quite unintended side effect. In eventually winning the confidence of those with whom they did business or those they professionally served, Quakers tended to prosper. In the swiftly expanding economy of the American colonies as well as in prosperous Britain, enlarging its empire and poised for the leadership of the industrial revolution, this prosperity spilled over into many Quaker families. With this wealth came the customary diseases of softening of the arteries of many of the young and the conservative note of caution that often crept into many well-to-do venerables among the Friends. Fred Tolles's book *Meetinghouse and Countinghouse* documents some of this tendency.

The question for Quakers has always been how to live *in* the world, as the Quakers have felt they must do, and yet not be taken over by the world. It is true that among Quakers there has been generous philanthropy, but a contemporary's words keep ringing in our ears when he says, "We dare not stop short with benevolence when God is calling for love." Sensitive consciences have led Quakers in different generations to carry out concerns for the care of the mentally troubled (William Tuke); for the prisoners (Elizabeth Fry); for the released slaves after the American Civil War (Levi Coffin); for the proper treatment of the Indians in the same period (Laurie Tatman); for the modest but sincere efforts to heal some of the wounds of war and violence (Franco-Prussian War, 1870; and after both World Wars, 1918 and 1945). But John Woolman's searching questions in his essay on *A Word of Remembrance and Caution to the Rich* still have an amazingly contemporary thrust even to those who may not qualify for the last word in the title: "May we look upon our treasures, the furniture of our houses, and our garments, and try whether the seeds of war have nourishment in these our possessions. Holding treasures in the self-pleasing spirit is a strong plant, the fruit whereof ripens fast. A day of outward distress is coming and Divine Love calls for us to prepare against it."[31] Matters concerning the accumulation and distribution of money and property and the security they represent are still as unresolved and troubling as they were when Woolman raised questions about them with his own generation in the eighteenth century. But their very presence as an active issue on the agenda seldom leaves Quakers for long, and a few strong souls in each generation touch the quick of the Society by the simplicity of their lives and their availability to answer the calls of need, which they sense and respond to.

---

31. John Woolman, *Journal*, Whittier Edition (Boston: Houghton Mifflin, 1871), Appendix, p. 307.

INTRODUCTION

In the course of our own century, most of the large Quaker fortunes in both Britain and America have disappeared. A careful scrutiny of Quakers who continue to worship in the Meetings that are carried on after the ancient pattern of silence and obedience would find that most of them are professional people: doctors, teachers, social workers, counselors, engineers, lawyers, and a few who may be in the arts and crafts or in various forms of business. They are for the most part people of the mid-to-upper layer of that elusive category called the "middle class." They often yearn for more blue-collar workers and members of ethnic minorities to join their ranks and wonder why so few of them are there.

In the eighteenth and nineteenth centuries, up to 1859 in Britain and even later in the United States, anyone who proposed to "marry out," that is, to marry other than a fellow Quaker, was labored with and if he or she persisted, was likely to be disowned. This practice seriously thinned the ranks of some of the most adventurous spirits, to say nothing of the barrier its genealogical tightness erected to prospective members who might have greatly strengthened its life.

When the decision finally came to permit marrying outside the Quaker membership, the close and intensively united community of Friends opened itself in a fresh way to a whole new increment of those who had not been brought up in Quaker families. Even so, there has been a minimum of proselytization; but now instead of being a hereditary club with a diminishing birth rate, Quakers welcome all who find that this way of worship and this way of life is what they have long been seeking. It has been said that you do not make Quakers, you discover them or they discover you.

People are drawn into the Society of Friends today through a number of doors: the form of worship, the commitment to simplicity in lifestyle, the accent on religious experience rather than creeds, the peace witness, and the implemented concern for the troubled areas of the world which the service bodies of the Society seek to serve. Interestingly enough, while many Quaker children ultimately continue their earlier connection as "birthright" Friends, the Society of Friends is becoming increasingly dependent for its membership and its leadership on those who enter it by "convincement," usually as adults. It has almost come to the point where it could be compared with the religious orders that have to renew themselves in each generation from men and women who feel called to join their ranks. This means

INTRODUCTION

that Quaker spirituality must be strong enough and articulate enough not only to draw persons who are meant to be there into their Meetings but, once they are there, to expand the aperture through which they originally came by the nurture and growth of the interior dimension from which all the rest, if it is genuine, must come.

Quaker Spirituality
Selected Writings

ABRIDGMENT OF

THE JOURNAL OF GEORGE FOX

GEORGE FOX
(1624–1691)

George Fox, whose life and witness were largely responsible for drawing together and setting the pattern of the spirituality of the Religious Society of Friends, was anything but a constant journal keeper. What is here called a Journal *is really an autobiography and is generally regarded as one of the great religious autobiographies in the English language.*

Fox had a prodigious memory and, in one of his long imprisonments in 1664, he either wrote or dictated a detailed account of the seventeen years of his adult life from 1647 to 1664. This is referred to as the Short Journal *and was used to refresh his mind when, a decade later, in 1674–1675, he dictated a fuller account to Thomas Lower, his stepson-in-law and devoted companion, who was the husband of one of Margaret Fell's daughters. This fuller account is called the* Spence Manuscript. *Thomas Ellwood, a gifted Quaker writer, was officially commissioned to take these manuscripts, together with copious letters, pastoral epistles, and other papers, and produce the first full account of Fox's life. This he accomplished in 1694, three years after Fox's death. The Ellwood edition of Fox's* Journal *was prefaced by a moving tribute to Fox written by William Penn.*

The sections of The Journal of George Fox *that follow are an abridgement or selection from the 760-page Nickalls edition published by the Cambridge University Press in 1952. This edition is regarded as the most accurate and readable one in existence today. The selections open with a few choice passages from William Penn's preface.*

WILLIAM PENN'S
PREFACE

*[Extracts from William Penn's Preface to the Original
Edition of George Fox's* Journal, *1694]*

HE WAS A MAN that God endued with a clear and wonderful
depth, a discerner of others' spirits, and very much a master of
his own. And though the side of his understanding which lay next to
the world, and especially the expression of it, might sound uncouth
and unfashionable to nice ears, his matter was nevertheless very
profound; and would not only bear to be often considered but the
more it was so the more weighty and instructing it appeared. And
abruptly and brokenly as sometimes his sentences would fall from
him about divine things, it is well known they were often as texts to
many fairer declarations. And indeed it showed, beyond all contradiction, that God sent him, that no arts or parts had any share in his
matter or manner of his ministry; and that so many great, excellent,
and necessary truths as he came forth to preach to mankind had
therefore nothing of man's wit or wisdom to recommend them; so
that as to man he was an original, being no man's copy. And his
ministry and writings show they are from one that was not taught of
man, nor had learned what he said by study. Nor were they notional
or speculative, but sensible and practical truths, tending to conversion and regeneration and the setting up of the kingdom of God in
the hearts of men; and the way of it was his work.   [xlii–xliii]

#   #

In his testimony or ministry, he much laboured to open Truth to
the people's understandings, and to bottom them upon the principal,

60

GEORGE FOX

Christ Jesus, the Light of the world, that by bringing them to something that was of God in themselves, they might the better know and judge of him and themselves. [xliii]

\# \#

But above all he excelled in prayer. The inwardness and weight of his spirit, the reverence and solemnity of his address and behaviour, and the fewness and fullness of his words have often struck even strangers with admiration, as they used to reach others with consolation. The most awful, living, reverent frame I ever felt or beheld, I must say, was his in prayer. And truly it was a testimony that he knew and lived nearer to the Lord than other men; for they that know him most will see most reason to approach him with reverence and fear.

He was of an innocent life, no busybody, nor self-seeker, neither touchy nor critical; what fell upon him was very inoffensive, if not very edifying. So meek, contented, modest, easy, steady, tender, it was a pleasure to be in his company. He exercised no authority but over evil, and that everywhere and in all, but with love, compassion, and long-suffering, a most merciful man, as ready to forgive as unapt to take or give an offence. Thousands can truly say he was of an excellent spirit and savour among them, and because thereof, the most excellent spirits loved him with an unfeigned and unfading love.

He was an incessant labourer; for in his younger time, before his many great and deep sufferings and travels had enfeebled his body for itinerant services, he laboured much in the word, and doctrine and discipline, in England, Scotland and Ireland, turning many to God, and confirming those that were convinced of the Truth, and settling good order as to church affairs among them.

I write by knowledge and not report; and my witness is true, having been with him for weeks and months together on divers occasions, and those of the nearest and most exercisiing nature, and that by night and by day, by sea and by land, in this and in foreign countries; and I can say I never saw him out of his place, or not a match for every service or occasion. [xlvii]

\# \#

Civil beyond all forms of breeding, in his behaviour; very temperate, eating little and sleeping less, though a bulky person.

Thus he lived and sojourned among us; and as he lived, so he died; feeling the same eternal power, that had raised and preserved him, in his last moments. So full of assurance was he that he triumphed over death; and so even to the last, as if death were hardly worth notice or a mention. [xlviii]

\# \#

I have done when I have left this short epitaph to his name. *Many sons have done virtuously in this day, but dear George thou excellest them all.* [xlviii]

William Penn

THE JOURNAL

1635   That all may know the dealings of the Lord with me, and the various exercises, trials, and troubles through which he led me.

I was born in the month called July in the year 1624, at Drayton-in-the-Clay in Leicestershire. My father's name was Christopher Fox; he was by profession a weaver, an honest man, and there was a Seed of God in him. The neighbours called him "Righteous Christer." My mother was an upright woman; her maiden name was Mary Lago, of the family of the Lagos and of the stock of the martyrs.

When I came to eleven years of age, I knew pureness and righteousness; for while I was a child I was taught how to walk to be kept pure. The Lord taught me to be faithful in all things, and to act faithfully two ways, viz., inwardly to God and outwardly to man, and to keep to "yea" and "nay" in all things. For the Lord showed me that though the people of the world have mouths full of deceit and changeable words, yet I was to keep to "yea" and "nay" in all things; and that my words should be few and savoury, seasoned with grace; and that I might not eat and drink to make myself wanton but for health, using the creatures in their service, as servants in their places, to the glory of him that hath created them.   [1]

#   #

Afterwards, as I grew up, my relations thought to have me a priest,[1] but others persuaded to the contrary; whereupon I was put to a man,[2] a shoemaker by trade, and that dealt in wool, and used

---

1. Fox applied the term priest to all professional preachers, ministers, and clergy, irrespective of the particular sect to which they belonged.
2. Probably George Gee of Mancetter, a neighboring village.

grazing, and sold cattle; and a great deal went through my hands. While I was with him, he was blessed; but after I left him he broke, and came to nothing. I never wronged man or woman in all that time, for the Lord's power was with me and over me, to preserve me. While I was in that service, I used in my dealings the word "verily," and it was a common saying among people that knew me, "If George says 'Verily' there is no altering him." When boys and rude people would laugh at me, I let them alone and went my way, but people had generally a love to me for my innocency and honesty. [2]

\#   \#

1644   Now during the time that I was at Barnet a strong temptation to despair came upon me. And then I saw how Christ was tempted, and mighty troubles I was in. And sometimes I kept myself retired in my chamber, and often walked solitary in the Chase there, to wait upon the Lord. And I wondered why these things should come to me; and I looked upon myself and said, "Was I ever so before?" [4]

\#   \#

1646   When I was come down into Leicestershire, my relations would have had me married, but I told them I was but a lad, and I must get wisdom. Others would have had me into the auxiliary band among the soldiery, but I refused; and I was grieved that they proffered such things to me, being a tender youth. Then I went to Coventry, where I took a chamber for a while at a professor's house till people began to be acquainted with me, for there were many tender people in that town.

And after some time I went into my own country again, and was there about a year, in great sorrows and troubles, and walked many nights by myself. [5]

\#   \#

I went to another ancient priest at Mancetter in Warwickshire and reasoned with him about the ground of despair and temptations, but he was ignorant of my condition; and he bid me take tobacco and sing psalms. Tobacco was a thing I did not love and psalms I was not in an estate to sing; I could not sing. Then he bid me come again and he would tell me many things, but when I came again he was angry and pettish, for my former words had displeased him. [5–6]

GEORGE FOX

# #

1647   I brought them Scriptures, and told them there was an anointing within man to teach him, and that the Lord would teach his people himself. [8]

# #

About the beginning of the year 1647, I was moved of the Lord to go into Derbyshire, where I met with some friendly people, and had many discourses with them. Then passing further into the Peak country, I met with more friendly people, and with some in empty, high notions. And travelling on through some parts of Leicestershire and into Nottinghamshire, there I met with a tender people, and a very tender woman whose name was Elizabeth Hooton; and with these I had some meetings and discourses. But my troubles continued, and I was often under great temptations; and I fasted much, and walked abroad in solitary places many days, and often took my Bible and went and sat in hollow trees and lonesome places till night came on; and frequently in the night walked mournfully about by myself, for I was a man of sorrows in the times of the first workings of the Lord in me. [9]

# #

Oh, the everlasting love of God to my soul when I was in great distress! When my troubles and torments were great, then was his love exceeding great. [10]

# #

Now after I had received that opening from the Lord that to be bred at Oxford or Cambridge was not sufficient to fit a man to be a minister of Christ, I regarded the priests less, and looked more after the dissenting people. And among them I saw there was some tenderness, and many of them came afterwards to be convinced, for they had some openings. But as I had forsaken all the priests, so I left the separate preachers also, and those called the most experienced people; for I saw there was none among them all that could speak to my condition. And when all my hopes in them and in all men were gone, so that I had nothing outwardly to help me, nor could tell what to do, then, Oh then, I heard a voice which said, "There is one, even Christ Jesus, that can speak to thy condition," and when I heard it my heart did leap for joy. Then the Lord did let me see why there was none upon the earth that could speak to my condition, namely, that I might give him all the glory; for all are concluded under sin, and shut up in unbelief as I had been, that Jesus Christ might have the pre-eminence, who enlightens, and gives grace, and faith and power. Thus, when God doth work who shall let [prevent] it? And this I knew experimentally.   [11]

\#   \#

And one day when I had been walking solitarily abroad and was come home, I was taken up in the love of God, so that I could not but admire the greatness of his love. And while I was in that condition it was opened unto me by the eternal Light and power, and I therein saw clearly that all was done and to be done in and by Christ, and how he conquers and destroys this tempter, the Devil and all his works, and is atop of him, and that all these troubles were good for me, and temptations for the trial of my faith which Christ had given me. And the Lord opened me that I saw through all these troubles and temptations. My living faith was raised, that I saw all was done by Christ, the life, and my belief was in him. And when at any time my condition was veiled, my secret belief was stayed firm, and hope underneath held me, as an anchor in the bottom of the sea, and anchored my immortal soul to its Bishop, causing it to swim above the sea, the world where all the raging waves, foul weather, tempests, and temptations are. But oh, then did I see my troubles, trials, and temptations more than ever I had done!   [14]

\#   \#

And therefore none can be a minister of Christ Jesus but in the eternal Spirit, which was before the Scriptures were given forth; for if they have not his Spirit, they are none of his.   [17]

\#   \#

Yet the work of the Lord went on in some, and my sorrows and troubles began to wear off and tears of joy dropped from me, so that I could have wept night and day with tears of joy to the Lord, in humility and brokenness of heart. And I saw into that which was without end, and things which cannot be uttered, and of the greatness and infiniteness of the love of God, which cannot be expressed by words. For I had been brought through the very ocean of darkness and death, and through the power and over the power of Satan, by the eternal glorious power of Christ. Even through that darkness was I brought, which covered over all the world, and which chained down all, and shut up all in death. And the same eternal power of God, which brought me through these things, was that which afterwards shook the nations, priests, professors, and people. Then could I say I had been in spiritual Babylon, Sodom, Egypt, and the grave; but by the eternal power of God I was come out of it, and was brought over it and the power of it, into the power of Christ. And I saw the harvest white, and the Seed of God lying thick in the ground, as ever did wheat that was sown outwardly, and none to gather it; and for this I mourned with tears. [21]

#　#

1648　In the year 1648, as I was sitting in a Friend's house in Nottinghamshire (for by this time the power of God had opened the hearts of some to receive the word of life and reconciliation), I saw there was a great crack to go throughout the earth, and a great smoke to go as the crack went; and that after the crack there should be a great shaking. This was the earth in people's hearts, which was to be shaken before the Seed of God was raised out of the earth. And it was so; for the Lord's power began to shake them, and great meetings we began to have, and a mighty power and work of God there was amongst people, to the astonishment of both people and priests. [22]

#　#

After this I went again to Mansfield, where was a great meeting of professors and people, and I was moved to pray, and the Lord's power was so great that the house seemed to be shaken. When I had done, some of the professors said it was now as in the days of the apostles, when the house was shaken where they were. [22–23]

#　#

And at a certain time, when I was at Mansfield, there was a sitting of the justices about hiring of servants; and it was upon me from the Lord to go and speak to the justices that they should not oppress the servants in their wages. So I walked towards the inn where they sat but finding a company of fiddlers there, I did not go in but thought to come in the morning, when I might have a more serious opportunity to discourse with them, not thinking that a seasonable time. But when I came again in the morning, they were gone, and I was struck even blind that I could not see. And I inquired of the innkeeper where the justices were to sit that day and he told me at a town eight miles off. My sight began to come to me again, and I went and ran thitherward as fast as I could. And then I was come to the house where they were, and many servants with them, I exhorted the justices not to oppress the servants in their wages, but to do that which was right and just to them; and I exhorted the servants to do their duties, and serve honestly, etc. And they all received my exhortation kindly, for I was moved of the Lord therein.   [26]

# #

Thus the work of the Lord went forward, and many were turned from the darkness to the light within the compass of these three years, 1646, 1647, and 1648. And divers meetings of Friends, in several places, were then gathered to God's teaching, by his light, spirit, and power; for the Lord's power brake forth more and more wonderfully.

Now was I come up in spirit through the flaming sword into the paradise of God. All things were new, and all the creation gave another smell unto me than before, beyond what words can utter. I knew nothing but pureness, and innocency, and righteousness, being renewed up into the image of God by Christ Jesus, so that I say I was come up to the state of Adam which he was in before he fell. The creation was opened to me, and it was showed me how all things had their names given them according to their nature and virtue. And I was at a stand in my mind whether I should practise physic for the good of mankind, seeing the nature and virtues of the creatures were so opened to me by the Lord. But I was immediately taken up in spirit, to see into another or more steadfast state than Adam's in innocency, even into a state in Christ Jesus, that should never fall. And the Lord showed me that such as were faithful to him in the power and light of Christ should come up into that state in which Adam was before he fell, in which the admirable works of the creation, and the virtues thereof, may be known, through the openings of that divine Word of wisdom and power by which they were made. Great things did the Lord lead me into, and wonderful depths were opened unto me, beyond what can by words be declared; but as people come into subjection to the spirit of God, and grow up in the image and power of the Almighty, they may receive the Word of wisdom, that opens all things, and come to know the hidden unity in the Eternal Being.   [27]

#   #

I was to direct people to the Spirit that gave forth the Scriptures, by which they might be led into all Truth, and so up to Christ and God, as they had been who gave them forth.   [34]

#   #

These things I did not see by the help of man, nor by the letter, though they are written in the letter, but I saw them in the light of the Lord Jesus Christ, and by his immediate Spirit and power, as did the holy men of God, by whom the Holy Scriptures were written. Yet I had no slight esteem of the Holy Scriptures, but they were very precious to me, for I was in that spirit by which they were given forth, and what the Lord opened in me I afterwards found was agreeable to them.   [34]

#   #

Moreover when the Lord sent me forth into the world, he forbade me to put off my hat to any, high or low; and I was required to "thee" and "thou" all men and women, without any respect to rich or poor, great or small. And as I travelled up and down, I was not to bid people "good morrow" or "good evening," neither might I bow or scrape with my leg to any one; and this made the sects and professions to rage. But the Lord's power carried me over all to his glory, and many came to be turned to God in a little time, for the heavenly day of the Lord sprang from on high, and brake forth apace by the light of which many came to see where they were.   [36]

#   #

1649   Oh, the rage and scorn, the heat and fury that arose! Oh, the blows, punchings, beatings, and imprisonments that we underwent for not putting off our hats to men! For that soon tried all men's patience and sobriety, what it was. Some had their hats violently plucked off and thrown away so that they quite lost them. The bad language and evil usage we received on this account are hard to be expressed, besides the danger we were sometimes in of losing our lives for this matter, and that, by the great professors of Christianity, who thereby discovered that they were not true believers. And though it was but a small thing in the eye of man, yet a wonderful confusion it brought among all professors and priests. But, blessed be the Lord, many came to see the vanity of that custom of putting off the hat to men, and felt the weight of Truth's testimony against it.   [37]

# #

Now after I was set at liberty from Nottingham gaol, where I had been kept prisoner a pretty long time, I travelled as before in the work of the Lord. And coming to Mansfield-Woodhouse, there was a distracted woman under a doctor's hand, with her hair loose all about her ears. He was about to let her blood, she being first bound, and many people being about her holding her by violence; but he could get no blood from her. And I desired them to unbind her and let her alone, for they could not touch the spirit in her, by which she was tormented. So they did unbind her; and I was moved to speak to her in the name of the Lord to bid her be quiet and still, and she was so. The Lord's power settled her mind, and she mended and afterwards received the Truth, and continued in it to her death. And the Lord's name was honoured, to whom the glory of all his works belongs.   [43–44]

# #

Now while I was at Mansfield-Woodhouse, I was moved to go to the steeplehouse there on a First-day, out of the meeting in Mansfield, and when the priest had done I declared the Truth to the priest and people. But the people fell upon me with their fists, books, and without compassion or mercy beat me down in the steeplehouse and almost smothered me in it, being under them. And sorely was I bruised in the steeplehouse, and they threw me against the walls and when that they had thrust and thrown me out of the steeplehouse, when I came into the yard I fell down, being so sorely bruised and beat among them. And I got up again and then they punched and thrust and struck me up and down and they set me in the stocks and brought a whip to whip me, but did not. And as I sat in the stocks they threw stones at me, and my head, arms, breast, shoulders, back, and sides were so bruised that I was mazed and dazzled with the blows. And I was hot when they put me in the stocks. After some time they had me before the magistrate, at a knight's house and examined me, where were many great persons, and I reasoned with them of the things of God and his teachings, and Christ's, and how that God that made the world did not well in temples made with hands; and of divers things of the Truth I spake to them, and they, seeing how evilly I had been used, set me at liberty. The rude people were ready to fall upon me with staves but the constable kept them off. And when they had set me at liberty, they threatened me with pistols, if ever I came again they would kill me and shoot me; and they would carry their pistols to the steeplehouse. And with threatening I was freed. And I was scarce able to go or well to stand, by reason of ill-usage. Yet with much ado I got about a mile from the town, and as I was passing along the fields Friends met me. I was so bruised that I could not turn in my bed, and bruised inwardly at my heart, but after a while the power of the Lord went through me and healed me, that I was well, glory be to the Lord for ever.   [44–45]

#   #

From Coventry I went to a place called Atherstone, and when I was two miles off it the bell rang upon a market day for a lecture, and it struck at my life, and I was moved to go to the steeplehouse. And when I came into it I found a man speaking, and as I stood among the people the glory and life shined over all, and with it I was crowned. And when the priest had done I spoke to him and the people the truth and the light which let them see all that ever they had done, and of their teacher within them, and how the Lord was come to teach them himself, and of the Seed Christ in them; how they were to mind that, and the promise that was to the Seed of God within them, which is Christ.   [47–48]

#   #

And as I was passing on Leicestershire I came to Twycross, where there were excise-men, and I was moved of the Lord to go to them and warn them to take heed of oppressing the poor, and people were much affected with it. Now there was in that town a great man, that had long lain sick and was given over by the physicians; and some Friends in the town desired me to go to see him. And I went up to him and was moved to pray by him; spoke to him in his bed, and the power of the Lord entered him that he was loving and tender.

And I left him and came down among the family in the house, and spake a few words to the people that they should fear the Lord and repent and prize their time and the like words, and there came one of his servants with a naked sword and run at me ere I was aware of him, and set it to my side, and there held it, and I looked up at him in his face and said to him, "Alack for thee, it's no more to me than a straw." And then he went away in a rage, with threatening words, and I passed away, and the power of the Lord came over all, and his master mended, according to my belief and faith that I had seen before. And he then turned this man away that run at me with the sword, and afterwards he was very loving to Friends; and when I came to that town again both he and his wife came to see me.   [49]

\#   \#

1650   There came an officer to me and took me by the hand and said I must go before the magistrates, and the other two that were with me, and so when we came before them about the first hour afternoon, they asked me why we came thither. I said God moved us to do so.   [51]

\#   \#

They put me in and out of the room from the first hour to the ninth hour at night in examinations, having me backward and forward, and said in a deriding manner that I was taken up in raptures, as they called it.

At last they asked me whether I was sanctified. I said, "Sanctified? yes," for I was in the paradise of God.

They said, had I no sin?

"Sin?" said I, "Christ my Saviour hath taken away my sin, and in him there is no sin."

They asked how we knew that Christ did abide in us.

I said, "By his Spirit that he has given us."

They temptingly asked if any of us were Christ.

I answered, "Nay, we are nothing. Christ is all."

They said, "If a man steal is it no sin?"

I answered, "All unrighteousness is sin."

And many such like words they had with me. And so they committed me as a blasphemer and as a man that had no sin, and committed another man with me to the House of Correction in Derby for six months.   [51–52]

GEORGE FOX

\#   \#

This was Justice Bennet of Derby that first called us Quakers because we bid them tremble at the word of God, and this was in the year 1650. And the justices gave leave that I should have liberty to go a mile. And I perceived their end, and I told the gaoler that if they would set me how far a mile was, I might walk in it sometimes, but it's like they thought I would go away. I told them I was not of that spirit; and the gaoler confessed it after, that they did it with that intent to have me gone away to ease the plague from them, and they said I was an honest man.   [58]

\#   \#

And when I was in the House of Correction my relations came to me and were much troubled that I should be in prison, for they looked upon it to be a great shame to them for me to be in gaol. It was a strange thing to be imprisoned then for religion. They went to the justice that cast me into prison, and would have been bound in one hundred pounds; and others in Derby, fifty pounds apiece, that I might have gone home with them and that I should come no more amongst them to declare against the priests. They had me up before the justice with them; and because I would not have them to be bound, for I was innocent from any ill behaviour and had spoken the word of life and Truth unto them, Justice Bennet got up into a rage; and as I was kneeling down to pray to the Lord to forgive him, he ran upon me with both his hands and struck me and cried, "Away with him, gaoler. Take him away, gaoler." And some thought I was mad because I stood for purity, perfection, and righteousness.   [60–61]

\#   \#

1651   And when I was in the House of Correction, there came a trooper to me and said, as he was sitting in the steeplehouse hearing the priest he was in an exceeding great trouble and the voice of the Lord came to him saying, "What, dost not thou know that my servant is in prison? Go to him for directions." And he came, and I spake to his condition and opened his understanding, and settled his mind in the light and spirit of God in himself; and I told him that which showed him his sin and troubled him, for it would show him his salvation; for he that shows a man his sins is he that takes it away. So the Lord's power opened to him, so that he began to have great

73

understanding of the Lord's Truth and mercies, and began to speak boldly in his quarters amongst the soldiers and others concerning Truth.   [64]

#   #

1651   My time being nearly out of being committed six months to the House of Correction, they filled the House of Correction with persons that they had taken up to be soldiers (during April 1651, the Commonwealth forces were actively strengthened, following the discovery of a Royalist plot) and then they would have had me to be a captain of them and the soldiers cried they would have none but me. So the keeper of the House of Correction was commanded to bring me up before the Commissioners and soldiers in the market place; and there they proffered me that preferment because of my virtue[3] as they said, with many other compliments, and asked me if I would not take up arms for the Commonwealth against the King. But I told them I lived in the virtue of that life and power that took away the occasion of all wars, and I knew from whence all wars did rise, from the lust according to James's doctrine.[4] Still they courted me to accept of their offer and thought that I did but compliment with them. But I told them I was come into the covenant of peace which was before wars and strifes were. And they said they offered it in love and kindness to me because of my virtue, and such like flattering words they used, and I told them if that were their love and kindness I trampled it under my feet. Then their rage got up and they said, "Take him away, gaoler, and cast him into the dungeon amongst the rogues and felons"; which they then did and put me into the dungeon amongst thirty felons in a lousy, stinking low place in the ground without any bed. Here they kept me a close prisoner almost a half year, unless it were at times; and sometimes they would let me walk in the garden, for they had a belief of me that I would not go away.

And in this time I was exceeding much oppressed with judges and magistrates and courts, and was moved to write to the judges concerning their putting men to death for cattle and for money and small things, several times, how contrary to the law of God it was. One time, I was under great sufferings in my spirit through it, and under the very sense of death; but when I came out of it, standing in

---

3. Meaning *valor*.
4. James IV:1.

the will of God a heavenly breathing arose in my soul to the Lord. Then did I see the heavens opened and the glory of God shined over all. Two men suffered [were hanged] for small things, and I was moved to admonish them for their theft and encourage them concerning their suffering, it being contrary to the law of God; and a little after they had suffered their spirits appeared to me as I was walking, and I saw the men were well.

And there was a young woman that was to be put to death for robbing her master; and judgment was given and a grave made for her and she carried to execution. I was made to write to the judge and to the jury about her, and when she came there though they had her upon the ladder with a cloth bound over her face, ready to be turned off, yet they had not power to hang her (as by the paper which I sent to be read at the gallows may be seen), but she was brought back again. And they came with great rage against me into the prison. Afterwards, in the prison this young woman came to be convinced of God's everlasting Truth. [64–66]

\# \#

So Worcester fight came on, and Justice Bennet sent the constables to press me for a soldier, seeing I would not accept of a command.[5] I told them I was brought off from outward wars. They came down again to give me press-money but I would take none. [67]

\# \#

They offered me money twice, but I would not take it. Then they were wroth, and I was committed close prisoner without bail or mainprize. Thereupon I writ to them again, directing my letter to Colonel Barton, who was a preacher, and the rest that were concerned in my commitment.[6]

Now when they had gotten me into Derby dungeon, it was the belief and saying of people that I should never come out: but I had faith in God, and believed I should be delivered in his time; for the Lord had said to me before, that I was not to be removed from that place yet, being set there for a service which he had for me to do. [67]

---

5. Cromwell's army passed near Derby toward the end of August 1651, gathering reinforcements everywhere, as it hurried south to intercept the Royalist Scottish army at Worcester on September 3.

6. Thomas Ellwood, p. 49; Bicent., i, 73.

QUAKER SPIRITUALITY

\# \#

They could not agree what to do with me; and sometime they would have me up before the Parliament, and another time they would have banished me to Ireland. At first they called me a deceiver and seducer and a blasphemer; and then when God brought his plagues upon them they said I was an honest and virtuous man. But their good report and bad report, their well or ill speaking was nothing to me; for the one did not lift me up, nor the other cast me down, praised be the Lord.

At length they were made to turn me out of gaol about the beginning of winter in the year 1651, who had been kept a year, within three weeks, in four prisons, the House of Correction, and at the town prison and the county gaol and dungeon, and then in the high gaol where I was kept till I was set freely at liberty. And this was in the month called October[7] in the Commonwealth's days. And then the light and truth and glory of the Lord flowed and spread abroad.   [70]

\# \#

The next day I came to Cranswick to Captain Pursloe's. And he went with me to Justice Hotham's, a pretty tender man, that had some experience of God's working in his heart. After that I had some discourse with him of the things of God, he took me into his closet, and said he had known that principle this ten year, and he was glad that the Lord did now publish it abroad to people. And so after a while there came in a priest with whom I had some discourse concerning the Truth, but his mouth was quickly stopped, for he was nothing but a notionist, and not in possession of what he talked of.   [74–75]

\# \#

And in the afternoon I went to the great high priest, their doctor, that Justice Hotham said he would send for to speak with me, to the steeplehouse three miles off, where he preached, and sat me down in the steeplehouse till the priest had done. And he took a text, which was, "Ho, every one that thirsteth, let him come freely, without money and without price." And so I was moved of the Lord God to

---

7. About October 8, 1651.

say unto him, "Come down, thou deceiver and hireling, for dost thou bid people come freely and take of the water of life freely, and yet thou takest three hundred pounds off them for preaching the Scriptures to them. Mayest thou not blush for shame? Did the prophet Isaiah and Christ so do that spoke those words and gave them forth freely? Did not Christ command his ministers, 'Freely you have received, freely give'?" And so the priest, like a man amazed, packed away.　　　　　　　　　　　　　　　　　　　　　　　　　　　　[76]

# #

I came to a stack of hay and lay in the haystack all night in the snow and rain, being but three days before the time called Christmas.　　　　　　　　　　　　　　　　　　　　　　　　　　　　[77]

# #

I passed to Cleveland amongst those people that had tasted of the power of God, but were all shattered to pieces and the heads of them turned Ranters. Now they had had great meetings, so I told them after that they had had such meetings they did not wait upon God to feel his power to gather their minds together to feel his presence and power and therein to sit to wait upon him, for they had spoken themselves dry and had spent their portions and not lived in that which they spake, and now they were dry. They had some kind of meetings but took tobacco and drank ale in them and so grew light and loose.　　　　　　　　　　　　　　　　　　　　　　　　　　[79]

# #

1652　　　And a great deal of people gathered about me and I declared the Truth and the word of life to them. And after, I went to an inn and desired them to let me have a lodging and they would not; and I desired them to let me have a little meat and milk and I would pay them for it, but they would not.　　　　　　　　　　　　　　　　[91]

# #

And after I was passed a pretty way out of the town I came to another house and desired them to let me have a little meat and drink and lodging for my money, but they would not neither but denied me. And I came to another house and desired the same, but they refused me also; and then it grew so dark that I could not see the highway; but I discovered a ditch and got a little water and refreshed myself and got over the ditch and sat amongst the furze bushes, being weary with travelling, till it was day.   [91]

# #

And I went to Gainsborough, and there, a Friend having been speaking in the market, the market and town were all in an up-roar.   [96]

# #

And in the eternal power of God I was moved of the Lord God to stand up atop of the table and tell them that Christ was in them except they were reprobates; and it was the eternal power of Christ and Christ that spake in me that time to them. And generally with one consent all the people did acknowledge the thing, and gave testimony to it, and confessed to it—yea, even the very professors and all them that were in a rage against me—and I said that if the power of God and the Seed spoke in man or woman it was Christ.   [96]

# #

And the next First-day I went to Tickhill and there the Friends of that side gathered together and there was a meeting; and a mighty brokenness with the power of God there was amongst the peo-ple.   [98]

# #

At night we came to a country house; and there being no ale-house near they desired us to stay there all night, where we had a good service for the Lord, declaring his Truth amongst them; for the Lord had said unto me if I did but set up one in the same spirit that the prophets and apostles were in that gave forth the Scriptures, he or she should shake all the country in their profession ten miles about them.   [103]

# #

And the next day we passed on, warning people as we met them of the day of the Lord that was coming upon them. As we went I spied a great high hill called Pendle Hill, and I went on the top of it with much ado, it was so steep; but I was moved of the Lord to go atop of it; and when I came atop of it I saw Lancashire sea; and there atop of the hill I was moved to sound the day of the Lord; and the

Lord let me see atop of the hill in what places he had a great people to be gathered. As I went down, on the hillside I found a spring of water and refreshed myself, for I had eaten little and drunk little for several days.   [103–104]

# #

And the Lord opened to me at that place, and let me see a great people in white raiment by a river's side coming to the Lord.   [104]

# #

And from thence I came to Ulverston and so to Swarthmoor to Judge Fell's.   [113]

# #

And so Margaret Fell[8] had been abroad, and at night when she came home her children told her that priest Lampitt and I disagreed; and it struck something at her because she was in a profession with him, though he hid his dirty actions from them. So at night we had a great deal of reasoning and I declared the Truth to her and her family.

And the next day Lampitt came again and I had a great deal of discourse with him before Margaret Fell, who soon then discerned the priest clearly, and a convincement came upon her and her family of the Lord's Truth. And there was a humiliation day shortly after, within a day or two, kept at Ulverston, and Margaret Fell asked me to go to the steeplehouse with her, for she was not wholly come off. I said, "I must do as I am ordered by the Lord," so I left her and walked into the fields, and then the word of the Lord came to me to go to the steeplehouse.   [114]

# #

Then I showed them that God was come to teach his people by his spirit and to bring them off all their old ways, religions, churches, and worship, for all their religions, and worship, and ways were but talking of other men's words, for they were out of the life and spirit that they were in that gave them forth.

One Justice Sawrey cried out, "Take him away"; and Judge Fell's

---

8. Margaret Fell (1614–1702), wife of Judge Thomas Fell. Her home now became the cradle of the new movement and she its nursing mother. In 1669 she married George Fox.

wife said to the officers, "Let him alone, why may not he speak as well as any other." [114–115]

\# \#

I returned to Swarthmoor again, where the Lord's power seized upon Margaret Fell and her daughter Sarah and several of them. [116]

\# \#

And after this Judge Fell was come home, and Margaret sent for me to return thither, and so I came through the country back to Swarthmoor again; and the priests and professors, and that envious Justice Sawrey, had incensed Judge Fell and Captain Sandys much against the Truth with their lies; and after dinner I answered him all his objections and satisfied him by Scripture so as he was thoroughly satisfied and convinced in his judgment. [118]

\# \#

After we had discoursed a pretty time together, Judge Fell was satisfied that I was the man; and he came also to see by the spirit of God in his heart over all the priests and teachers of the world and did not go to hear them for some years before he died; for he knew it was the Truth, and that Christ was the teacher of his people and their saviour. [118]

\# \#

Richard Farnsworth and James Nayler were come to Swarthmoor also to see me and the family. (And James Nayler was under a fast fourteen days.) And Judge Fell, for all the opposition, let the meeting be kept at his house and a great meeting was settled there in the Lord's power to the tormenting of the priests and professors (which has remained above twenty years to this day), he being satisfied of the Truth. After I had stayed awhile and the meeting was settled, I went to Underbarrow and had a great meeting there and from thence to Kellet, and had a great meeting at Robert Widders's and many were convinced there, where several came from Lancaster and some from York.

And there was a captain stood up after the meeting was done and asked me where my leather breeches were, and I let the man run on awhile and at last I held up my coat and said, "Here are my leather breeches which frighten all your priests and professors."

And Margaret Fell had a vision of a man in a white hat that should come and confound the priests, before my coming into those parts.

And a man had a vision of me that a man in leather breeches should come and confound the priests, and this man's priest was the first that was confounded and convinced. And a great dread there was amongst the priests and professors concerning the man in leather breeches.   [119]

# #

And after, I came up to Swarthmoor again, and there came up four or five priests, and I asked them whether any of them could say they ever had a word from the Lord to go and speak to such or such a people and none of them durst say so. But one of them burst out into a passion and said he could speak his experiences as well as I; but I told him experience was one thing but to go with a message and a word from the Lord as the prophets and the apostles had and did, as I had done to them, this was another thing.

Could any of them say they had such a command or word from the Lord at any time? But none of them could answer to it. But I told them the false prophets and false apostles and anti-christs could use the words and speak of other men's experiences that never knew or heard the voice of God and Christ; and such as they might get the good words and experience of others. This puzzled them much and laid them open.   [123]

# #

About this time, 1652, Christopher Taylor,[9] another minister, Thomas Taylor's brother, was convinced also of Truth; and they both became ministers of the gospel and great sufferers they were; and they came to know the word of the Lord and were commanded to go to many steeplehouses and markets and places and preach Christ freely. Also John Audland and Francis Howgill and John Camm[10]

---

9. Christopher Taylor (c. 1620–1686) opened a school at Waltham Abbey, Essex; he later emigrated to Pennsylvania.

10. John Camm (1605–1657), early publisher of Quakerism, especially in Bristol.

came forth to be faithful ministers, and Edward Burrough, and Richard Hubberthorne,[11] and Miles and Stephen Hubbersty and Miles Halhead and several others, and so continued till their deaths, and multitudes were turned to the Lord.

And James Nayler travelled up and down in many places amongst the people that were convinced. At last he and Francis Howgill were cast into Appleby gaol by the malicious priests and magistrates. And Francis Howgill and Edward Burrough died prisoners for the Lord's Truth.   [124–125]

# #

They fell so upon Friends in many places that they could hardly pass the highways, stoning and beating and breaking their heads. And then the priests began to prophesy again that within a half year we should be all put down and gone.

And about a fortnight after, I went into Walney Island and James Nayler went with me and we stayed overnight at a little town on this side called Cocken, and had a meeting where there was one convinced. And in the evening there came a man who bound himself with an oath that he would shoot me with a pistol, many people being in the fold. And the people of the house went forth. And after a while I walked forth, the power of the Lord was so mighty to the chaining of them in the yard that the man of the house, being a professor, was so tormented and terrified that he went into a cellar to his prayers. And after I went into the house when Truth was come over them. And there was a raw man of the house, seeing the Truth had come over, he fell to speaking and let up their spirits. And so I walked out of the house into the yard again and fell a-speaking; and then the fellow drew his pistol. And he snapped his pistol at me but it would not go off, though he struck fire. And some held him and some carried me away, and so through the power of the Lord God I escaped. So the Lord's power came over them all, though there was a great rage in the country.   [130]

# #

And Justice Sawrey and Justice Thompson of Lancaster granted forth a warrant for me, but Judge Fell, coming home, they did not

---

11. Richard Hubberthorne (1628–1662), a leading preacher of Quakerism, especially in Norwich and London.

serve it upon me, for he was out of the country all this time that I was thus abused and cruelly used. [131–132]

\# \#

And Judge Fell asked me to give him a relation of my persecution and I told him they could do not otherwise, they were in such a spirit; and they manifested their priests' fruits and profession and religion. So he told his wife that I made nothing of it and spoke as a man that had not been concerned; for the Lord's power healed me again. [132]

\# \#

And after this I went to Lancaster with Judge Fell to the Sessions where John Sawrey aforesaid, and Justice Thompson had given forth a warrant to apprehend me.

So I appeared at the Sessions upon the hearing of it, but was never apprehended by it. And there I met Colonel West, another justice. [133]

\# \#

And Colonel West stood up who had long been weak, and blessed the Lord and said he never saw so many sober people and good faces together all the days of his life. He said that the Lord had healed him that day, for he had been sick, and he said, "George, if thou hast anything to say to the people, thou mayest freely declare it in the open Sessions." So I was moved of the Lord to speak, and as soon as I began, priest Marshall, their orator, goes his ways. And this I was moved to declare, that the Scriptures were given forth by the spirit of God and all people must first come to the spirit of God in themselves by which they might know God and Christ, of whom the prophets and the apostles learnt; and by the same spirit they might know the holy Scriptures and the spirit which was in them that gave them forth; so that spirit of God must be in them that come to know them again, but which spirit they might have fellowship with the Son and the Father and with the Scriptures and one with another, and without it they cannot know neither God, nor Christ, nor the Scriptures, nor have fellowship one with another. [136]

\# \#

Your teacher is within you; look not forth; it will teach you lying in bed, going abroad, to shun all occasion of sin and evil.

\#   \#

1653   And so after a while I visited many meetings in Lancashire, and so came back to Swarthmoor again.

And then James Milner and Richard Myers went out into imaginations. And a company followed them. And I was in a fast about ten days, my spirit being greatly exercised on Truth's account. And as Judge Fell and Colonel Benson were in Swarthmoor Hall talking of the news in the News Book, of Parliament, etc., I was moved to tell them that before that day fortnight the Long Parliament should be broken up and the Speaker plucked out of his chair. And that day fortnight Colonel Benson came again and was speaking to Judge Fell and said that now he saw that George was a true prophet; for Oliver had broken up the Parliament by that time.[12] And many openings I had of several things which would be too large to utter.   [147]

\#   \#

And great threatenings there were in Cumberland that if ever I came there they would take away my life; but when I heard of it I went into Cumberland to one Miles Wennington into the same parish but they had not power to touch me.

And also about this time Anthony Pearson, a great persecutor of Friends, was convinced at Appleby, over whose head they carried a sword when he went to the Bench. And coming over to Swarthmoor, I being at Colonel West's they sent for me and Colonel West said, "Go, George, for it may be of great service to the man"; and the Lord's power reached him.   [148]

\#   \#

So I called all people to the true teacher, out of the hirelings such as teach for the fleece and make a prey upon the people, for the Lord was come to teach his people himself by his spirit, and Christ saith, "Learn of me; I am the way" which doth enlighten every man that cometh into the world, that all through him might believe: and so to learn of him who had enlightened them, who was the Light.

[149–150]

\#   \#

---

12. The Long Parliament, which first met on November 3, 1640, was broken up on April 20, 1653.

GEORGE FOX

And I brought them all to the spirit of God in themselves, by which they might know God and Christ and the Scriptures and to have heavenly fellowship in the Spirit; now the everlasting Gospel was preached again that brought life and immortality to light, and the day of the Lord was come, and Christ was come to teach his people himself and how they might find their teacher within, when they were in their labours and in their beds.

The Lord had given me a spirit of discerning by which I many times saw the states and conditions of people, and would try their spirits.   [155]

\#   \#

And the next day we came through that country into Cumberland again where we had a general meeting of many thousands of people atop of a hill, near Langlands. Heavenly and glorious it was and the glory of the Lord did shine over all, and there were as many as one could well speak over, there was such a multitude. Their eyes were kept to Christ their teacher and they came to sit under their vine, that afterwards a Friend in the ministry, Francis Howgill, went amongst them, and when he was moved to stand up amongst them he saw they had no need of words for they was all sitting down under their teacher Christ Jesus; so he was moved to sit down again amongst them without speaking anything.

So great a convincement there was in Cumberland, Bishoprick, Northumberland, Yorkshire, Westmorland, and Lancashire, and the plants of God grew and flourished so by heavenly rain, and God's glory shined upon them, that many mouths the Lord opened to his praise, yea to babes and sucklings he ordained strength.   [168]

\#   \#

But at the first convincement, when Friends could not put off their hats to people nor say "you" to a particular, but "thee" and "thou"; and could not bow nor use the world's salutations, nor fashions, nor customs, many Friends, being tradesmen of several sorts lost their custom at the first; for the people would not trade with them nor trust them, and for a time Friends that were tradesmen could hardly get enough money to buy bread. But afterwards people came to see Friends' honesty and truthfulness and "yea" and "nay" at a word in their dealing, and their lives and conversations did preach and reach to the witness of God in all people, and they knew and saw

85

that for conscience sake towards God, they would not cozen and cheat them, and at last that they might send any child and be as well used as themselves, at any of their shops.

So then things altered so that all the enquiry was, where was a draper or shopkeeper or tailor or shoemaker or any other tradesman that was a Quaker; insomuch that Friends had double the trade, beyond any of their neighbours. And if there was any trading they had it, insomuch that then the cry of all the professors and others was "If we let these people alone they will take the trading of the nation out of our hands."   [169–170]

# #

1654 And so when the churches were settled in the north, the Lord had raised up many and sent forth many into his vineyard to preach his everlasting Gospel, as Francis Howgill and Edward Burrough to London, John Camm and John Audland to Bristol through the countries, Richard Hubberthorne and George Whitehead towards Norwich, and Thomas Holme into Wales, a matter of seventy ministers did the Lord raise up and send abroad out of the north countries.   [174]

# #

All Friends be low, and keep in the life of God to keep you low.   [176]

# #

And so after I had visited the churches in the north and all were settled under God's teaching, and the glory of the Lord shined over them, I passed from Swarthmoor to Lancaster, and so through many towns, and felt I answered the witness of God in all people, though I spoke not a word. So I left the north fresh and green under Christ their teacher. And I came up into Yorkshire.   [177]

# #

I was preserved in the everlasting Seed that never fell nor changes.   [178]

# #

1655 And after I went to Leicester, and from Leicester to Whetstone;[13] and before the meeting began there came a matter of seven-

---

13. Whetstone, about five miles from Leicester.

teen troopers of Colonel Hacker's[14] regiment with his marshall, and
they took me up before the meeting.

Colonel Hacker asked me again if I would go home and stay at
home; I told him if I should promise him so, that would manifest that
I was guilty of something, for to go home and make my home a
prison; and if I went to meetings they would say I brake their order;
but I told them I should go to meetings as the Lord ordered me, and
therefore could not submit to that, but said we were a peaceable
people.

"Well then," said Colonel Hacker, "I will send you tomorrow by
six o'clock to my Lord Protector by Captain Drury, one of his life-
guard."   [191–192]

# #

And when I was at London he left me at the Mermaid and went
and told Oliver Cromwell of me.

And I gave forth a paper and bid him carry it to Oliver, which is
here as followeth:

Dear Friend,

This is the word of the Lord God to thee. Live in the
wisdom of the life of God, that with it thou mayest be ordered
to his glory, and order his creatures to his glory. And be still
and silent from thy own wisdom, wit, craft, subtilty, or policy
that would arise in thee, but stand single to the Lord, without
any end to thyself. Then God will bless thee and prosper thee
in his ways; thou wilt feel his blessing in thy generation.

And with thy mind stayed upon the Lord, thou wilt be
kept in perfect peace, without any intent to thyself, to the
glory of God. And there wilt thou feel no want, nor never a
failing, nor forsaking, but the presence of the Lord God of life
with thee. For now the state of this present age is, that the
Lord is bringing his people into the life the Scriptures were
given forth from, in which life people shall come to have unity
with God, with Scriptures and one with another, for the
establishing righteousness, truth, and peace, in which is the
kingdom of God.

---

14. Colonel Francis Hacker (d. 1660) lived at Withcote Hall, near Oakham.

From a lover of thy soul and eternal good.
George Fox.   [194–195]

# #

And after a few days I was had before Oliver Cromwell by Captain Drury.

Upon the Fifth-day of the First-month Captain Drury who brought George Fox up to London by order from Colonel Hacker did come to the inn into the chamber where George Fox lay and said that it was required of George Fox from Oliver Cromwell that he would promise that he would not take up a sword against the Lord Protector or the Government as it is now; and that George Fox would write down the words in answer to that which the Protector required, and for George Fox to set his hand to it.

The Fifth-day of the First-month George Fox was moved of the Lord to give out these words following which were given to Oliver Cromwell. And George Fox was then presently brought before him by Captain Drury.

George Fox to Oliver Cromwell, *1654*.[15]

I, who am of the world called George Fox, do deny the carrying or drawing of any carnal sword against any, or against thee, Oliver Cromwell, or any man. In the presence of the Lord God I declare it.

God is my witness, by whom I am moved to give this forth for the Truth's sake, from him whom the world calls George Fox; who is the son of God who is sent to stand a witness against all violence and against all the works of darkness, and to turn people from the darkness to the light, and to bring them from the occasion of the war and from the occasion of the magistrate's sword, which is a terror to the evil doers who act contrary to the light of the Lord Jesus Christ, which is a praise to them that do well, a protection to them that do well and not evil. Such soldiers as are put in that place no false accusers must be, no violence must do, but be content with their wages; and the magistrate bears not the sword in vain.

From under the occasion of that sword I do seek to bring people. My weapons are not carnal but spiritual, and "my kingdom is not of this world," therefore with a carnal weapon I

---

15. 1655 (by modern calendar).

do not fight, but am from those things dead; from him who is not of the world, called of the world by the name George Fox. And this I am ready to seal with my blood. [197–198]

# #

From him who to all your souls is a friend, for establishing of righteousness and cleansing the land of evil doers and a witness against all wicked inventions of men and murderous plots, which answered shall be with the light in all your consciences, which makes no covenant with death, to which light in you all I speak, and am clear.

G.F.

who is of the world called George Fox, who a new name hath which the world knows not.

We are witnesses of this testimony, whose names in the flesh are called

Thomas Aldam
Robert Craven

He brought me in before him before he was dressed, and one Harvey[16] (that had come amongst Friends but was disobedient) waited upon him.

And so when I came before him[17] I was moved to say, "Peace be on this house"; and I bid him keep in the fear of God that he might receive wisdom, that by it he might be ordered, that with it he might order all things under his hand to God's glory. And I spake much to him of Truth, and a great deal of discourse I had with him about religion, wherein he carried himself very moderately; but he said we quarrelled with the priests, whom he called ministers. [198–199]

# #

And I told him the prophets, Christ, and the apostles declared freely; and they declared against them that did not declare freely; such as preached for filthy lucre and divined for money and preached for hire and were covetous and greedy like the dumb dogs that could never have enough; and such priests as did bear rule by their means

---

16. Charles Harvey, groom of the bed-chamber.
17. The meeting took place March 6, 1655.

and the people that loved to have it so. Now they that have the same spirit that Christ, and the prophets, and apostles had could not but declare against all such now as they did then. And several times he said it was very good, and truth, and I told him that all Christendom so called had the Scriptures but they wanted the power and spirit that they had that gave them forth; and therefore they were not in fellowship with the Son, nor with the Father, nor with the Scriptures, nor one with another.

And many more words I had with him. And many people began to come in, that I drew a little backward, and as I was turning he catched me by the hand and said these words with tears in his eyes, "Come again to my house; for if thou and I were but an hour in a day together we should be nearer one to the other," and that he wished me no more ill than he did to his own soul. And I told him if he did he wronged his own soul; and so I bid him hearken to and hear God's voice that he might stand in his counsel and obey it; if he did so, that would keep him from hardness of heart, and if he did not hear God's voice his heart would be hardened. And he said it was true. So I went out, and he bid me come again. And then Captain Drury came out after me and told me his Lord Protector said I was at liberty and might go whither I would, "And," says he, "my Lord says you are not a fool," and said he never saw such a paper in his life as I had sent him before by him. Then I was brought into a great hall, where the Protector's gentlemen were to dine; and I asked them what they did bring me thither for. They said, it was by the Protector's order, that I might dine with them. I bid them let the Protector know I would not eat a bit of his bread, nor drink a sup of his drink. When he heard this, he said that there was a people risen, meaning us, that he could not win either with honour, high places, nor gifts, but all other people he could. For we did not seek any of their places, gifts, nor honours, but their salvation and eternal good, both in this nation and elsewhere. But it was told him again that we had forsook our own, and were not like to look for such things from him.   [200]

# #

The Lord's power went over the nation insomuch that many Friends were moved to go into most parts up and down the nation about this time, and into Scotland to sound forth the everlasting Gospel; and the glory of the Lord was set over all to his everlasting praise.

And a great convincement there was in London, and many in Oliver Protector's house and family.[18]

And I went to see him again but could not get to him, the officers began to be so rude.   [202]

And sometimes they would turn up my coat and see for my leather breeches and then they would be in a rage.   [202]

# #

Truth hath been talked of, but now it is possessed. Christ hath been talked of, but now he is come and is possessed.   [204]

# #

What a world is this: ... they have lost the hidden man of the heart, and the meek and quiet spirit, which is of the Lord, of great price.   [205]

# #

So the hearts of the people were opened by the spirit of God and they were turned from the hirelings to Christ Jesus their shepherd who had purchased them without money and would feed them without money or price. And Nicholas Beard and many others were convinced that day, that came to hear the dispute. And so the Lord's power came over all and his day many came to see. And abundance of Ranters and professors there were that had been so loose in their lives that they began to be weary of it and had thought to have gone into Scotland to have lived privately, and the Lord's Truth catched them all and their understandings were opened by his light, spirit, and power, through which they came to be settled upon the Lord; and so became very good Friends in the Truth and became very sober men, that great blessing and praising the Lord there was amongst them, and admiration in the country.   [211–212]

# #

And after this I passed to Cambridge that evening, and when I came into the town it was all in an uproar, hearing of my coming, and the scholars were up, and were exceeding rude. But I kept on my horse-back and rid through them in the Lord's power. "Oh!" said

---

18. Charles Harvey (for a time), Mary Saunders, Lettice Shane, and Theopholis Green are known to have been Quakers.

they, "he shines, he glisters" but they unhorsed Captain Amor Stoddard before he could get to the inn; and when we were in the inn they were exceeding rude in the inn, and in the courts and in the streets. The miners, and colliers, and cartmen could never be ruder.

And there John Crook met us at the inn. And the people of the house asked me what I would have for supper, as is the usual way of inns. "Supper," said I, "were it not that the Lord's power was over these rude scholars it looked as if they would make a supper of us and pluck us to pieces"; for they knew I was so against their trade, which they were there as apprentices to learn, the trade of preaching, that they raged as bad as ever Diana's craftsmen did against Paul.

[218–219]

# #

And this year came out the Oath of Abjuration from Oliver Protector,[19] by which many Friends suffered. And several Friends went to speak with him but he began to harden. And sufferings increasing upon Friends by reason that envious magistrates made use of that oath as a snare to catch Friends in, who they knew could not swear at all.   [220]

# #

God kept Friends over the rage of people; and great spoiling of goods there was upon Friends for tithes by the Independent and Presbyterian priests and some Baptist priests that had gotten into steeplehouses, as the books of sufferings will declare. So I went into Leicestershire where Colonel Hacker said if I came down there he would imprison me again, though Oliver Protector had set me at liberty; but I came down to Whetstone where his troopers had taken me before; and Colonel Hacker's wife and his marshall came to the meeting and were convinced. And the glorious, powerful day of the Lord was set over all, and many were convinced that day at that meeting, where were two Justices of Peace, Peter Price and Walter Jenkins, that came out of Wales, that were convinced and came to be ministers of Christ.   [222]

---

19. On April 26, 1655, a Proclamation required persons suspected to be Roman Catholics to take an oath abjuring papal authority and doctrine, upon pain of imprisonment and forfeiture of estate. This occurred at the time of Fox's visit to London.

GEORGE FOX

#　#

And they told me there were some Baptists and a Baptist woman sick, and John Rush went along to visit her. And when we came there were a-many people in the house that were tender about her; and they told me she was not a woman for this world, and if I had anything to comfort her concerning the world to come I might speak to her. So I was moved of the Lord God to speak to her and the Lord raised her up that she was well, to the astonishment of the town and country. Her husband's name was Baldock. And so we went to our inn again, and there were two desperate fellows fighting so that none durst come nigh them to part them, but I was moved in the Lord's power to go to them, and when I had loosed their hands, I held one by one hand and the other by the other hand; and I showed them the evil of their doings, and convinced them, and reconciled them each to other that they were loving and very thankful, so that people admired at it.   [228–229]

#　#

After awhile I went out of the city and left James Nayler behind me in London. And as I parted from him I cast my eyes upon him, and a fear struck in me concerning him.   [229–230]

#　#

1656　And from thence we passed into Cornwall, a dark country, through many desperate services and great opposition, but through the power of the Lord we came over all.   [235]

#　#

About this time I was moved to give forth the following exhortation to Friends in the ministry: [262]

#　#

Be patterns, be examples in all countries, places, islands, nations, wherever you come; that your carriage and life may preach among all sorts of people, and to them. Then you will come to walk cheerfully over the world, answering that of God in every one; whereby in them ye may be a blessing, and make the witness of God in them to bless you. Then to the Lord God you will be a sweet savour and a blessing.   [263]

\#   \#

And when I was in prison in Cornwall there was a Friend went to Oliver Cromwell and offered his body to him for to go to lie in Doomsdale prison for me or in my stead, that he would take him and let me go at liberty, and it so struck him and came over him that he said to his great men and his Council, "Which of you would do so much for me if I was in the same condition?"   [264–265]

\#   \#

And from Launceston we came through the countries to Exeter, where many Friends were in prison, and amongst the rest James Nayler, for a little before the time we were set at liberty, James ran out into imaginations, and a company with him; and they raised up a great darkness in the nation.   [268]

\#   \#

That night that we came to Exeter, I spoke with James Nayler, for I saw he was out and wrong and so was his company.

Shortly after Fox's unhappy visit with Nayler in which Fox sensed that he "ran out into imaginations and a company with him," Nayler was released from Exeter prison and travelled to Bristol. The 1656 Nayler incident in Bristol, although ever so sketchily dealt with in Fox's Journal, was a major crisis both for the young and vulnerable Society of Friends and for Fox as its guide. Urged on by a number of adoring women followers, James Nayler had ridden into Bristol with his companions singing "Holy, Holy, Holy, Lord God of Israel" and flinging their cloaks in the mire for his horse to walk on, symbolizing the coming of Christ into Jerusalem. Nayler was arrested together with his companions and while the companions were later released, Nayler was kept in prison and charged with blasphemy. When tried, he staunchly denied "James Nayler to be Christ but said that Christ was in him." After a long trial in Parliament itself, Nayler was found to be guilty of blasphemy. His cruel punishment included two public whippings across the city of London with over 300 whip strokes each, and having his tongue bored through with a hot iron and his forehead branded with a B.

GEORGE FOX

Next to George Fox, James Nayler had been, perhaps, the most effective voice in sharing the Quaker message and this incident was a hard blow to the credibility of the Quaker witness. It confirmed the accusations of instability and illuminist fanaticism of which the enemies of the swiftly spreading Quaker movement had long accused it. In the course of Nayler's punishment, which he bore with the bravest of courage, he repented utterly and publicly of this incident and its effect in blunting the witness to his experience of Christ within, that he had given years of his life to proclaim.

George Fox had further distanced himself from James Nayler in the pain of this happening. The word of the London Yearly Meeting's Christian Faith and Practice on the outcome of this incident can scarcely be improved upon. "Having publicly abjured his follies in several statements, he sought to be reconciled with Fox who was lying ill and exhausted in Reading." Rebuffed, Nayler wrote to Margaret Fell: "My spirit was quieted in that simplicity in which I went, in that to return . . . and so His will is our peace." William Dewsbury was at least instrumental in bringing about a reconciliation between Nayler and Fox and Nayler resumed his Quaker service, "living in great self-denial and very jealous of himself."

Out of this brokenness came such a sense of God's forgiveness and of humility and tenderness that the closing years of his life have touched Friends to the core. Once again, the above source tells of the final scene of his life and quotes a saying of Nayler's that is especially precious to Friends and that follows this statement: "In 1660 he set out on foot for the North, intending to go home to his wife and children. He was seen by a friend of Hertford, sitting by the wayside in meditation; and passed on through Huntingdon, where another friend saw him in such an awful frame as if he had been redeemed from the earth and a stranger on it, seeking a better country and inheritance. Some miles beyond Huntingdon, he was robbed and bound, and found towards evening in a field. He was taken to a Friend's house near King's Ripton, and passed away in the peace of God towards the end of October, 1660."

James Nayler's last words, spoken about two hours before his departure out of this life were:

There is a spirit which I feel that delights to do no evil, nor to revenge any wrong, but delights to endure all things, in hope to enjoy its own in the end. Its hope is to outlive all wrath and contention, and to weary out all exaltation and cruelty, or whatever is of a nature contrary to itself. It sees to the end of all temptations. As it bears no evil in itself, so it conceives none in thoughts to any other. If it be betrayed, it bears it, for its ground and spring is the mercies and forgiveness of God. Its crown is meekness, its life is everlasting love unfeigned; it takes its kingdom with entreaty and not with contention, and keeps it by lowliness of mind. In God alone it can rejoice, though none else regard it, or can own its life. It is conceived in sorrow, and brought forth without any to pity it, nor doth it murmur at grief and oppression. It never rejoiceth but through sufferings; for with the world's joy it is murdered. I found it alone, being forsaken. I have fellowship therein with them who lived in dens and desolate places in the earth, who through death obtained this resurrection and eternal holy life.[20]

A ND FROM THENCE (Exeter) we came to Bristol the Seventh-day night, to Edward Pyott's house, and it was noised over the town that I was come; and I had never been there before. And on the First-day morning I went to the meeting in Broadmead, and a great meeting there was, and quiet. And in the afternoon notice was given of a meeting to be in the orchard.   [269–270]

#   #

And so for many hours did I declare the word of life amongst them in the eternal power of God that by him they might come up into the beginning and be reconciled to God. And I showed them the types and figures and shadows of Christ in the time of the law, and showed them how that Christ was come that ended the types and shadows, and tithes and oaths, and denied swearing and set up "yea" and "nay" instead of it, and a free teaching. And now he was come to teach people himself, and how that his heavenly day was springing

---

20. See also Kenneth Boulding, *The Nayler Sonnets*, reprinted from *Inward Light*, 1944.

from on high. And I was moved to pray in the mighty power of the Lord and the Lord's power came over all. [271]

\# \#

And from thence we passed to London, and when we came near Hyde Park we saw a great clutter of people. And we espied Oliver Protector coming in his coach, and I rid up to his coach-side. But some of his life-guard would have put me away, but he forbade them. So I rid down by his coach-side with him declaring what the Lord gave me to say unto him of his condition, and of the sufferings of Friends in the nation, and how contrary this persecution was to Christ and to the apostles and Christianity. And I rid by his coach till we came to [St.] James Park gate, and he desired me to come to his house.

And the next day one of Oliver's wife's maids, Mary Saunders, came up to me to my lodgings and said that her master came to her and said he could tell her some good news. And she asked him what it was, if it were good that was well. And he said unto her George Fox was come to town: and she said that was good news indeed but could hardly believe it: but he told her how I met him and rid from Hyde Park down to James Park with him.

So the Lord's power came over all; and Friends were glad and the Lord had the glory and the praise.

And so Edward Pyott and I went to Whitehall after a time and when we came before him there was one Dr. John Owen, Vice-Chancellor of Oxford, with him; so we were moved to speak to Oliver Cromwell concerning the sufferings of Friends and laid them before him and turned him to the light of Christ who had enlightened every man that cometh into the world: and he said it was a natural light, and we showed him the contrary, and how it was divine and spiritual from Christ the spiritual and heavenly man, which was called the life in Christ, the Word and the light in us. And the power of the Lord God riz in me, and I was moved to bid him lay down his crown at the feet of Jesus. [274–275]

\# \#

And in this year 1656 the Lord's Truth was finely planted over this nation and many thousands were turned to the Lord; and seldom under a thousand in prison in the nation for tithes and going to the steeplehouses, and for contempts and not swearing and not putting off their hats. And Oliver Protector began to harden and several Friends were turned out of their offices of justices and other offices.   [280]

# #

1657   And so I visited the meetings up and down in London; and some of them were troubled with rude people and apostates that had run out with James Nayler. And I was moved to write to Oliver Cromwell, and laid before him the sufferings of Friends in the nation and in Ireland.

And I was moved again to go and speak to Oliver Protector when there was a talk of making him King. And I met him in the Park and told him that they that would put on him an earthly crown would take away his life.

And he asked me, "What say you?"

And I said again, they that sought to put him on a crown would take away his life, and bid him mind the crown that was immortal.

And he thanked me after I had warned him of many dangers and how he would bring a shame and a ruin upon himself and his posterity, and bid me go to his house. And then I was moved to write to him and told him how he would ruin his family and posterity and bring darkness upon the nation if he did so. And several papers I was moved to write to him.   [289]

# #

I had for some time felt drawings in my spirit to go into Scotland.   [315]

# #

After some time we came to John Crook's house where a General Yearly Meeting for the whole nation was appointed to be held. This meeting lasted three days, and many Friends from most parts of the nation came to it, so that the inns and towns around were filled, for a matter of three or four thousand people were at it. And although there was some disturbance by some rude people that had run out from Truth, yet the Lord's power came over all, and a glorious meeting it was. The everlasting Gospel was preached, and many received it, which brought life and immortality to light in them, and shined over all.

Then I was moved by the power and spirit of the Lord, to open unto them the promise of God, how that it was made to the Seed, not to seeds, as many, but to one, which Seed was Christ; and that all people, both males and females, should feel this Seed in them, which was heir of the promise; that so they might all witness Christ in them, the hope of glory, the mystery which had been hid from ages and generations, which was revealed to the apostles, and is revealed again now, after this long night of apostacy.   [339]

#   #

About this time she, they called the Lady Claypole,[21] was very sick and troubled in mind, and nothing could comfort her. And I was moved of the Lord to write a paper and send it to her to be read unto her.

Friend,

Be still and cool in thy own mind and spirit from thy own thoughts, and then thou wilt feel the principle of God to turn thy mind to the Lord God, whereby thou wilt receive his strength and power from whence life comes, to allay all tempests, against blusterings and storms. That is it which moulds up into patience, into innocency, into soberness, into stillness, into stayedness, into quietness, up to God, with his power.   [346]

#   #

Therefore be still a while from thy own thoughts, searching, seeking, desires and imaginations, and be stayed in the principle of God in thee, to stay thy mind upon God, up to God; and thou wilt find strength from him and find him to be a present help in time of trouble, in need, and to be a God at hand. And it will keep thee humble being come to the principle of God, which hath been transgressed; which humble, God will teach in his way, which is peace; and such he doth exalt. And now as the principle of God in thee hath been transgressed, come to it, to keep thy mind down low, up to the Lord God; and deny thyself. And from thy own will, that is, the earthly, thou must be kept. Then thou wilt feel the power of God, that will bring nature into his course, and to see the glory of the

---

21. Elizabeth Cromwell (1629–1658), second daughter of the Protector.

first body. And there the wisdom of God will be received, which is Christ, by which all things were made and created, in wisdom to be preserved and ordered to God's glory. There thou wilt come to receive and feel the physician of value, which clothes people in their right mind, whereby they may serve God and do his will. [346–347]

#   #

Looking down at sin, and corruption, and distraction, you are swallowed up in it; but looking at the light that discovers them, you will see over them. That will give victory; and you will find grace and strength; and there is the first step of peace. That will bring salvation; and see to the beginning and the glory that was with the Father before the world began; and so come to know the Seed of God which is heir of the promise of God, and the world which hath no end; unto the power of an endless life, which power of God is immortal, which brings up the soul, which is immortal, up to the immortal God, in whom it doth rejoice. So in the name and power of the Lord Jesus Christ, strengthen thee.

G.F.

And she said it settled and stayed her mind for the present. And many Friends got copies of it, both in England and Ireland, to read it to distracted people; and it settled several of their minds, and they did great service with it both in England and Ireland. [349]

#   #

And many Friends being in prisons at this time, a matter of two hundred were moved to go to the Parliament to offer up themselves to lie in the same dungeons where their friends lay, that they that were in prison might go forth and not perish in the stinking dungeons and gaols. And this we did in love to God and our brethren that they might not die in prison, and in love to them that cast them in, that they might not bring innocent blood upon their own heads which would cry to the Lord, and bring his wrath and vengeance and plagues upon them.

And then the Parliaments would be in a rage and sometimes send them word that they would whip them and send them home again;

and many times soon after the Lord would turn them out and send them home, who had not power to do good in their day. And when the Long Parliament sat I was moved to send several papers to them and speak to them how the Lord was bringing a day of darkness upon them all that should be felt. [349]

\# \#

One time, as I was going into the country, and two Friends with me, when I was gone a little above a mile out of the city, there met me two troopers who took me and the Friends that were with me prisoners and brought us to the Mews and there kept us. They were Colonel Hacker's men, but the Lord's power was so over them that they did not take us before any officers, but shortly after set us at liberty again.

And the same day, I took boat and went to Kingston, and from thence I went afterwards to Hampton Court, to speak with the Protector about the sufferings of Friends. I met him riding into Hampton-Court Park, and before I came at him he was riding in the head of his life-guard, I saw and felt a waft of death go forth against him, and he looked like a dead man. When I had spoken to him of the suffering of Friends and warned him as I was moved to speak to him, he bid me come to his house. So I went to Kingston, and the next day went up to Hampton Court. But when I came, he was very sick, and Harvey told me, who was one of his men that waited on him, that the doctors were not willing I should come in to speak with him. So I passed away, and never saw him no more.

From Kingston I went to Isaac Penington's, in Buckinghamshire, where I had appointed a meeting, and the Lord's truth and power came over all.

And after I had visited Friends in London and in the country thereaways I went into Essex. And there I had not been long before I heard Oliver Protector was dead. And then I came up to London again when Richard, his son, was made Protector. [350]

\# \#

And there was great persecution about seven miles off London. The rude people usually came out of several parishes so that they beat, abused, and bruised Friends exceedingly. And one day they beat and abused about eighty Friends that went out of London to a

101

meeting, and tore their coats and cloaks off their backs and threw them into ditches and ponds, and all moiled them with dirt.   [352]

\#   \#

And great sufferings I had about this time; and great confusion and distraction there was amongst the powers and people.

And after a while I passed to Reading, and was under great sufferings and exercises, and in a great travail in my spirit for ten weeks' time. For I saw how the powers were plucking each other to pieces. And I saw how many men were destroying the simplicity and betraying the Truth. And a great deal of hypocrisy, deceit, and strife was got uppermost in people, that they were ready to sheath their swords in one another's bowels.   [353-354]

\#   \#

And this time, towards 1659, the powers had hardened themselves, persecuting Friends, and had many of them in prison, and were crucifying the Seed, Christ, both in themselves and others. And at last they fell a-biting and devouring one another until they were consumed one of another; who had turned against and judged that which God had wrought in them and showed them. So, God overthrew them, and turned them upside down, and brought the King over them, who were always complaining that the Quakers met together to bring in King Charles, whereas Friends did not concern themselves with the outward powers.   [354]

\#   \#

So when I had travailed with the witness of God which they had quenched, and I had gotten through with it and over all that hypocrisy, and saw how that would be turned under and down, and that life would rise over it, I came to have ease, and the light, power, and spirit shined over all. And in this day many of our old envious persecutors were in great confusion.

I had a sight and sense of the King's return a good while before, and so had some others. For I several times writ to Oliver Cromwell and told him, while he was persecuting God's people, those he looked upon as his enemies were preparing to come upon him. Several rash spirits would have bought Somerset House that we might have meetings in it, but I was moved of the Lord to forbid them so to do, for I did foresee the King's coming in again at that time. [355]

\# \#

1660 And great fears and troubles were in many people and a looking for the King Charles II coming in, and that all things should be altered; but I told them the Lord's power and light was over all and shined over all, and that the fear would only take hold of the hypocrites and such as had not been faithful to God, our persecutors. For in my travail and sufferings at Reading when people were at a stand and could not tell what might come in nor who might rule, I told them the Lord's power was over all, for I had travailed through it, and his day shined, whosoever should come in; and all would be well whether the King came in or no, to them that loved God and were faithful to him; and so I bid all Friends to fear none but the Lord, and keep in his power which is over all. [362–363]

\# \#

And I had a General Meeting at Edward Pyott's near Bristol where there were many thousands of people, for beside Friends from many parts thereabouts some of the Baptist and Independent teachers came to it and all was quiet, for most of the sober people came out of Bristol to it. And the people that stayed in the city said the city looked naked, the sober people were so gone forth to this meeting. And the Lord's everlasting Seed, Christ Jesus, was set over all that day. [366–367]

\# \#

And at this meeting some Friends did come out of most parts of the nation, for it was about business of the church both in this nation and beyond the seas. For when I was in the north, several years before, I was moved to set up that meeting, for many Friends suffered and their goods were spoiled wrongfully, contrary to the law. And so several Friends that had been justices and magistrates and that did understand the law came there and were able to inform Friends, and to gather up the sufferings that they might be laid before the justices and judges.

And justices and captains had come to break up this meeting, but when they saw Friends' books and accounts of collections concerning the poor, how that we did take care one county to help another, and to provide for our poor that none of them should be chargeable to their parishes, etc., and took care to help Friends beyond the seas, the justices and officers were made to confess that we did their work and Friends desired them to come and sit with them then. [373]

# #

And then they began to imprison and persecute Friends because that we would not give them tithes, and many thousands of our Friends in their days suffered imprisonments. And many thousand pounds worth of goods were taken away from them, so that they made many widows and fatherless, for many died in prison that they had caused to be cast into prison. [392]

# #

1661   Though Oliver Cromwell at Dunbar fight had promised to the Lord that if he gave him the victory over his enemies he would take away tithes or else let him be rolled into his grave with infamy, when the Lord had given his victory and he came to be chief, he confirmed the former laws that if people did not set forth their tithes they should pay treble, and this to be executed by two justices of peace in the country upon the oath of two witnesses. [394]

# #

There were about seven hundred Friends in prison in the nation, upon contempts to Oliver's and Richard's government; and when the King came in he set them all at liberty. It was said there was something drawn up that we should have our liberty, only it wanted signing. And then the Fifth-Monarchy people rose and a matter of thirty of them made an insurrection in London.[22] On the First-day there were glorious meetings and the Lord's truth shined over all and his power was set over all. And at midnight, soon after, the drums beat and they cried, "Arms, arms!" which caused the trained bands and soldiers to arise, both in the city and country.

And I got up out of bed, and in the morning took boat and came down to Whitehall stairs and went through Whitehall; and they looked strangely upon me; and I went to the Pall Mall. And all the city and suburbs were up in arms and exceeding rude; all people were

---

22. Begun Sunday night, January 6–7, 1661, ended January 9.

against us and they cried, "There is a Quaker's house, pluck it down."
And divers Friends came thither to me; and as a Friend, one Henry
Fell, was going to a General Meeting at Major Beard's, the soldiers
knocked him down and he had been killed if the Duke of York had
not come by. And all the prisons were soon after filled with Friends
and many died in prison, they being so thronged up. And many inns
were full, both in cities, towns, and country; and it was hard for any
sober people to stir for several weeks' time.   [394–395]

# #

Margaret Fell went to the King and told him what work there
was in the city and nation and showed him that we were a peaceable
innocent people and that we must keep our meetings as we used to do
and that it concerned him to see that peace was kept, that so no blood
might be shed.

And all the posts were laid open to search all letters, so that none
could pass; but we heard of several thousands of our Friends that
were cast into prison, and Margart Fell carried the account to the
King and Council. And the third day after we had an account of
several thousands more that were cast into prison, and she went and
laid them also before the King and his Council; and they wondered
how we could have such intelligence, seeing they had given such
strict charge for the intercepting all letters; but the Lord did so order
it that we had an account as aforesaid, notwithstanding all their
stoppings. And then we drew up another declaration and got it
printed, and sent some of them to the King and Council. And they
were sold up and down the streets and at the Exchange, which
declaration is as followeth:

This Declaration was given unto the King upon the 21st day
of the 11th Month, *1660* [January 1661].

*A Declaration from the harmless and innocent people of God,
called Quakers, against all plotters and fighters in the world,* for
the removing the ground of jealousy and suspicion from
both magistrates and people in the kingdom, concerning
wars and fightings. And also something in answer to that
clause of the King's late Proclamation which mentions the
Quakers, to clear them from the [5th Monarchy] plot and the
fighting which therein is mentioned, and for the clearing
their innocency.

QUAKER SPIRITUALITY

Our principle is, and our practices have always been, to seek peace and ensue it and to follow after righteousness and the knowledge of God, seeking the good and welfare and doing that which tends to the peace of all. We know that wars and fightings proceed from the lusts of men (as Jas iv. 1–3), out of which lusts and the Lord hath redeemed us, and so out of the occasion of war. The occasion of which war, and war itself (wherein envious men, who are lovers of themselves more than lovers of God, lust, kill, and desire to have men's lives and estates) ariseth from the lust. All bloody principles and practices, we, as to our own particulars, do utterly deny, with all outward wars and strife and fightings with outward weapons, for any end or under any pretence whatsoever. And this is our testimony to the whole world. [398–399]

# #

That the spirit of Christ, by which we are guided, is not changeable, so as once to command us from a thing as evil and again to move unto it; and we do certainly know, and so testify to the world, that the spirit of Christ, which leads us into all Truth, will never move us to fight and war against any man with outward weapons, neither for the kingdom of Christ, nor for the kingdoms of this world. [399–400]

# #

For this we can say to the whole world, we have wronged no man's person or possessions, we have used no force nor violence against any man, we have been found in no plots, nor guilty of sedition. When we have been wronged, we have not sought to revenge ourselves, we have not made resistance against authority, but wherein we could not obey for conscience' sake, we have suffered even the most of any people in the nation. We have been accounted as sheep for the slaughter, persecuted and despised, beaten, stoned, wounded, stocked, whipped, imprisoned, haled out of synagogues, cast into dungeons and noisome vaults where many have died in bonds, shut up from our friends, denied

needful sustenance for many days together, with other the
like cruelties. [401]

\# \#

And this is both our principle and practice, and hath been from
the beginning, so that if we suffer, as suspected to take up arms or
make war against any, it is without any ground from us; for it neither
is, nor ever was in our hearts, since we owned the Truth of God;
neither shall we ever do it, because it is contrary to the spirit of
Christ, his doctrine, and the practice of his apostles, even contrary to
him for whom we suffer all things, and endure all things.

And whereas men come against us with clubs, staves, drawn
swords, pistols cocked, and do beat, cut and abuse us, yet we never
resisted them, but to them our hair, backs, and cheeks have been
ready. It is not an honour to manhood nor to nobility to run upon
harmless people who lift not up a hand against them, with arms and
weapons. [401–402]

\# \#

And there was a great darkness both in the city and country; but
this declaration of ours cleared the air and laid the darkness, and the
King gave forth after this a little proclamation that no soldiers should
go to search any house but with a constable.

And at the execution of these Monarchy Men they cleared us
from having any hand in their plot.

And after the light had shined over all, though many thousands
were imprisoned up and down the nation, all gaols being full, the
King gave forth after this a declaration that Friends should be set at
liberty without paying fees. And so the Truth, with great labour,
travail, and care, came over all, for Margaret [Fell] and Thomas
Moore went often to the King and he was tender towards them.

[404]

\# \#

Friends, your sufferings, all that are or have been of late in
prison, I would have you send up an account of them, how things are
amongst you, which is to be delivered unto the King and his Council;
for things are pretty well here after the storm. [405]

QUAKER SPIRITUALITY

\#   \#

Oh, the daily reproaches and beatings in highways because we would not put off our hats, and for saying "thou" to people; and the priests spoiling our goods because we could not put into their mouths and give them tithes, besides casting in prison as the records and books of sufferings testify, and besides the great fines in courts for not swearing. But with them for all these things the Lord God did plead. [406]

\#   \#

And I was moved to write to those justices and to tell them did we ever resist them when they took our ploughs and plough-gear, our cows and horses, our corn and cattle, and kettles and platters from us, and whipped us, and set us in the stocks, and cast us in prison, and all this for serving and worshiping of God in spirit and truth and because we could not conform to their religions, manners, customs, and fashions. Did we ever resist them? Did we not give them our backs and our cheeks and our faces to spit on, and our hair to pluck at? [406–407]

\#   \#

And before this time we received account from New England that they had made a law to banish the Quakers out of their colonies, upon pain of death in case they returned; and that several Friends, so banished, returning were taken and hanged,[23] and that divers more were in prison, in danger of the like sentence. And when they were put to death, as I was in prison at Lancaster, I had a perfect sense of it, as though it had been myself, and as though the halter had been put about my neck.

But as soon as we heard of it, Edward Burrough went to the King, and told him there was a vein of innocent blood opened in his dominions, which, if it were not stopped, would overrun all. To which the King answered, "But I will stop that vein." Edward Burrough said, "Then do it speedily, for we do not know how many may soon be put to death." The King answered, "As speedily as ye

---

23. William Robinson and Marmaduke Stevenson were put to death at Boston, October 27, 1659; Mary Dyer on June 1, 1660; William Leddra on March 14, 1661.

will. Call," said he to some present, "the secretary, and I will do it presently." The secretary being called, a mandamus was forthwith granted. A day or two after, Edward Burrough going again to the King, to desire the matter might be expedited, the King said he had no occasion at present to send a ship thither, but if we would send one, we might do it as soon as we would. Edward Burrough then asked the King if it would please him to grant his deputation to one called a Quaker, to carry the mandamus to New England. He said, "Yes, to whom ye will." Whereupon Edward Burrough named one Samuel Shattuck (as I remember) who, being an inhabitant of New England, was banished by their law to be hanged if he came again; and to him the deputation was granted. Then we sent for one Ralph Goldsmith, an honest Friend, who was master of a good ship, and agreed with him for £300, goods or no goods, to sail in ten days. He forthwith prepared to set sail, and with a prosperous gale, in about six weeks time arrived before the town of Boston in New England upon a First-day morning, called Sunday. With him went many passengers, both of New and Old England, that were Friends whom the Lord did move to go to bear their testimony against those bloody persecutors, who had exceeded all the world in that age in their persecutions.

The townsmen at Boston, seeing a ship come into the bay with English colours, soon came on board, and asked for the captain. Ralph Goldsmith told them he was the commander. They asked him if he had any letters. He said, "Yes." They asked if he would deliver them. He said, "No, not to-day." So they went a-shore and reported there was a ship full of Quakers, and that Samuel Shattuck was among them, who they knew was, by their law, to be put to death for coming again after banishment; but they knew not his errand, nor his authority.

So all being kept close that day, and none of the ship's company suffered to land, next morning, Samuel Shattuck, the King's deputy, and Ralph Goldsmith, the commander of the vessel, went on shore; and sending back to the ship the men that landed them, they two went through the town to the governor John Endicott's door, and knocked. He sent out a man to know their business. They sent him word their business was from the King of England, and they would deliver their message to none but the governor himself. Thereupon they were admitted to go in, and the governor came to them, and having received the deputation and the mandamus, he laid off his hat,[24] and looked upon them. Then going out, he bid the Friends follow him. So he went to the deputy-governor, and after a short consultation, came out to the Friends, and said, "We shall obey his Majesty's commands," as by the order may be seen, and the relation in William Coddington's book, who is governor of Rhode Island and a Friend. After this, the master gave liberty to the passengers to come on shore, and presently the noise of the business flew about the town, and the Friends of the town and the passengers of the ship met together to offer up their praises and thanksgivings to God, who had so wonderfully delivered them from the teeth of the devourer. While they were thus met, in came a poor Friend who, being sentenced by their bloody law to die, had lain some time in irons, expecting execution. This added to their joy, and caused them to lift up their hearts in high praises to God, who is worthy for ever to have the praise, the glory, and the honour; for he only is able to deliver, and to save, and to support all that sincerely put their trust in him.

[411–413]

\# \#

1662 Now there being very many Friends in prison in the nation, Richard Hubberthorne and I drew up a paper concerning them, and got it delivered to the King, that he might understand how we were dealt with by his officers.

\# \#

1663
[*After word of Edward Burrough's death in prison, George Fox*] wrote the following lines for the staying and settling of Friends' minds;

Friends,
Be still and wait in your own conditions, and settled in the Seed of God that doth not change, that in that ye may feel dear Edward Burrough among you in the Seed, in which and by which he begat you to God, with whom he is; and that in the Seed ye may all see and feel him, in the which is unity in the

---

24. I.e., before the King's representative.

life with him. And so enjoy him in the life that doth not change, but which is invisible.

G.F.   [437]

\#   \#

1664   And after the meeting was done I came over the Sands to Swarthmoor.   [456]

\#   \#

And the next day a lieutenant of a foot company came with his sword and pistol to take me, and I told him I knew his message and errand the night before, and so had given up myself to be taken; for if I would have escaped their imprisonment I might have been forty miles off before they came; but I was an innocent man and so mattered not what they could do unto me.   [457]

\#   \#

And so I was kept in prison until the Assizes.

And when they and the jury were sworn, the judge asked me whether I had refused the oath, the last Assizes.

And I said that I never took oath in my life, and Christ the saviour and judge of the world saith, "Swear not at all."   [474]

\#   \#

The judge said you refused it [the oath] at the Assizes and I can tender the oath to any man now and praemunire[25] him for not taking it, and he said they might bring me in guilty, I denying the oath.   [475]

\#   \#

He spoke to the jury, and the jury brought in for the King, "Guilty."   [476]

\#   \#

So presently they set me aside, and Margaret Fell was called, who had a great deal of good service among them. Many more words

---

25. Forfeiture of property.

were spoken concerning the Truth. And so the court broke up near the second hour.

And in the afternoon we were brought up to have our sentence passed upon us. And Margaret Fell desired that judgment and sentence might be deferred till the next morning.　　　　　　[476]

\#　\#

Then the judge bid the gaoler take me away, and I was had away to my chamber and they passed away from the court. And the Truth and power of the Lord God was glorious over all. And many spirits were crossed grievously in their envy and malice. And Margaret Fell they praemunired, and he passed sentence upon her.　　　　[484]

\#　\#

1665　　And so they committed me again to close prison. And Colonel Kirby gave order to the gaoler that no flesh alive must come at me for I was not fit to be discoursed with by men.

So I was put up in a smoky tower where the smoke of the other rooms came up and stood as a dew upon the walls, where it rained in also upon my bed and the smoke was so thick as I could hardly see a candle sometimes, and many times I was locked under three locks; and the under-gaoler would hardly come up to unlock one of the upper doors; the smoke was so thick that I was almost smothered with smoke and so starved with cold and rain that my body was almost numbed, and my body swelled with the cold.

And many times when I went to stop out the rain off me in the cold winter season, my shift would be as wet as muck with rain that came in upon me. And as fast as I stopped it the wind, being high and fierce, would blow it out again; and in this manner did I lie all that long cold winter till the next Assizes.　　　　　　[484–485]

\#　\#

And often they threatened to hang me over the wall and the officers often in their rage would bid the soldiers shoot me and run me through, and the deputy governor said that the King, knowing I had a great interest in the people, had sent me thither, that if any stir was in the nation they might hang me over the walls to keep the people down.　　　　　　[494]

GEORGE FOX

\# \#

1666 But at last the governor came under some trouble having sent out a privateer who had taken some ships that were not enemies' ships but their friends and so came under trouble, after which he grew somewhat more friendly to me.

And I desired him when he came to London, he being a Parliament man, that he would speak to Esquire Marsh and to Sir Francis Cobb and some others, and tell them that I was a prisoner, and for what, and how long I had lain in prison, and he did so.

And when he came down again he told me that Esquire Marsh, that was one of the King's esquires of his body, said he would go one hundred miles barefoot for my liberty, he knew me so well, and that several others spoke well of me. So the governor was very loving to me.

And after a while John Whitehead brought an order from the King for my release.   [501]

\# \#

And so after I had passed through many counties and had large meetings, visiting Friends and my relations, I came at last to London.

But I was so weak with lying about three years in cruel and hard imprisonments, my joints and my body were so stiff and benumbed that I could hardly get on my horse. Neither could I well bend my knees, nor hardly endure fire nor eat warm meat: I had been so long kept from it.

And so after I had visited Friends' meetings in London, which were large and precious, I walked into the ruins of the city that was burnt, which I saw lying according as the word of the Lord came to me concerning it several years before.   [510]

\# \#

1667 Blessed be the Lord. And though I was very weak, yet I travelled up and down in the service of the Lord.   [511]

\# \#

And then I was moved of the Lord God to set up and establish five Monthly Meetings of men and women in the city of London, besides the Women's Meeting and the Quarterly Meeting, to admonish, and exhort such as walked disorderly or carelessly, and not according to Truth; and to take care of God's glory.

And the Lord opened to me and let me see what I must do, and how I must order and establish the Men's and Women's Monthly and Quarterly Meetings in all the nation, and write to other nations, where I came not, to do the same. [511]

\# \#

1668 And as I was lying in my bed the word of the Lord came to me that I must go back to London. And Alexander Parker and several others came to me the next morning, and I asked them what they felt. And they asked me what was upon me, and I told them I felt I must return to London, and they said it was upon them the same. And so we gave up to return to London, for which way the Lord moved us and led us we went in his power. [517]

\# \#

Then I came to Waltham and established a school there for teaching of boys, and ordered a women's school to be set up at Shacklewell to instruct young lasses and maidens in whatsoever things were civil and useful in the creation. [520]

\# \#

1669 Now I was moved of the Lord to go over into Ireland, to visit the Seed of God in that nation. [536]

\# \#

When we came on shire in Ireland, the earth and the very air smelt with the corruption of the nation and gave another smell than England to me, with the corruption and the blood and the massacres and the foulness that ascended. [537]

\# \#

Now the Province of Munster's Meeting (to which General Meeting of Cork belongs) and Men's Meeting were over, wherein the power of the Lord was so great that Friends in the power and spirit of the Lord brake out into singing, many together with an audible voice making melody in their hearts; at this time I was moved to declare to Friends in the ministry. [541]

GEORGE FOX

\#   \#

I passed to other meetings, where the power of the Lord God and his spirit was wonderfully manifested to the refreshing of Friends, and from thence to the Foxe's country, who claimed kindred, but I told them that my kindred were they that stood in the life and power of God. [542]

\#   \#

And a good, weighty people there is, and true, and tender, and sensible of the power of the Lord God, and his Truth in that nation (Ireland) worthy to be visited; and very good order they have in their meetings, and they stand up for righteousness and holiness, that dams up the way of wickedness. Oh, the sufferings and trials gone through, by reason of the bad spirits! The Lord have the glory, whose power went over them, like a tide that covers the earth. [549]

\#   \#

And there [Bristol] Margaret Fell and her daughters and sons-in-law met me, where we were married. Margaret Fell was come to visit her daughter Yeamans.

I had seen from the Lord a considerable time before that I should take Margaret Fell to be my wife. And when I first mentioned it to her she felt the answer of life from God thereunto. But though the Lord had opened this thing unto me, yet I had not received a command from the Lord for the accomplishment of it then. Wherefore I let the thing rest, and went on in the work and service of the Lord as before, according as the Lord led me, travelling up and down in this nation and through the nation of Ireland. But now, after I was come back from Ireland and was come to Bristol and found Margaret Fell there, it opened in me from the Lord that the thing should be now accomplished.

And after we had discoursed the thing together I told her if she also was satisfied with the accomplishing of it now she should first send for her children, which she did. And when the rest of her daughters were come I was moved to ask the children and her sons-in-law whether they were all satisfied and whether Margaret had answered them according to her husband's will to her children, she being a widow, and if her husband had left anything to her for the assistance of her children, in which if she married they might suffer

115

loss, whether she had answered them in lieu of that and all other things. And the children made answer and said she had doubled it, and would not have me to speak of those things. I told them I was plain and would have all things done plainly, for I sought not any outward advantage to myself.

And so when I had thus acquainted the children with it, and when it had been laid before several meetings both of the men and women, assembled together for that purpose, and all were satisfied, there was a large meeting appointed of purpose in the meetinghouse at Broad Mead in Bristol, the Lord joining us together in the honourable marriage in the everlasting covenant and immortal Seed of life, where there were several large testimonies borne by Friends.

[554–555]

\# \#

After this I stayed in Bristol about a week and then passed with Margaret into the country to Olveston, where Margaret passed homewards towards the north and I passed on in the work of the Lord into Wiltshire, where I had many large and precious meetings.   [555]

\# \#

1670   And whilst I was in the country I heard that Margaret was haled out of her house and carried to Lancaster prison again, an order being gotten from the King and Council to fetch her back into prison again upon her old praemunire, though she was discharged from that imprisonment by an order from the King and his Council the year before.

As soon as I was got to London, I hastened Thomas Lower's wife Mary, and Sarah Fell (two of my wife's daughters) to the King, to acquaint him how their mother was dealt with, and see if they could get a full discharge for her that she might enjoy her estate and liberty without molestation. This was somewhat difficult at first to get, but by diligent attendance on it they at length got an order from the King that their mother should not be molested nor disquieted in the enjoyment of her estate nor house.

[557–558]

\# \#

After I had been in the country, as I came up the streets in London the drums beat for every household to send forth a soldier into the trained bands, to be in readiness, the Act against seditious conventicles being then come into force,[26] and was turned upon us who of all people were free from sedition and tumult. Whereupon I writ the declaration before mentioned, showing from the preamble and terms of the said Act, that we were not such a people, nor our meetings such meetings as were described in that Act.[27]   [558]

\# \#

And as I was going toward Rochester I lighted and walked down a hill: and a great weight and oppression fell on my spirit. So I got on my horse again, but my weight and oppression was so as I was hardly able to ride ... and very much loaden and burdened with the world's spirits.   [569]

\# \#

But at last I lost my hearing and sight so as I could not see nor hear. And I said unto Friends that I should be as a sign to such as would not see, and such as would not hear the Truth. And in this condition I continued a pretty while. And several people came about me, but I felt their spirits and discerned, though I could not see them, who was honest-hearted and who was not.

And several Friends that were doctors came and would have given me physic but I was not to meddle with their things. And under great sufferings and groans and travails, and sorrows and oppressions, I lay for several weeks.   [570]

\# \#

And one time, when they had given me up, several went away and said they would not see me die; and others said I would be still enough by such a time; and it was all over London and in the country that I was past hopes of recovery and that I was deceased.   [570]

\# \#

And there I lay at the widow Dry's all that winter, warring with the evil spirits, and could not endure the smell of any flesh meat.

[570]

---

26. The second Conventicle Act came into force May 10, 1670. It forbade, under heavy penalties, meetings of more than five persons.

27. *A Declaration from the People of God, called Quakers, against all Seditious Conventicles.*

QUAKER SPIRITUALITY

# #

And at this time there were great persecutions and there had been searching for me at London, and some meetinghouses plucked down and broken up with soldiers. Sometimes they would come with a troop of horse and a company of foot, and they would break their swords and muskets, carbines and pikes, with beating Friends and wounding abundance, so that the blood stood like puddles in the streets. And Friends were made to stand, by the Lord's power. And some of the formalists would say if Friends did not stand the nation would run into debauchery. [572]

# #

So in my deep misery I saw things beyond words to utter; and I saw a black coffin but I passed over it.

And at last I overcame these spirits and men-eaters though many times I was so weak that people knew not whether I was in the body or out. And many precious Friends came far and nigh to see me and attended upon me and were with me; and towards the spring I began to recover and to walk up and down, to the astonishment of Friends and others.

But they all saw and took notice that as the persecutions ceased I came from under my travails and sufferings. [573]

Since chapters 23 and 24 of the Journal *have been pieced together out of several sources, it would seem wise simply to summarize their account of George Fox's American journey where he travelled in the ministry from 1671 to 1673. Leaving England in August 1671, George Fox and a group of his close companions crossed the Atlantic and spent some seven months in Barbados and Jamaica before they made the crossing to Virginia, arriving there in April 1672. From Virginia, using Indian guides and where possible horses and small boats, they made their way north through bogs and swamps and trackless forests to Boston. They then retraced their course and extended it as far as Carolina before returning to Virginia in order to embark for England. They arrived in Bristol some two months short of two years from the date of their departure.*

GEORGE FOX

In the course of this perilous journey, stops were made to isolated Friends and to help in the ordering of the small Friends groups that they encountered. In addition to nurturing Friends, Fox was called upon in almost every populated region to speak to large groups of colonists who were of many denominations and of none. In not a few of these there were vigorous public encounters with local religious leaders. Fox did not neglect the Indians and on several occasions met with their Kings in moving conversations. Uneasy over the slavery that he found, especially in the Caribbean, he warned the owners of slaves to treat them with generous concern and to free them after thirty years of servitude.

At the close of his return journey to England, the Journal *contains what is almost a prayer of thanksgiving that in its outpouring of gratitude does not conceal what the journey had cost him:*

1673 The great Lord God of heaven and earth and creator of all, who is over all, carried us by his high hand and mighty power and wisdom over all, and through many dangers and perils by sea and land; and perils of deceitful professors without possession, who were as the raging waves of the sea, but made a calm; and perils of wolves, bears, tigers, and lions; and perils of rattlesnakes and other venomous creatures of like poisonous nature; and perils through great swamps, and bogs, and the wilderness, where no way was, but for such-like creatures, where we travelled and lodged in the nights by fires; and perils over great bays, creeks, and rivers, in open small boats and small canoes; and perils in great storms and tempests in the ocean, which many times were beyond words to utter; and great perils through the Indian countries in the woods or wildernesses by maneaters, some whereof lay in wait for some of our company that passed from us, but they were discovered, for the Lord's power gave them dominion over all; and great perils by night through the cold, rain, frosts, snow, in lying in the woods and wilderness several nights together until some of our company had their hands and fingers benumbed, whenas some of the world at such times have had their noses and some their fingers and toes frozen off (I was an eye witness of some of these things); and perils of robbers by land and pirates by sea, these troublesome times, whereof the sea abounds. [661]

119

QUAKER SPIRITUALITY

#   #

The Lord was our convoy; the Lord God steered our course; the Lord God, who rides upon the wings of the wind, ordered our winds for us. [662]

#   #

[*Notified of his return to Bristol, the reunion with his family and Friends is swiftly described:*]

And Margaret (Fell), and Thomas Lower (her son-in-law) with two of her daughters, Sarah Fell and Rachel Fell, came up to Bristol to me out of the North, and John Rous and William Penn and his wife, and Gerald Roberts came down from London to see us; and many Friends from several parts of the nation came to see us at the fair.

Glorious, powerful meetings we had there, and the Lord's infinite power and life was over all. I was moved to declare: God was the first teacher, in Paradise; and whilst man kept under his teaching he was happy.... They that come to be renewed up again into the divine heavenly image, in which man was first made, will know the same God, that was the first teacher of Adam and Eve in Paradise, to speak to them now by his son who changes not. Glory be to his name for ever. [665–666]

#   #

The clearness of persons proposing marriage more closely and strictly inquired into in the wisdom of God; and all the members of the spiritual body, the Church, might watch over and be helpful to each other in love.

And after the Women's Meetings were settled in those countries, and I had many precious meetings amongst Friends.... [668]

#   #

And after I had stayed a while in London I passed with Margaret and Rachel Fell into the country to Hendon and from thence to William Penn's at Rickmansworth in Hertfordshire, where Thomas Lower came to us the next day to accompany us on our journey northward. [670]

GEORGE FOX

\#   \#

And as I was sitting at supper that night before the morning I went away, I felt I was taken, yet said nothing to anybody of it then. [670]

\#   \#

At Armscote in Tredington parish, we had a very large and precious meeting in his barn and the Lord's powerful presence was amongst us.

And after the meeting was done and Friends many of them gone, as I was sitting in the parlour with some Friends, discoursing, there came one Justice Parker and a priest called Rowland Harris, priest of Honington, to the house. Though there was no meeting when they came, yet Henry Parker took me, and Thomas Lower for company with me; and though he had nothing to lay to our charge, sent us both to Worcester gaol by a strange sort of mittimus. . . . [670–671]

\#   \#

Being thus made prisoners, without any probable appearance of being released before the Quarter Sessions at soonest, we got some Friends to accompany my wife and her daughter into the north, and we were conveyed to Worcester gaol. [671]

\#   \#

1674
[*In a letter of George Fox to George Whitehead and others in London:*]
(At the Sessions) the chairman stood up and said, "You Mr. Fox are a famous man and all this may be true that you have said. But, that we may be better satisfied, will you take the Oath of Allegiance and Supremacy?" Then I told them it was a snare; and then they caused the oath to be read. And when they had done I told them, I never took an oath in my life. [674]

\#   \#

And when I was speaking what I could say instead of the oath they cried, "Give him the book." And I said, "The book

121

says, 'Swear not at all' ''; and then they cried, "Take him away gaoler, take him away." [676]

\#　\#

Thomas Lower, though he is at liberty, won't leave me, but stays with me in prison till he see what may be done concerning me. So no more but my love,
George Fox [677]

\#　\#

After I had been a prisoner at Worcester, soon after the Sessions were over I was removed to London by a *habeas corpus* for the sheriff to bring me up to the King's Bench bar. [681]

\#　\#

(Nine months later: Oct. *1674*)
Endeavours were used to get me released, at least for a time, till I was grown stronger; but the way of effecting it proved difficult and tedious; for the King was not willing to release me by any other way than a pardon, being told he could not legally do it; and I was not willing to be released by a pardon, which he would readily have given me, because I did not look upon that way as agreeable with the innocency of my cause. [701]

\#　\#

After this, my wife went to London, and spoke to the King, laying before him my long and unjust imprisonment, with the manner of my being taken, and the justices' proceedings against me in tendering me the oath as a snare, whereby they had praemunired me; so that I being now his prisoner, it was in his power and at his pleasure to release, which she desired. The King spoke kindly to her, and referred her to the lord-keeper, to whom she went, but could not obtain what she desired; for he said the King could not release me otherwise than by a pardon; and I was not free to receive a pardon, knowing I had not done evil. [701]

\#　\#

1675
[*In the King's court in London his case was finally brought before Judge Hale, the Chief Justice.*]

GEORGE FOX

I was set at liberty the 12th day of the 12th month 1674 [February 1675] by the Lord Chief Justice Hale, upon a trial of the errors in my indictment, without receiving any pardon or coming under any obligation or engagement at all. And the Lord's everlasting power went over all to his glory and praise, and to the magnifying of his name for ever, Amen. Thus from the 17th of 10th month [December] 1673, was I kept a prisoner and tossed to and from Worcester to London and from London to Worcester again three times, and so kept a prisoner till the 12th of 12th month 1674 [February 1675], being one year and near two months. [705]

#　#

And so when I was set at liberty, having been very weak, I passed to Kingston after I had visited Friends in London. And after I had stayed a while there and visited Friends I came to London again. And I writ a paper to the Parliament and sent several books to them. And several papers out of divers parts of the nation were sent up to the King and Parliament from Friends. And a great book against swearing was given to them, which so influenced many of them it was thought they would have done something for our relief therein if they had sat longer. [706]

#　#

The Truth sprang up first, to us so as to be a people to the Lord, in Leicestershire in 1644, in Warwickshire in 1645, in Nottinghamshire in 1646, in Derbyshire in 1647, and in the adjacent counties in 1648, 1649, and 1650; and in Yorkshire in 1651, and in Lancashire and Westmorland in 1652, and in Cumberland, Bishoprick, and Northumberland in 1653, in London and most parts of the nation and Scotland and Ireland in 1654. And in 1655 many went beyond seas, where Truth also sprang up. And in 1656 Truth broke forth in America and in many other places.

And the Truth stood all the cruelties and sufferings that were inflicted upon Friends by the Long Parliament and then by Oliver Protector, and all the Acts that Oliver Protector made, and his Parliaments, and his son Richard after him, and the Committee of Safety.

And after, it withstood and lasted out all the Acts and Proclamations, since 1660 that the King came in. And still the Lord's Truth is

123

over all and his Seed reigns and his Truth exceedingly spreads unto this year 1676. [709]

George Fox died in 1691, some fifteen years after the concluding of his Journal. *In the Nickalls edition of the* Journal, *these later years in Fox's life are covered by an able essay written by the late Henry J. Cadbury. Fox spent less than two of these later years (1678–1680) at Swarthmoor Hall in the North of England. For the balance of the time, he used London as his base and both counselled and personally participated in strengthening the structure and especially the spiritual nurture of the vast cluster of Monthly Meetings that were spread like a net over Britain. His moving epistles continued to rouse Friends and his ministry and prayers that sprang up in the meetings for worship did not wane in their power to the very end of his life. In these later years he shared in two visits to the Continent (1677 and 1684), travelling with seasoned Friends and visiting principally the Netherlands and a few cities in Northwestern Germany. The Dutch Yearly Meeting was established in the first of these visits.*

George Fox encouraged his fellow Quaker William Penn in his concern to establish a colony in America that was referred to as "A Holy Experiment." In 1681, King Charles II was persuaded to settle a sizable debt that was owed to the estate of Penn's deceased father, Admiral Penn, by granting to William Penn the proprietorship of a vast tract of land in America which was to become known as Pennsylvania. William Penn left England on August 13, 1682, in order to set up his new colony. He was accompanied and followed by thousands of Quakers whom he had invited to leave their homelands in order to colonize the new territory whose constitution promised full religious liberty to all.

As late as 1686 there were still 1460 Quakers in prison in Britain. This persistent persecution countered by the unbending refusal of Friends to give up their right to worship in their own way, which Fox and his companions bravely maintained, kept swelling the numbers of British Friends who chose to cross the ocean in order to be free to follow their inward Guide and to raise their families in a climate where their Quaker testimonies were respected.

George Fox lived to see Britain's bloodless revolution of

GEORGE FOX

1688 and a lessening of pressure upon his Quaker movement in the years that followed. A careful study of British history in this period from 1660–1689 would be compelled to make more than a footnote of the sizable influence exerted by the unflinching, nonviolent Quaker willingness to suffer for full religious freedom to worship God as they were drawn to do in securing the new freedom for all which the revision of the laws in 1689 accomplished.

George Fox died in 1691 at the age of 67. Two of his exclamations at the very close of his life have been preserved. "Now I am clear. I am fully clear." "All is well. The Seed of God reigns over all, and over death itself. And though I am weak in body, yet the power of God is over all, and the Seed reigns over disorderly spirits."

A SELECTION OF PASSAGES FROM

THE EPISTLES OF
GEORGE FOX

THE EPISTLES

To that of God in you both I speak, and do beseech you both for the Lord's sake to return within, and wait to hear the voice of the Lord there; and waiting there, and keeping close to the Lord, a discerning will grow, that you may distinguish the voice of the stranger when ye hear it. . . . Oh! be faithful, be faithful to the Lord in that ye know.   Epistle 5 (*1652*)

Stand still in that which shews and discovers; and there doth strength immediately come: And stand still in the light and submit to it, and the other will be hush'd and gone; and then content comes. And when temptations and troubles appear, sink down in that which is pure, and all will be hush'd and fly away.   Epistle 10 (*1652*)

None of you be sayers [only] but doers of the word.   Epistle 13 (*1652*)

Know one another in the power of an endless life which doth not change ... keep your meetings in that which changeth not, that nothing but Christ may reign in you.   Epistle 23 (*1653*)

O Friends, mind the Seed of God and the life of Christ! And take heed of being hurried with many thoughts, but live in that which goes over them all, that in it ye may reign and live in the Seed of God.   Epistle 52 (*1653*)

Your strength is, to stand still, that ye may receive refreshings: that ye may know how to wait, and how to walk before God, by the spirit within you. . . . And Friends, everywhere meet together, . . . and watch over one another in that which is eternal, and see everyone, that your words be from the eternal life.   Epistle 43 (*1653*)

The kernel is [to be found] within, the husk without. . . . They are outsiders who feed on outsides.   Epistle 46 (*1653*)

For the saints, which were to honor all men, they were in that of God, which did reach to that of God in all men.   Epistle 53 (*1653*)

All Friends, be low and in the life of God dwell to keep you low.   Epistle 62 (*1654*)

Wait all on the Lord, that ye may be settled and stayed in the Lord. . . . No creature can read the Scriptures to profit thereby, but who come to the light and Spirit that gave them forth.   Epistle 65 (*1654*)

Live in the Seed, and there ye will feel the ministry of the life and spirit in your own particulars, in which ye may be serviceable to others, that are without, and among yourselves.   Epistle 84 (*1655*)

Take heed of wronging the world or anyone in bargains, or overreaching them: but dwell in the cool, sweet, and holy power of the Lord God, and in righteousness, that it may run down amongst you; and that will keep you low. . . . There is the danger and temptation to you, of drawing your minds into your business, and clogging them with it; so that you can hardly do anything in the service of God, but there will be crying, my business, my business, and your minds will go into the things, and not over the things . . . and so when your minds are got into the riches, and cumbered therewith, ye go back into that ye were before . . . then that mind that is cumbered, it will fret, being out of the power of God.   Epistle 131 (*1656*)

All Friends everywhere, meet together, and in the measure of God's spirit wait, that with it all your minds may be guided up to God and to receive wisdom from God. . . . And Friends, meet togeth- er; . . . and know one another in that which is eternal, in the Light which was, before the world was. . . . And if ye turn from this Light, ye grow strange; and so neglecting your meetings, ye grow cold, and your minds run into the earth, and grow weary and slothful and careless, and heavy and sottish, and dull and dead.   Epistle 149 (*1657*)

And none go beyond the measure of the spirit of God, nor quench it; for where it is quenched, it cannot try things. So if you have anything upon them to speak, in the life of God stand up, and speak it, if it be but two or three words, and sit down again; and keep in the life, that ye may answer that of God in every man upon the earth.   Epistle 150 (*1657*)

And when Friends have finished their business, sit down and continue a while, quietly, and wait upon the Lord to feel him; and go not beyond the power, but keep in the power, by which God Al- mighty may be felt among you.   Epistle 162 (*1658*)

To all the . . . chosen and faithful, who are the gold tried in the fire . . . who have been tried by goods spoiling, by bonds, by whip- pings, by mockings and reproaches . . . and some have been tried by death; and ye have proved to be pure gold, that hath come out brighter and brighter. Who have not feared the waves of the seas, nor the winds; who fears not the storms or the weather; whose anchor holds, which is the hope, the mystery, which anchors the soul which is immortal, to the immortal God.   Epistle 167 (*1658*)

All Friends everywhere, who are dead to carnal weapons, and have beaten them to pieces, stand in that which takes away the occasions of wars, in the power which saves men's lives, and destroys none, nor would have others.   Epistle 177 (*1659*)

And your growth in the Seed is in the silence, where ye may find a feeding of the bread of life . . . and there is innocence and simplicity of heart and spirit is lived in and the life is fed on.   Epistle 181 (*1659*)

And Friends, take heed of blending yourselves with the outward powers of the earth.   Epistle 188 (*1659*)

And it may be, there will be a time of shearing and clipping; but the earth is the Lord's and the fullness thereof. So mind him to be your portion, and the Seed, Christ your all, and your life; and fear not the losing the fleece, for it will grow again . . . in him sit down in life and peace and rest. Epistle 194 (*1660*)

Lay hands upon no man suddenly, I warn you and charge you all in the presence of the living God, but touch the witness of God in everyone.   Epistle 195 (*1660*)

And know the power and life of God in one another, which gave forth the Scriptures, which was before the Scripture was: which life had unity in. So in the life, God Almighty preserve you.   Epistle 197 (*1660*)

In this your day of trial, . . . though ye have not a foot of ground to stand upon, yet ye have the power of God to skip and to leap in;

standing in that which is your life, that is everlasting. . . . And prisons, fetters, dungeons, and sufferings, what are they to you? . . . for ye are met and gathered into the fold of Christ Jesus . . . and he being among you felt, and in you all, ye will have every one of you, in your own particular, joy, peace, comfort, consolation, assurance, confidence, and satisfaction. . . . You who know the Shepherd and his crook, which plucks you out, he shows you the pastures of life in which you must feed.   Epistle 206 (*1661*)

In the power of God and his immortal Seed dwell.   Epistle 209 (*1661*)

Keep low in the power . . . and live up in the seed which was before the devil was.   Epistle 212 (*1661*)

Above all things take heed of judging one another, for in that ye may destroy one another, and leave one another behind, and drive one another back into the world, and eat out the good of one another . . . so go on in the Truth, answering it in every one in the inward parts and in the power of God . . . in that is your life.   Epistle 219 (*1662*)

[There is] no knowing the Scriptures but by the same Holy Ghost that moved the Holy men to give them forth . . . to know a fellowship with Christ in his death and sufferings is above the fellowship of bread and wine, which will have an end; but the fellowship of the Gospel and the Holy Spirit hath no end.   Epistle 230 (*1663*)

Therefore in Christ that never fell, the peace and rest, and light and life and the power of Truth live.   Epistle 232 (*1664*)

If you do not go forth from the Light, Spirit, and Truth within, the Light you will feel to guide and lead you, and instruct you and by it you may have immortality put upon you: and be not ashamed of Christ Jesus the light, and life and teacher; nor of his spirit to lead you.   Epistle 238 (*1664*)

For people must not be always talking, and hearing, but they must come into obedience to the great God of heaven and earth. Epistle 248 (*1666*)

Mind the hidden man of the heart . . . keep justice and truth in all your dealings and tradings, in equity, in yea and nay . . . that they may preach to all that you have to deal withal, answering the equal principle in all. . . . And so, walk in the Light as children of the Light, and of the day.   Epistles 250–251 (*1667*)

And God having given them his dominion and flavor, lose it not, but rather increase it in the life; for at first ye know that many could not take so much money in your trade as to buy bread with; all people stood aloof to you, when you stood upright . . . but now you, through your life, come to answer that of God in all, they say, they will trust you before their own people, knowing that you will not cheat, nor wrong, nor cozen, nor oppress them: for the cry is now amongst them that are without, where is there a Quaker of such and such a trade? So they will deal with Friends before they will deal with their own. O therefore Friends, who have purchased this through great sufferings, lose not this great favor which God hath given you, but that you may answer the witness of God in every man, which witnesseth to your faithfulness, that they may glorify your Father on your behalf.   Epistle 251 (*1667*)

Wait in his power and Light, that ye may be children of the Light, by believing in the Light which is the life in Christ; that you may be grafted into him, the true root, and built upon him, the true foundation.   Epistle 288 (*1672*)

Let your lives and conversation preach, that with a measure of

the spirit of God you may reach to that of God in all. Epistle 319
(*1675*)

Dear Friends, with my love to you and all of the rest of the
faithful Friends in bonds; and my desire is to the Lord, that ye all
may stand faithful and valiant in his glorious name, and for his holy
peaceable truth now in this day of storm and tempest. . . . I am a
witness for God in all my sufferings and imprisonments and hailing
before magistrates about sixty times, about this thirty-sixth year.

And so, Friends, when you are tried, you may come forth more
precious than gold that is tried in the fire; and keep the word of
patience. . . . Epistle 377 (*1682*)

(Epistle to all who go to plant new farms in America)

In all places where you do outwardly live and settle, invite all the
Indians, and their Kings, and have meetings with them, or they with
you; so that you may make inward plantations with the light and
power of God and the grace, truth, and spirit of Christ, and with it
you may answer the light of truth, and spirit of God, in the Indians,
their Kings and their people; and so by it you may make heavenly
plantations in their hearts for the Lord, and so beget them in God,
that they may serve and worship him, and spread the truth abroad;
and so that you may all be kept warm in God's love, power, and zeal,
for the honor of his name. Epistle 379 (*1682*)

(Epistle to Charlestown in Carolina telling of situations of Quakers in
Britain in *1683*)

We are here under great persecution, betwixt thirteen and fourteen hundred in prison; an account of which hath been lately delivered to the King. Besides the great spoil and havoc which is made of
Friends' goods, by informers; and besides the great spoil of about
two-thirds of our estates, and upon the Twenty-Pound a month Acts
(levies) for not going to the Steeple-house; and besides many being
imprisoned and praemunired for not swearing allegiance, both men,
women, widows, and maids: and many are fined and sent into prison
as rioters, for meeting to worship God, and we are kept out of our
meetings in streets and highways and many places of the land, and

beaten and abused. And therefore prize the liberty, both natural and spiritual, that you enjoy. And many are cast into prison because they cannot pay the priests' tithes. So that at present we are under great sufferings, persecutions, and imprisonments; but the Lord's power is over all, and that supports his people.   Epistle 386 (*1683*)

I say again if it please the Lord and be his will to try you in stinking prisons and dungeons, Brideswells, houses of correction, and suffer you to be put in such places ... I say the Lord can sanctifie such places ... his people are all in the hand, and under the wings of Christ... Pray for the enemies that put you there; and if they curse and hate you, you are to bless them, and do good to them.... Keep under the wing of Christ and in him is your sanctuary and saviour who destroys the destroyer, and is over all the first and the last. Epistle 398 (*1684*)

Dispatch business quickly, and keep out of long debates and heats ... be swift to hear, and slow to speak, and let it be in the grace, which seasons all words.   Epistle 418 (*1690*)

Dear Friends, something was upon me to write unto you, that such among Friends who marry, and provide great dinners, that instead thereof, it will be good savour on such occasions, that they may be put in mind at such time, to give some thing to the poor that be widows and fatherless, and such like, to make them a feast, or to refresh them: and this I look upon, would be a very good savour, to feast the poor that cannot feast you again ... and would be a means to keep the mind to the Lord; and in remembrance of the poor; for they that give to the poor lend to the Lord and the Lord will repay them.   Epistle 419 (*1690*)

SELECTIONS FROM

THE LETTERS OF
ISAAC PENINGTON

ISAAC PENINGTON
(*1616–1679*)

*Before turning to the letters of Isaac Penington, it may be well to
frame them with a glimpse, at least, into the life of this deeply
committed Friend and his wife Mary. Isaac Penington was born
in 1616. His grandfather had been a wealthy London merchant
and his father one of the leading Puritan statesmen of Britain.
The father had been a member of Parliament, Lord High Sheriff
of London, and twice the Lord Mayor of London. His wealth and
position made it natural for Isaac Penington to attend the University of Cambridge and the way to the highest society was open
to him. He did not marry until he was thirty-eight years old. His
bride was Lady Mary Springett, a beautiful and sensitive woman
who had married when she was eighteen and had lost her husband—a gallant young colonel in Cromwell's army—a year after
the marriage when she was carrying their child. It was this child,
the lovely Gulielma Springett, called Guli, who was later to
marry the young William Penn. Mary Penington had lost both
parents when she was three and was brought up by relatives.
When she came of age she inherited large estates and was a
wealthy woman so that she and Isaac Penington had the most
ample provision for any life position they might choose when
they married in 1654. They settled in Chalfont St. Giles, an
attractive part of Buckinghamshire, some twenty miles from
London.*

*Both Isaac and Mary Penington were seekers, travelers in
the spiritual life. They had tasted of different religious offerings
but found none of their religious connections satisfying. Both
were yearning always for more inward religion than they had
discovered. There were centrifugal as well as centripetal forces*

that played on their first encounters with Quakers during the third year of their marriage. They were used to gentler manners than they found among these meetings and there were many things that put them off, yet they recognized a fierce sincerity and a centering down in the Friends that drew them.

Penington wrote of this period, "I set myself against taking up the cross to the language, fashion, and custom and honours of the world: for my station and connections in the world made it very hard; but I never had peace or quiet in my mind till the Lord, by the stroke of his judgments, brought me off from these things." It was not until 1658 that the Peningtons met George Fox and heard him preach. Isaac Penington's witness to the crumblings of his inner hesitations that took place after this year and a half of weighing the matter are moving to read: "I felt the dead quickened, the Seed raised insomuch that my heart (in the certainty of light and clearness of true sense) said, 'This is he, this is he, there is no other. This is he whom I have waited for and sought from my childhood, who was always near me and often begotten life in my heart. But I knew him not distinctly, nor how to receive him or dwell with him. And then in this sense (in the meltings and breakings of the spirit) was I given up to the Lord to become his, both in waiting for the further revealing of his Seed in me and to serve him in the life and power of the Seed.'" Again he cries out: "I have met with my God; I have met with my Saviour; and he hath not been present with me without his salvation. But I have felt the healings drop upon my soul from under his wings. I have met with the true knowledge, the knowledge of life . . . which my soul hath rejoiced in, in the presence of the Lord. I have met the Seed's Father, in the Seed I have felt him my Father."

At last they were inwardly reached and cost them what it might, and the prospect was that it would cost them perhaps all of their property and even their freedom (with prison the lot of so many Friends), they knew they must throw in their lot with these people. William Penn, their future son-in-law, in a tribute to Isaac Penington at his death said, "But to the glory of the living God and praise of this man's memory, let me say neither his worldly station (the most considerable of any that closed in with this way of religion) nor the contradictions it gave to former conceptions, nor the debasement it brought upon his learning or *wisdom, nor yet the reproach and loss of all that attended his public espousal of it did deter him from embracing it." And the same could be said for Mary Penington. Her large wealth was nibbled away by relatives who used her refusal to take the oath as a means of keeping her from appearing in court against their claims. Even the property at Chalfont St. Giles was confiscated.*

Isaac Penington was in prison for seventeen weeks in 1661–1662 in Aylesbury Gaol for worshiping God in his own house. On this occasion there were sixty other Friends in prison with him. When he was released they went straight ahead with meetings twice a week in his home. He was in prison again for a month for accompanying the body of a deceased Friend to the grave. In 1665 he was forcibly taken from sitting in a Quaker meeting and sent to Aylesbury for sixteen weeks. On the order of the Earl of Bridgewater he was sent to Aylesbury for nine months in 1665–1666. This was followed by another two years in the same prison by the order of the same earl. In 1670 he went to visit Friends in the Reading Gaol and was himself seized and kept in prison for one and three-quarters years between 1670 and 1672. Because he was always of frail health and highly sensitive, these periods of incarceration in Gaols as they were run at this time were a great cross to him, but he bore it all cheerfully and many of the letters in this selection carry the dateline of one of these prisons.

Thomas Ellwood, who lived in the Penington family as a tutor for the years 1662–1669, says of Penington, "I think not of him without delight." The word that described this gentle, tender, loving Friend, Isaac Penington, with great discernment was, "He was not stiff or stout in the defense of his own building." And he had little ill to speak about his persecutors. Mary Penington's complete sharing of her husband's witness made possible his courageous struggle for religious liberty. Isaac Penington died in 1679 and Mary Penington, who was five years his junior, died in 1682.

Letters have a way of drawing out of the one who writes them a genuine entry into the life of another. Often enough this pierces deeply into the life of the recipient and unsheathes the inward reaches of the being of the writer more tellingly than a conversation between them might do. For the shyness and reticence at sharing on the interior level of experience in each other's company seems to fall away under the spell of an intimate letter. These selections from the letters of Isaac Penington are nearly all taken from his letters of spiritual guidance both to those within the Society of Friends and those outside that sought his counsel. Although they were written well over three hundred years ago they are marked by this penetrating intimacy that makes them not only authentic but capable of carrying to many readers in our own day a sense that the letters are speaking to their condition.

The selected letters have been taken from the second London edition, 1828. Where any identification of the date and the recipient of the letter exists, it is given.

THE LETTERS

To Thomas Walmsley   *1670*

It is not enough to hear of Christ, or read of Christ; but this is the thing, to feel him my root, my life, my foundation; and my soul engrafted into him, by him who hath power to engraft.

\# \#

O Friend, I beseech thee, mind this; come, O come to the true root! come to Christ indeed! Rest not in an outward knowledge; but come to the inward life, the hidden life, and receive life from him who is the life; and then abide in and live to God in the life of his Son.

To Bridget Atley   *No date*

He hath changed, and doth change thy spirit daily; though it be as the shooting up of the corn, whose growth cannot be discerned at present by the most observing eye, but it is very manifest afterwards that it hath grown. My heart is refreshed for thy sake, rejoicing in the Lord's goodness towards thee; and that the blackness of darkness begins to scatter from thee, though the enemy be still striving the same way to enter and distress thee again. But wait to feel the relieving measure of life, and heed not distressing thoughts, when they rise ever so strongly in thee; nay, though they have entered thee, fear them not, but *be still awhile, not believing in the power which thou feelest they have over thee,* and it will fall on a sudden.

\# \#

And oh, learn daily more and more, to trust and hope in him, and not to be afrighted with any amazement, nor to be taken up with the sight of the present thing; but wait for the shutting of thy own eye upon every occasion, and for the opening of the eye of God in thee, and for the sight of things therewith as they are from him.

To Bridget Atley   *1665*

Thou must join in with the beginnings of life and be exercised with the day of small things, before thou meet the great things, wherein is the clearness and satisfaction of the soul. The rest is at noonday; but, the travels begin at the breakings of day, wherein are but glimmerings, or little light, wherein the discovery of good and evil are not manifest and certain; yet *there* must the traveller begin and travel, and in his faithful travel (in much fear and trembling lest he should err) the light will break in on him more and more.

To the Friend of Francis Fines   *No date*

The sum and substance of true religion doth not stand in getting a notion of Christ's righteousness, but in feeling the power of the endless life, receiving the power, and being changed by the power. And where Christ is, there is his righteousness.

#   #

Christ was anointed and sent of God, a Saviour, to destroy the works of the Devil, to break down all rule and authority contrary to God in man; for his work is in the heart. There he quickens, there he raiseth, there he brings into death that which is to die, raising the seed immortal, and bringing the creature into subjection to it. Now, to feel the power that doth this, and to feel this wrought by the power, this is far beyond all talk about justification and righteousness. Hither would I have thee come, out of the talk, out of the outwardness of knowledge, into the thing itself, and into the trueness of the new and living knowledge which is witnessed here.

#   #

That charge of thine on us, that we deny the person of Christ, and make him nothing but a light or notion, a principle in the heart of man, is very unjust and untrue; for we own that appearance of him in his body of flesh, his sufferings and death, and his sitting at the Father's right hand in glory: but then we affirm, that there is no true knowledge of him, or union with him, but in the seed or principle of his life in the heart, and that *therein* he appears, subdues sin, and reigns over it, in those that understand and submit to the teaching and government of his Spirit.

ISAAC PENINGTON

To Friends of Truth in the
Two Chalfonts   *Aylesbury Prison, 1666*

The Seed which God hath sown in you is pure and precious. Oh, that it may be found living in you, and ye abiding in it. Oh, that no other seed may at any time usurp authority over it; but that ye may know the authority and pure Truth which is of God, and therein stand, in the pure dominion, over all that is against him.

#   #

O my dear Friends, that there may be kept down in you which is forward to judge, to approve or disapprove; and may the weighty judgment of the Seed be waited for. And Oh, do not judge, do not judge, before the light of the day shine in you and give forth the judgment; but stand and walk in fear and humility, and tenderness of spirit, and silence of flesh.

#   #

From your brother and companion in the faith, patience, and afflictions of the Seed,

To a Friend   *1673*

O my Friend, mind this precious Truth inwardly, this precious grace inwardly, the precious life inwardly, the precious light inwardly, the precious power inwardly, the inward word of life, the inward voice of the Shepherd in the heart, the inward seed, the inward salt, the inward leaven, the inward pearl, &c. whereby Christ effects this. Distinguish between words *without* concerning the thing, and the thing itself *within;* and wait and labour then to know, understand, and be guided by, the motives, leadings, drawings, teachings, quickenings, &c. of the thing itself within.

To Nathaniel Stonar   *1671*

If thou wilt have life, thou must come to that which gives life. If thou wilt come into the ministration of the New Testament, thou must come into the spirit and power; and now the letter of the Scriptures in the Spirit and power which wrote them, if ever thou know them aright.

QUAKER SPIRITUALITY

#   #

And oh, that thou also might feel quickenings of life and true leadings.

To Catharine Pordage   *1671*
I make little of the illumination of the understanding without subjection to him that illuminateth.

#   #

The troubled soul is not only to go to the Lord but it must be taught by him how to go to him. The Lord is the teacher.... It is not the great and main work to be found *doing*, but to be found doing *aright*, from the true teachings and from the right spirit.... A little praying from God's spirit and in that which is true and pure is better than thousands of vehement desires in one's own will and after the flesh. For as long as a man prays thus, that which should die in him lives in his very prayer; and how shall it ever be destroyed, if it get food and gain strength there? ... It is not thy proper work to look out at the way or think it hard (for it is not so to the true Seed), but to be travelling it in faithfulness as thou art drawn and led; and this will save thee much sorrow.

To Catharine Pordage and Another   *1671*
It is your proper state to wait daily, not for comforts, not for refreshments (that day is to come afterwards), but for convictions and reproofs of that in you which is contrary to God.... You must die to your own wisdom if ever ye will be born of a walk in the wisdom of God.... If ye will ever know the spirit of the Lord, ye must meet with him as a searcher and reprover in your hearts.

To an Unknown Correspondent   *1671*
Then, as God gives the knowledge, he requires obedience which is to be learned of God in the new spirit of life.

To Thomas and Ann Mudd   *1672*
While I was there with you, true living breathings did spring up in my heart to the Lord for you. Last First-day, my wife had a letter of George Fox sent her which I read that night. In the reading of it I

had many thoughts respecting you, and a desire that ye peruse it; which I sent unto you the next day for that end. Now this morning you were upon my heart and several things rose up in me in reference to you.... One was that ye keep steadfast in that holy testimony to draw from outward and dead knowledge, and out of dead practices and worships after man's own conceivings into an inward principle, and into worship in spirit and in truth, both inwardly in the heart, and outwardly in the assemblies of God's gathering.... [Another], that ye be daily exercised, guided, and your heart opened and quickened by the principle and spirit of Truth; that so ye may know what it is to walk with the Lord and to feel the power of the Lord; and to be led by him out of and away from the mysterious workings of the power and spirit of darkness inwardly.

To Widow Hemmings   1673
O my friend, that thou mightst feel more and more the truth in the inward parts and be more and more established therein.... Oh! The Lord God prosper his own seed and holy plantation in thy heart and keep thee in the meek, lowly, humble, poor, and tender spirit, unto which is his mercy and blessing.

To Widow Hemmings   1675
There is a river, a sweet, still, flowing river, the streams whereof will make glad thy heart. And learn but in quietness and stillness to retire to the Lord, and wait upon him; in whom thou shalt feel peace and joy, in the midst of thy troubles from the cruel and vexatious spirit of this world. So wait to know thy work and service to the Lord, in thy place and station; and the Lord make thee faithful therein, and thou wilt want neither help, support nor comfort.

Thy Friend in the truest, sincerest, and most constant love.

To Dulcibella Laiton   1677
There is a pure seed of life which God hath sown in thee; Oh, that it might come through, and come over all that is above it, and contrary to it. And for that end, wait daily to feel it, and to feel thy mind subdued by it, and joined to it. Take heed of looking out in the reasonings of thy mind, but dwell in the feeling sense of life; and then, that will arise in thee more and more, which maketh truly wise,

and gives power, and brings into the holy authority and dominion of life.

\#   \#

Come out of the knowledge and comprehension about things, into the feeling life; and let that be thy knowledge and wisdom, which thou receivest and retainest in the feeling life; and that will lead thee into the footsteps of the flock, without reasoning, consulting, or disputing.

To S. W.   *1678*
O my dear Friend, let not any part of thy life lie in notions above the Seed, but let it all lie in the Seed itself, in thy waiting upon the Lord for its arisings in thee, and in thy feeling its arisings. Oh, what becomes of flesh, and self, and self-righteousness, when this lives in the heart. My religion, which I now daily bless my God for, began in this Seed; which, when I first felt, and discerningly knew from the Lord, my cry to him was, Oh, this is it I have longed after and waited for! Oh, unite my soul to thee in this for ever! This is thy Son's gift from thee, thy Son's grace, thy Son's Truth, thy Son's life, thy Son's Spirit.

\#   \#

Here Christ is formed in the soul, of a truth; here the black garments of unrighteousness, yea, of man's righteousness too, are put off, and the white raiment put on; here the holy image is brought forth in the heart, even the image of the dear Son, which partakes of the divine nature of the Father; here the soul is new created in Christ Jesus.

To S. W.   *1678*
Oh, my Friend, there is an ingrafting into Christ, a being formed and new created in Christ, a living and abiding in him, and a growing and bringing forth fruit through him unto perfection. Oh, mayst thou experience all these things; and, that thou mayst so do, wait to know life, the springings of life, the separations of life inwardly from all that evil which hangs about it, and would be springing up and mixing with it, under an appearance of good; that life may come to live fully in thee, and nothing else. And so, sink very low, and become

very little, and know little; yea, know no power to believe, act, or suffer any thing for God, but as it is given thee, by the springing grace, virtue, and life of the Lord Jesus. For, grace is a spiritual inward thing, an holy Seed, sown by God, springing up in the heart. People have got a notion of grace, but know not the thing. Do not thou matter the notion, but feel the thing; and know thy heart more and more ploughed up by the Lord, that his Seed's grace may grow up in thee more and more, and thou mayst daily feel thy heart as a garden, more and more enclosed, watered, dressed, and delighted in by him.

This is a salutation of love from thy Friend in the Truth, which lives and changes not.

To Lady Conway   No date

Oh, wait to feel the Seed, and the cry of thy soul in the breathing life of the Seed, to its Father, with its sweet, kindly, and natural subjection to him. And wait for the risings of the power in thy heart, in the Father's seasons, and for faith in the power, that thou mayst feel inward healing, of all the inward wounds which the Lord makes in thy soul, through his love to thee for thy good.

To Abraham Grimsden   No date

It is easy to profess and make a show of Truth, but hard to come into it. It is very hard to the earthly mind, to part with that which must be parted with for it, before the soul can come to possess and enjoy it. Profession of Truth, without the life and power, is but a slippery place, which men may easily slide from; nay, indeed, if men be not in the life and power, they can hardly be kept from that which will stain their profession. The Lord, who searcheth the heart, knows how it is with thee: oh, consider thy ways, and fear before him, and take heed of taking his name in vain, for he will not hold such guiltless.

To One under Divine Visitation   No date

Oh! look not after great things: small breathings, small desires after the Lord, if true and pure, are sweet beginnings of life. Take heed of despising "the day of small things," by looking after some great visitation, proportionable to thy distress, according to thy eye. Nay, thou must become a child, thou must lose thy own will quite by degrees. Thou must wait for life to be measured out by the Father, and be content with what proportion, and at what time, he shall please to measure.

Oh! be little, be little, and then thou wilt be content with little: and if thou feel now and then a check or a secret smiting, in *that* is the Father's love; be not over wise, nor over eager in thy own willing, running, and desiring, and thou mayst feel it so; and by degrees come to the knowledge of thy Guide, who will lead thee step by step in the path of life, and teach thee to follow, and in his own season powerfully judge that which cannot nor will not follow. Be still, and wait for light and strength, and desire not to know or comprehend, but to be known and comprehended in the love and life, which seeks out, gathers, and preserves the lost sheep.

I remain thy dear Friend, and a well-wisher to thy soul in the love of my Father.

To Joseph Wright   *No date*

I was weary and sick at heart of opinions, and had not the Lord brought that to my hand which my soul wanted, I had never meddled with religion more. But, as I felt that in my heart which was evil and not of God, so the Lord God of my life pointed me to that of him in my heart which was of another nature, teaching me to wait for and know his appearance there; in subjection whereto, I experience him stronger than the strong man that was there before; and by his power he hath separated me from that within, which separated me from him before; and thus being separated, truly I feel union with him, and his blessed presence every day, which, what it is unto me, my tongue cannot utter.

To The Women's Meeting at John Mannock's   *1678*

And mind, Friends, what is now upon me to you; it is one thing to sit waiting to feel the power, and to keep within the limits of the power thus far; and another, yea, and harder, to feel and keep within the sense and limits of the power, when ye come to act. Then, your reasonings, your wisdom, your apprehensions, have more advantage to get up in you, and to put themselves forth. Oh, therefore, watch narrowly and diligently against the forward part, and keep back to the life, which though it rise more slowly, yet acts more surely and safely for God.

Oh, wait and watch to feel your keeper keeping you within the holy bounds and limits, within the pure fear, within the living sense, while ye are acting for your God; that ye may only be his instruments, and feel him acting in you.

\# \#

And take heed of the quickness and strength of reason, or of the natural part, which avails little: but wait for the evidence and demonstration of God's Spirit, which reaches to the witness and doth the work. Are they in a snare? are they overtaken in a fault? yea, are they in measure blinded and hardened, so that they can neither see nor feel, as to this particular? Retire, sit still awhile, and travail for them. Feel how life will arise in any of you, and how mercy will reach towards them, and how living words, from the tender sense, may be reached forth to their hearts deeply by the hand of the Lord for their good. And, if ye find them at length bowing to the Lord, oh, let tender compassion help them forwards; that what hath been so troublesome and groundedly dissatisfactory in the progress, may at length have a sweet tissue for their good, and our joy and rejoicing in the Lord.

\# \#

Your Friend and Brother in the tender Truth, and in pure love and precious life.

On Prayer in Families   *No date*
Ye must come out of your knowledge, into the feeling of an inward principle of life, if ever ye be restored to the true unity with God, and to the true enjoyment of him again. Ye must come out of the knowledge and wisdom ye have gathered from the Scriptures, into a feeling of the things there written of, as it pleaseth the Lord to open and reveal them in the hidden man of the heart.

To a Parent   *1665*
I have not much freedom to write at present, yet the spirit of thy letter doth so strongly draw, that I cannot be wholly silent.

This, therefore, in the uprightness, fear, and tenderness of my heart, I say to thee.

There is a pure principle of life in the heart, from whence all good springs. This thou art to mind in thyself; and this thou art to wait on the Lord to be taught, and enabled by him to reach to in thy children; that thou mayst be an instrument in his hand to bring them into the fear of him, which is acceptable to him, and will be profitable to them. Mind therefore its leadings in thy heart, and wait to be acquainted with its voice there.

#   #

And as to thy children, daily feel the need of instruction from the Almighty, to govern and direct them, and wait daily to receive it from him; and what thou receivest, give forth in fear, and wait for his carrying it home and working it upon their hearts. For he is a Father, and hath tenderness, and gives true wisdom to every condition of his people that wait upon him; so as he may be known to all daily, and they able to be nothing without him.

Breathe unto the Lord, that thy heart may be single, thy judgment set straight by his principle of life in thee, and thy children guided to, and brought up in the sense of the same principle. As for praying, they will not need to be taught that outwardly; but if a true sense be kindled in them, though never so young, from that sense will arise breathing to him that begat it, suitable to their state; which will cause growth and increase of that sense and life in them.

Thus in the plainness of my heart have I answered thee, according to the drawings and freedom which I found there, which I dare not exceed, who am thy unfeigned Friend, though outwardly unknown.

To E. Terry on Disputes   *No date*

As touching disputes, indeed I have no love to them; Truth did not enter my heart that way, nor do I expect to propagate it in others that way; yet, sometimes a necessity is laid upon me for the sake of others. And truly, when I do feel a necessity, I do it in great fear; not trusting in my spear or bow, I mean in strong arguments or wise considerations, which I (of myself) can gather or comprehend; but I look up to the Lord for the guidance, help, and demonstration of his Spirit, that way may be made thereby in men's hearts for the pure seed to be reached to, wherein the true conviction and thorough conversion of the soul to God is witnessed. I had far rather be feeling Christ's life, Spirit, and power in my own heart, than disputing with others about them.

ISAAC PENINGTON

The Friends of Both the Chalfonts *1667*

Now, my dear Friends, ye know somewhat of this, and ye know
the way to it. Oh, be faithful, be faithful, —travel on, travel on; let
nothing stop you; but wait for and daily follow the sensible leadings
of that measure of life, which God hath placed in you, which is one
with the fulness, and into which the fulness runs daily and fills it,
that it may run into you and fill you.

\# \#

Thus, my dear Friends, let us retire, and dwell in the peace
which God breathes, and lie down in the Lamb's patience and stillness, night and day, which nothing can wear out or disturb: and
so the preservation of the poor and needy shall be felt to be in his
name, and glory shall be sung to his name over all. . . .

To the Independents of Canterbury *No date*

It pleased the Lord, after many years, when my hope nearly
failed, to visit me in a wonderful manner, breaking my heart in
pieces, giving me to feel his pure living power, and the raising of his
holy Seed in my heart thereby; insomuch, that I cried out inwardly
before him, "This is He, this is He whom I have sought after and so
much wanted! This is the pearl, this is the holy leaven! Do what thou
wilt with me, afflict me how thou wilt, and as long as thou pleasest, so
that at length I may be joined with this, and become one with this!"
So, the eye of my understanding was from that day anointed, and I
saw and felt the pure life of the Son made manifest in me; and the
Father drew me to him as to a living stone, and hath built my soul
upon him, and brought me to Mount Zion, and the holy city of our
God; where the river of life sends forth its streams, which refresh and
make glad the holy city, and all the tabernacles that are built on God's
holy hill.

\# \#

Oh, that ye might inwardly know these things! Turn in, turn in.
Mind what stirs in your hearts; what moves against sin, what moves
towards sin. The one is the Son's life, the Son's grace, the Son's
Spirit; the other is the spirit and nature which is contrary thereto. If
ye could come but to the sense of this, and come to a true inward
silence, and waiting, and turning at the reproofs of heavenly wisdom,

and know the heavenly drawings into that which is holy and living, ye would soon find the Lord working in your hearts.

To Catharine Pordage on Prayer   *1671*

Prayer is a gift; and he that receiveth it, must first come to the sense of his own inability; and so wait to receive; and perhaps begin, but with a groan or sigh from the true Spirit, and thus grow in ability from the same Spirit, denying the ability which is after the flesh: this latter abounds in many, who mistake and err in judgment, not waiting on the Lord to be enabled by him rightly to judge and distinguish between flesh and spirit, but are many times willingly ignorant in this particular, —it will cost so dear to come to a true understanding therein.

#   #

The troubled soul is not only to go to the Lord, but it must be taught by him *how* to go to him. The Lord is the teacher, and *this* is a great lesson, which the soul cannot learn of itself, but as it is taught by him. Men abound in their several ways in religion, in that which God is arising to scatter and confound; so that, it is not the great and main work to be found *doing*, but to be found doing *aright*, from the true teachings, and from the right Spirit.

In the time of great trouble there may be life stirring underneath, and a true and tender sense, and pure desires, in which there may be a drawing nigh and breathing of heart to the Lord; but, in the time of trouble and great darkness, may not a man easily desire amiss, and pray amiss, if he have not his guide. A little praying from God's Spirit, and in that which is true and pure, is better than thousands of vehement desires in one's own will, and after the flesh.

To the Women Friends at Armscot   *1678*

In your meetings together to do service for the Lord, be every one of you very careful and diligent in watching to his power, that ye may have the sensible living feeling of it, each of you, in your own hearts, and in the hearts one of another; and that ye may keep within the limits of it, and not think, or speak, or act beyond it. And know, Oh, wait more and more to know, how to keep that silence which is of the power, that, in every one of you, what the power would have silent may be silent. Oh, take heed of the forwardness of the flesh, the wisdom of the flesh, the will of the flesh, the talkativeness of the flesh;

keep them back, oh, let them for ever be kept back in every one of you, by the presence and virtue of the power.

The power is the authority and blessing of your meetings, and therein lies your ability to perform what God requires; be sure ye have it with you. Keep back to the life, keep low in the holy fear, and ye shall not miss of it. You will find it easy to transgress, easy to set up self, easy to run into sudden apprehensions about things, and one to be of this mind and another of that; but feel the power to keep down all this, and to keep you out of all this; every one watching to the life, when and where it will arise to help you, and that ye may be sensible of it when it doth arise, and not in a wrong wisdom oppose it, but be one with it. And thus, if any thing should arise from the wrong wisdom in any, ye may be sensible of it, not defiled or entangled with it, but abiding in that which sees through it and judges it; that so life may reign, in your hearts and in your meetings, above that which will be forward, and perking over the life, if ye be not very watchful.

#　#

There is that near you which will guide you; O! wait for it, and be sure ye keep to it; that being innocent and faithful, in following the Lord in the leadings of his power, his power may plead your cause in the hearts of all his tender people hereabouts; and they may see and acknowledge, that your meetings are of God, —that ye are guided by him into that way of service in his holy fear, in which he himself is with you, and by the movings of his Holy Spirit in your hearts, hath engaged you. Be not hasty either in conceiving any thing in your minds, or in speaking it forth, or in any thing ye are to do; but feel him by his Spirit and life going along with you, and leading you into what he would have any of you, or every one of you do. If ye be in the true feeling sense of what the Lord your God would have done, and join with what is of God, as it riseth in any, or against any thing that is not of God, as it is made manifest among you; ye are all in your places and proper services, obeying the blessed will and doing the blessed work of the Lord your God.

To M. Hiorns　　　　　　　　　　　　　　　　　　　*1679*

Now this advice ariseth in my heart. Oh, keep cool and low before the Lord, that the Seed, the pure living Seed, may spring more and more in thee, and thy heart be united more and more to the Lord therein. Coolness of spirit is a precious frame, and the glory of the Lord most shines therein, in its own lustre and brightness; and when the soul is low before the Lord it is still near the Seed, and preciously in its life one with the Seed. And when the Seed riseth, thou shalt have liberty in the Lord to rise with it; only take heed of that part which will be outrunning it, and getting above it, and so not ready to descend again, and keep low in the deeps with it.

# #

Postscript: Now, feel the child's nature, which chooseth nothing, but desires the fulfilling of the Father's will in it. I cannot desire to enjoy any thing (saith the nature of the true birth) but as the Father, of himself, pleaseth to give me to enjoy. There is a time to want as well as to abound, while we are in this world. And the times of wanting, as well as abounding, are greatly advantageous to us.

# #

So, be still and quiet, and silent before the Lord, not putting up any request to the Father, nor cherishing any desire in thee, but in the Seed's lowly nature and purely springing life; and the Lord give thee the clear discerning, in the lowly Seed, of all that springs and arises in thy heart.

Thou didst read precious things of the Seed, when thou *wast* here, *written outwardly;* oh, that thou *mightst* read the same things *written inwardly* in thy own heart; which that thou mayst do, become as a weaned child, not exercising thyself in things too high or too wonderful for thee. Every secret thing, every spiritual mystery, but what God opens to thee, is too high and wonderful for thee. And if the Lord at any time open to thee deep mysteries, fear before the Lord, and go no further into them than the Lord leads thee. The error is still in the *comprehending knowing mind,* but never in the lowly weighty seed of life; —whither the Lord God of my life more and more lead thee, and counsel thee to take up thy dwelling-place there, daily instructing thee so to do. For the greatest as well as the least must be daily taught of the Lord, both in ascending and descending, or they will miss their way; yea, they must be daily *taught* of him to be silent before him, and know [what it is] to be *still* in *him,* or they will be apt to miss in either.

This from thy Friend,

ISAAC PENINGTON

This is our religion; to feel that which God begets in our hearts preserved alive by God, to be taught by him to know him, to worship, and live to him, in the leadings and by the power of his Spirit;

#   #

There is life, there is peace, there is joy, there is righteousness, there is health, there is salvation, there is power of redemption in the Seed; yea, there is so. But thy soul wants and doth not enjoy these things. Well, but how mayst thou come to enjoy them? There is no way, but union with the Seed; knowing the Seed, hearing the voice of the Seed, learning of and becoming subject to the Seed.

ABRIDGMENT OF

THE JOURNAL OF
JOHN WOOLMAN

JOHN WOOLMAN
(*1720–1772*)

Over the years, John Woolman's Journal *has become an American classic. It would be difficult to find, among the many journals that appeared in the ranks of the Quakers who flourished in colonial America in the eighteenth century, one that could compare with it. It was the favorite of Charles Lamb, who wrote, "Get the writings of John Woolman by Heart." In 1871, the poet Whittier issued a little-changed edition of the* Journal *adding a long informative introduction. This Whittier edition went through a number of printings. It was not by accident that Harvard's president, Charles William Eliot, selected Woolman's* Journal *for the "Five Foot Book Shelf" he edited early in this century. The edition that has been chosen here for abridgment was made by Phillip Moulton and published by the Oxford University Press in 1971. It is generally regarded as the most carefully researched and edited version of the* Journal *that we possess.*

Although the Journal *is written with restraint and a strong note of understatement that is not absent from other Quaker journals of that period, it is able to communicate a plain and honest account of a "collected" life. Woolman had his seasons of lower visibility, of getting away from the root, of running ahead of or lagging behind his Inward Guide. Yet he knew his way back, and he used what he knew. The flashes of sanctity that his* Journal, *with all its modesty, unveil are always enclosed in the earthy humanity of the husband and father, the tailor and orchardman, the respected member of a small colonial New Jersey town and a beloved member of his own Quaker meeting. His frankness about his own human—all too human—hesitations and their overcoming add to the authenticity of the* Journal.

Woolman's Journal *is not only the story of a "collected" man but it is the recounting of the way in which a Quaker "concern" may unfold within a man's heart, and if attended to and followed out, may not only reshape his own life as its vehicle but spread to others, and become a transforming power in the history of his time. In his concern to right the wrong of holding slaves, Woolman confronted a custom that was as fully accepted among many of the Quakers in his generation as the ownership of stocks and bonds or a bank account that bore interest might be in our own.*

As was customary among Friends, Woolman always secured a minute from his local meeting to travel in the ministry, taking a companion with him when he made his periodic journeys first into Maryland, Virginia, and Carolina, later to New England. He visited meetings and Quaker families, bringing his quiet but often painful message asking for the freeing of any slaves that Quakers might hold and the provision for their future well-being.

He began these journeys in 1746. By the time of his early death in 1772, his faithfulness to his concern and the widespread support of those who associated themselves with him had opened the Quakers of colonial America to a new dimension of their responsibility to their black brothers and had all but cleared Quaker membership of the holding of slaves. In the course of his traveling in the ministry on this spiritually centered social mission, the Journal *reveals the outlines of a highly creative, nonviolent approach to the resolution of conflict, an approach that is striking in its contemporary relevance.*

CHAPTER I

1720–1742   I have often felt a motion of love to leave some hints in writing of my experience of the goodness of God, and now, in the thirty-sixth year of my age, I begin this work. I was born in North-ampton, in Burlington County in West Jersey, A.D. 1720, and before I was seven years old I began to be acquainted with the operations of divine love. Through the care of my parents I was taught to read near as soon as I was capable of it, and as I went from school one Seventh-day, I remember, while my companions went to play by the way, I went forward out of sight; and sitting down, I read the twenty-second chapter of the Revelations: "He showed me a river of water, clear as crystal, proceeding out of the throne of God and the Lamb, etc." And in reading it my mind was drawn to seek after that pure habitation which I then believed God had prepared for his servants. The place where I sat and the sweetness that attended my mind remains fresh in my memory.

This and the like gracious visitations had that effect upon me, that when boys used ill language it troubled me, and through the continued mercies of God I was preserved from it.   [23]

# #

Another thing remarkable in my childhood was that once, going to a neighbor's house, I saw on the way a robin sitting on her nest; and as I came near she went off, but having young ones, flew about and with many cries expressed her concern for them. I stood and threw stones at her, till one striking her, she fell down dead. At first I was pleased with the exploit, but after a few minutes was seized with horror, as having in a sportive way killed an innocent creature while she was careful for her young. I beheld her lying dead and thought those young ones for which she was so careful must now perish for

want of their dam to nourish them; and after some painful considerations on the subject, I climbed up the tree, took all the young birds
and killed them, supposing that better than to leave them to pine
away and die miserably, and believed in this case that Scripture
proverb was fulfilled, "The tender mercies of the wicked are cruel"
[Prv. 12:10]. I then went on my errand, but for some hours could
think of little else but the cruelties I had committed, and was much
troubled.

Thus he whose tender mercies are over all his works hath placed
a principle in the human mind which incites to exercise goodness
toward every living creature; and this being singly attended to,
people become tender-hearted and sympathizing, but being frequently and totally rejected, the mind shuts itself up in a contrary disposition.

About the twelfth year of my age, my father being abroad, my
mother reproved me for some misconduct, to which I made an
undutiful reply; and the next First-day as I was with my father
returning from meeting, he told me he understood I had behaved
amiss to my mother and advised me to be more careful in future. I
knew myself blamable, and in shame and confusion remained silent.
Being thus awakened to a sense of my wickedness, I felt remorse in
my mind, and getting home I retired and prayed to the Lord to
forgive me, and do not remember that I ever after that spoke unhand-
somely to either of my parents, however foolish in other things.

Having attained the age of sixteen years, I began to love wanton
company, and though I was preserved from profane language or
scandalous conduct, still I perceived a plant in me which produced
much wild grapes. Running in this road I found many like myself,
and we associated in that which is reverse to true friendship.

But in this swift race it pleased God to visit me with sickness, so
that I doubted of recovering. And then did darkness, horror, and
amazement with full force seize me, even when my pain and distress
of body was very great. I thought it would have been better for me
never to have had a being than to see the day which I now saw. I was
filled with confusion, and in great affliction both of mind and body I
lay and bewailed myself. I had not confidence to lift up my cries to
God, whom I had thus offended, but in a deep sense of my great folly
I was humbled before him, and at length that word which is as a fire
and a hammer broke and dissolved my rebellious heart. And then my

cries were put up in contrition, and in the multitude of his mercies I found inward relief, and felt a close engagement that if he was pleased to restore my health, I might walk humbly before him.

After my recovery this exercise remained with me a considerable time; but by degrees giving way to youthful vanities, they gained strength, and getting with wanton young people I lost ground. The Lord had been very gracious and spoke peace to me in the time of my distress, and I now most ungratefully turned again to folly, on which account at times I felt sharp reproof but did not get low enough to cry for help. I was not so hardy as to commit things scandalous, but to exceed in vanity and promote mirth was my chief study. Still I retained a love and esteem for pious people, and their company brought an awe upon me. [24–26]

# #

In a while I resolved totally to leave off some of my vanities, but there was a secret reserve in my heart of the more refined part of them, and I was not low enough to find true peace. Thus for some months I had great trouble, there remaining in me an unsubjected will which rendered my labours fruitless, till at length through the merciful continuance of heavenly visitations I was made to bow down in spirit before the Lord.

I kept steady to meetings, spent First-days after noon chiefly in reading the Scriptures and other good books, and was early convinced in my mind that true religion consisted in an inward life, wherein the heart doth love and reverence God the Creator and learn to exercise true justice and goodness, not only towards all men but also towards the brute creatures; that as the mind was moved on an inward principle to love God as an invisible, incomprehensible being, on the same principle it was moved to love him in all his manifestations in the visible world; that as by his breath the flame of life was kindled in all animal and sensitive creatures, to say we love God as unseen and at the same time exercise cruelty towards the least creature moving by his life, or by life derived from him, was a contradiction in itself.

I found no narrowness respecting sects and opinions, but believed that sincere, upright-hearted people in every Society who truly loved God were accepted of him.

As I lived under the Cross and simply followed the openings of Truth, my mind from day to day was more enlightened; my former acquaintance was left to judge of me as they would, for I found it safest for me to live in private and keep these things sealed up in my own breast.

While I silently ponder on that change wrought in me, I find no language equal to it nor any means to convey to another a clear idea of it. I looked upon the works of God in this visible creation and an awfulness covered me; my heart was tender and often contrite, and a universal love to my fellow creatures increased in me. This will be understood by such who have trodden in the same path. [27–29]

# #

Now though I had been thus strengthened to bear the Cross, I still found myself in great danger, having many weaknesses attending me and strong temptations to wrestle with, in the feeling whereof I frequently withdrew into private places and often with tears besought the Lord to help me, whose gracious ear was open to my cry.

All this time I lived with my parents and wrought on the plantation, and having had schooling pretty well for a planter, I used to improve myself in winter evenings and other leisure times. And being now in the twenty-first year of my age, a man in much business shopkeeping and baking asked me if I would hire with him to tend shop and keep books. I acquainted my father with the proposal, and after some deliberation it was agreed for me to go.[28]

At home I had lived retired, and now having a prospect of being much in the way of company, I felt frequent and fervent cries in my heart to God, the Father of Mercies, that he would preserve me from all taint and corruption, that in this more public employ I might serve him, my gracious Redeemer, in that humility and self-denial with which I had been in a small degree exercised in a very private life.

The man who employed me furnished a shop in Mount Holly, about five miles from my father's house and six from his own, and there I lived alone and tended his shop. Shortly after my settlement here I was visited by several young people, my former acquaintance, who knew not but vanities would be as agreeable to me now as ever;

---

28. Additional sentence crossed out by Woolman in MS. A: "I had for a considerable time found my mind less given to husbandry than heretofore, having often in view some other way of living." A similar statement appears in MS. C.

The employer may have been John Ogburn; he seems to have retired prior to 1747, in which year he sold Woolman some property which included a small shop.

and at these times I cried to the Lord in secret for wisdom and strength, for I felt myself encompassed with difficulties and had fresh occasion to bewail the follies of time past in contracting a familiarity with a libertine people. And as I had now left my father's house outwardly, I found my Heavenly Father to be merciful to me beyond what I can express.

By day I was much amongst people and had many trials to go through, but in evenings I was mostly alone and may with thankfulness acknowledge that in those times the spirit of supplication was often poured upon me, under which I was frequently exercised and felt my strength renewed.   [29–30]

#   #

After a while my former acquaintance gave over expecting me as one of their company, and I began to be known to some whose conversation was helpful to me. And now, as I had experienced the love of God through Jesus Christ to redeem me from many pollutions and to be a succour to me through a sea of conflicts, with which no person was fully acquainted, and as my heart was often enlarged in this heavenly principle, I felt a tender compassion for the youth who remained entangled in snares like those which had entangled me. From one month to another this love and tenderness increased, and my mind was more strongly engaged for the good of my fellow creatures.

I went to meetings in an awful frame of mind and endeavoured to be inwardly acquainted with the language of the True Shepherd. And one day being under a strong exercise of spirit, I stood up and said some words in a meeting, but not keeping close to the divine opening, I said more than was required of me; and being soon sensible of my error, I was afflicted in mind some weeks without any light or comfort, even to that degree that I could take satisfaction in nothing. I remembered God and was troubled, and in the depth of my distress he had pity upon me and sent the Comforter. I then felt forgiveness for my offense, and my mind became calm and quiet, being truly thankful to my gracious Redeemer for his mercies. And after this, feeling the spring of divine love opened and a concern to speak, I said a few words in a meeting, in which I found peace. This I believe was about six weeks from the first time, and as I was thus humbled and disciplined under the Cross, my understanding became more strengthened to distinguish the language of the pure Spirit which inwardly moves upon the heart and taught [me] to wait in silence sometimes many weeks together, until I felt that rise which prepares the creature to stand like a trumpet through which the Lord speaks to his flock.

In the management of my outward affairs I may say with thankfulness I found Truth to be my support, and I was respected in my master's family, who came to live in Mount Holly within two years after my going there.

About the twenty-third year of my age, I had many fresh and heavenly openings in respect to the care and providence of the Almighty over his creatures in general, and over man as the most noble amongst those which are visible. And being clearly convinced in my judgment that to place my whole trust in God was best for me, I felt renewed engagements that in all things I might act on an inward principle of virtue and pursue worldly business no further than as Truth opened my way therein.

About the time called Christmas I observed many people from the country and dwellers in town who, resorting to the public houses, spent their time in drinking and vain sports, tending to corrupt one another, on which account I was much troubled. At one house in particular there was much disorder, and I believed it was a duty laid on me to go and speak to the master of that house. I considered I was young and that several elderly Friends in town had opportunity to see these things, and though I would gladly have been excused, yet I could not feel my mind clear.

The exercise was heavy, and as I was reading what the Almighty said to Ezekiel respecting his duty as a watchman, the matter was set home more clearly; and then with prayer and tears I besought the Lord for his assistance, who in loving-kindness gave me a resigned heart. Then at a suitable opportunity I went to the public house, and seeing the man amongst a company, I went to him and told him I wanted to speak with him; so we went aside, and there in the fear and dread of the Almighty I expressed to him what rested on my mind, which he took kindly, and afterward showed more regard to me than before. In a few years after, he died middle-aged, and I often thought that had I neglected my duty in that case it would have given me great trouble, and I was humbly thankful to my gracious Father, who had supported me herein.

My employer, having a Negro woman, sold her and directed me to write a bill of sale, the man being waiting who bought her. The thing was sudden, and though the thoughts of writing an instrument of slavery for one of my fellow creatures felt uneasy, yet I remembered I was hired by the year, that it was my master who directed me to do it, and that it was an elderly man, a member of our Society, who bought her; so through weakness I gave way and wrote it, but at the executing it, I was so afflicted in my mind that I said before my master and the Friend that I believed slavekeeping to be a practice inconsistent with the Christian religion. This in some degree abated my uneasiness, yet as often as I reflected seriously upon it I thought I should have been clearer if I had desired to be excused from it as a thing against my conscience, for such it was. And some time after this a young man of our Society spake to me to write an instrument of slavery, he having lately taken a Negro into his house. I told him I was not easy to write it, for though many kept slaves in our Society, as in others, I still believed the practice was not right, and desired to be excused from writing [it]. I spoke to him in good will, and he told me that keeping slaves was not altogether agreeable to his mind, but that the slave being a gift made to his wife, he had accepted of her.   [30–33]

CHAPTER II

1743–1748   Having now been several years with my employer,
and he doing less at merchandise than heretofore, I was thoughtful of
some other way of business, perceiving merchandise to be attended
with much cumber in the way of trading in these parts. My mind
through the power of Truth was in a good degree weaned from the
desire of outward greatness, and I was learning to be content with
real conveniences that were not costly, so that a way of life free from
much entanglements appeared best for me, though the income was
small. I had several offers of business that appeared profitable, but did
not see my way clear to accept of them, as believing the business
proposed would be attended with more outward care and cumber
than was required of me to engage in. I saw that a humble man with
the blessing of the Lord might live on a little, and that where the
heart was set on greatness, success in business did not satisfy the
craving, but that in common with an increase of wealth the desire of
wealth increased. There was a care on my mind to so pass my time as
to things outward that nothing might hinder me from the most
steady attention to the voice of the True Shepherd.

My employer, though now a retailer of goods, was by trade a
tailor and kept a servant man at that business; and I began to think
about learning the trade, expecting that if I should settle, I might by
this trade and a little retailing of goods get a living in a plain way
without the load of great business. I mentioned it to my employer and
we soon agreed on terms, and then when I had leisure from the affairs
of merchandise, I worked with his man. I believed the hand of
Providence pointed out this business for me and was taught to be
content with it, though I felt at times a disposition that would have
sought for something greater. But through the revelation of Jesus
Christ, I had seen the happiness of humility, and there was an earnest
desire in me to enter deep into it; and at times this desire arose to a

degree of fervent supplication, wherein my soul was so environed with heavenly light and consolation that things were made easy to me which had been otherwise.

In the year [*blank*] my employer's wife died. She was a virtuous woman and generally beloved of her neighbours; and soon after this he left shopkeeping and we parted. I then wrought at my trade as a tailor, carefully attended meetings for worship and discipline, and found an enlargement of gospel love in my mind and therein a concern to visit Friends in some of the back settlements of Pennsylvania and Virginia. And being thoughtful about a companion, I expressed it to my beloved friend Isaac Andrews, who then told me that he had drawings there and also to go through Maryland, Virginia, and Carolina. After considerable time passed and several conferences with him, I felt easy to accompany him throughout, if way opened for it. I opened the case in our Monthly Meeting, and Friends expressing their unity therewith, we obtained certificates to travel as companions—his from Haddonfield and mine from Burlington.   [35–36]

# #

So we took the meetings in our way through Virginia, were in some degree baptized into a feeling sense of the conditions of the people, and our exercise in general was more painful in these old settlements than it had been amongst the back inhabitants. But through the goodness of our Heavenly Father, the well of living waters was at times opened, to our encouragement and the refreshment of the sincere-hearted.

We went on to Perquimans River in North Carolina, had several meetings which were large, and found some openness in those parts and a hopeful appearance amongst the young people. So we turned again to Virginia.   [37]

# #

Two things were remarkable to me in this journey.[29] First in regard to my entertainment: When I ate, drank, and lodged free-cost with people who lived in ease on the hard labour of their slaves, I felt uneasy; and as my mind was inward to the Lord, I found, from place to place, this uneasiness return upon me at times through the whole

---

29. MS. C adds: "having been out three months and four days and travelled by estimation fifteen hundred miles."

visit. Where the masters bore a good share of the burden and lived frugal, so that their servants were well provided for and their labour moderate, I felt more easy; but where they lived in a costly way and laid heavy burdens on their slaves, my exercise was often great, and I frequently had conversation with them in private concerning it. Secondly, this trade of importing them from their native country being much encouraged amongst them and the white people and their children so generally living without much labour was frequently the subject of my serious thoughts. And I saw in these southern provinces so many vices and corruptions increased by this trade and this way of life that it appeared to me as a dark gloominess hanging over the land; and though now many willingly run into it, yet in future the consequence will be grievous to posterity! I express it as it hath appeared to me, not at once nor twice, but as a matter fixed on my mind. [38]

#   #

The winter following died my eldest sister, Elizabeth Woolman, Jr., of the smallpox, aged 31 years. She was from her youth of a thoughtful disposition and very compassionate to her acquaintance in their sickness or distress, being ready to help as far as she could. [39]

#   #

Of late I found drawings in my mind to visit Friends in New England, and having an opportunity of joining in company with my beloved friend Peter Andrews, we, having obtained certificates from our Monthly Meeting, set forward 16th day, 3rd month, 1747, and reached the Yearly Meeting on Long Island. [40]

#   #

In this journey I may say in general we were sometimes in much weakness and laboured under discouragements, and at other times, through the renewed manifestations of divine love, we had reasons of refreshment wherein the power of Truth prevailed.

We were taught by renewed experience to labour for an inward stillness, at no time to seek for words, but to live in the spirit of Truth and utter that to the people which Truth opened in us. My beloved companion and I belonged both to one meeting, came forth in the ministry near together, and were inwardly united in the work. He was about thirteen years older than I, bore the heaviest burden, and was an instrument of the greatest use. [41]

CHAPTER III

1749–1756   About this time believing it good for me to settle, and thinking seriously about a companion, my heart was turned to the Lord with desires that he would give me wisdom to proceed therein agreeable to his will; and he was pleased to give me a well-inclined damsel, Sarah Ellis, to whom I was married the 18th day, 8th month, 1749.

In the fall of the year 1750 died my father Samuel Woolman with a fever, aged about sixty years. In his lifetime he manifested much care for us his children, that in our youth we might learn to fear the Lord, often endeavouring to imprint in our minds the true principles of virtue, and particularly to cherish in us a spirit of tenderness, not only towards poor people, but also towards all creatures of which we had the command.

After my return from Carolina I made some observations on keeping slaves, which I had some time before shown him, and he perused the manuscript, proposed a few alterations, and appeared well satisfied that I found a concern on that account. And in his last sickness as I was watching with him one night, he being so far spent that there was no expectation of his recovery, but had the perfect use of his understanding, he asked me concerning the manuscript, whether I expected soon to offer it to the Overseers of the Press, and after some conversation thereon said, "I have all along been deeply affected with the oppression of the poor Negroes, and now at last my concern for them is as great as ever."

By his direction I had wrote his will in a time of health, and that night he desired me to read it to him, which I did, and he said it was agreeable to his mind. He then made mention of his end, which he believed was now near, and signified that though he was sensible of many imperfections in the course of his life, yet his experience of the power of Truth and of the love and goodness of God from time to time, even till now, was such that he had no doubt but that in leaving this life he should enter into one more happy.

The next day his sister Elizabeth came to see him and told him of the decease of their sister Anne, who died a few days before. He then said, "I reckon sister Anne was free to leave this world." Elizabeth said she was. He then said, "I also am free to leave it," and being in great weakness of body said, "I hope I shall shortly go to rest." He continued in a weighty frame of mind and was sensible till near the last.   [44–45]

# #

About this time a person at some distance lying sick, his brother came to me to write his will. I knew he had slaves, and asking his brother, was told he intended to leave them as slaves to his children. As writing is a profitable employ, as offending sober people is disagreeable to my inclination, I was straitened in my mind; but as I looked to the Lord, he inclined my heart to his testimony, and I told the man that I believed the practice of continuing slavery to this people was not right and had a scruple in mind against doing writings of that kind: that though many in our Society kept them as slaves, still I was not easy to be concerned in it and desired to be excused from going to write the will. I spake to him in the fear of the Lord, and he made no reply to what I said, but went away; he also had some concerns in the practice, and I thought he was displeased with me.

In this case I had a fresh confirmation that acting contrary to present outward interest from a motive of divine love and in regard to truth and righteousness, and thereby incurring the resentments of people, opens the way to a treasure better than silver and to a friendship exceeding the friendship of men.   [45–46]

# #

The manuscript before-mentioned having lain by me several years, the publication of it rested weightily upon me, and this year I offered it to the Overseers of the Press, who, having examined and made some small alterations in it, ordered a number of copies thereof to be published by the Yearly Meeting stock and dispersed amongst Friends.   [47]

# #

JOHN WOOLMAN

Scrupling to do writings relative to keeping slaves having been a means of sundry small trials to me, in which I have so evidently felt my own will set aside that I think it good to mention a few of them. Tradesmen and retailers of goods, who depend on their business for a living, are naturally inclined to keep the good will of their customers; nor is it a pleasant thing for young men to be under a necessity to question the judgment or honesty of elderly men, and more especially of such who have a fair reputation. Deep-rooted customs, though wrong, are not easily altered, but it is the duty of everyone to be firm in that which they certainly know is right for them. A charitable, benevolent man, well acquainted with a Negro, may, I believe, under some certain circumstances keep him in his family as a servant on no other motives than the Negro's good; but man, as man, knows not what shall be after him, nor hath he any assurance that his children will attain to that perfection in wisdom and goodness necessary in every absolute governor. Hence it is clear to me that I ought not to be the scribe where wills are drawn in which some children are made absolute masters over others during life.

About this time an ancient man of good esteem in the neighbourhood came to my house to get his will wrote. He had young Negroes, and I asking him privately how he purposed to dispose of them, he told me. I then said, "I cannot write thy will without breaking my own peace," and respectfully gave him my reasons for it. He signified that he had a choice that I should have wrote it, but as I could not consistent with my conscience, he did not desire it, and so he got it wrote by some other person. And a few years after, there being great alterations in his family, he came again to get me to write his will. His Negroes were yet young, and his son, to whom he intended to give them, was since he first spoke to me, from a libertine become a sober young man; and he supposed that I would have been free on that account to write it. We had much friendly talk on the subject and then deferred it, and a few days after, he came again and directed their freedom, and so I wrote his will.

Near the time the last-mentioned friend first spoke to me, a neighbour received a bad bruise in his body and sent for me to bleed him, which being done he desired me to write his will. I took notes, and amongst other things he told me to which of his children he gave his young Negro. I considered the pain and distress he was in and knew not how it would end, so I wrote his will, save only that part concerning his slave, and carrying it to his bedside read it to him and then told him in a friendly way that I could not write any instruments by which my fellow creatures were made slaves, without bringing trouble on my own mind. I let him know that I charged nothing for what I had done and desired to be excused from doing the other part in the way he proposed. Then we had a serious conference on the subject, and at length, he agreeing to set her free, I finished his will.

Having found drawings in my mind to visit Friends on Long Island, and having got a certificate from our Monthly Meeting, I set off 12th day, 5th month, 1756. [50–51]

\#   \#

The Lord I believe hath a people in those parts who are honestly concerned to serve him, but many I fear are too much clogged with the things of this life and do not come forward bearing the Cross in such faithfulness as the Almighty calls for.

My mind was deeply engaged in this visit, both in public and private; and at several places where I was, on observing that they had slaves, I found myself under a necessity in a friendly way to labour with them on that subject, expressing as way opened the inconsistency of that practice with the purity of the Christian religion and the ill effects of it manifested amongst us. [52]

\#   \#

Until the year 1756 I continued to retail goods, besides following my trade as a tailor, about which time I grew uneasy on account of my business growing too cumbersome. I began with selling trimmings for ¿arments and from thence proceeded to sell clothes and linens, and at length having got a considerable shop of goods, my trade increased every year and the road to large business appeared open; but I felt a stop in my mind.

Through the mercies of the Almighty I had in a good degree learned to be content with a plain way of living. I had but a small family, that on serious consideration I believed Truth did not require me to engage in much cumbrous affairs. It had been my general practice to buy and sell things really useful. Things that served chiefly to please the vain mind in people I was not easy to trade in, seldom did it, and whenever I did I found it weakened me as a Christian.

The increase of business became my burden, for though my

natural inclination was toward merchandise, yet I believed Truth required me to live more free from outward cumbers and there was now a strife in my mind between the two; and in this exercise my prayers were put up to the Lord, who graciously heard me and gave me a heart resigned to his holy will. Then I lessened my outward business, and as I had opportunity told my customers of my intentions that they might consider what shop to turn to, and so in a while wholly laid down merchandise, following my trade as a tailor, myself only, having no apprentice. I also had a nursery of apple trees, in which I employed some of my time—hoeing, grafting, trimming, and inoculating.

In merchandise it is the custom where I lived to sell chiefly on credit, and poor people often get in debt, and when payment is expected, not having wherewith to pay, their creditors often sue for it at law. Having often observed occurrences of this kind, I found it good for me to advise poor people to take such goods as were most useful and not costly.   [53–54]

#   #

As the least degree of luxury hath some connection with evil, for those who profess to be disciples of Christ and are looked upon as leaders of the people, to have that mind in them which was also in him, and so stand separate from every wrong way, is a means of help to the weaker. As I have sometimes been much spent in the heat and taken spirits to revive me, I have found by experience that in such circumstance the mind is not so calm nor so fitly disposed for divine meditation as when all such extremes are avoided, and have felt an increasing care to attend to that Holy Spirit which sets right bounds to our desires and leads those who faithfully follow it to apply all the gifts of divine Providence to the purposes for which they were intended. Did such who have the care of great estates attend with singleness of heart to this Heavenly Instructor, which so opens and enlarges the mind that men love their neighbours as themselves, they would have wisdom given them to manage without finding occasion to employ some people in the luxuries of life or to make it necessary for others to labour too hard. But for want of steadily regarding this principle of divine love, a selfish spirit takes place in the minds of people, which is attended with darkness and manifold confusions in the world.

In the course of my trading being somewhat troubled at various law suits about collecting money which I saw going forward, on applying to a constable he gave me a list of his proceeding for one year as follows—to wit, served 267 warrants, 103 summonses, and 79 executions. As to writs served by the sheriff, I got no account of them.

I once had a warrant for an idle man who I believed was about to run away, which was the only time I applied to the law to recover money.

Though trading in things useful is an honest employ, yet through the great number of superfluities which are bought and sold and through the corruption of the times, they who apply to merchandise for a living have great need to be well experienced in that precept which the prophet Jeremiah laid down for his scribe: "Seekest thou great things for thyself? Seek them not" [Jer 45:5].   [54–55]

#   #

A paragraph from "A Copy of a Letter
Wrote to a Friend"

I find that to be a fool as to worldly wisdom and commit my cause to God, not fearing to offend men who take offense at the simplicity of Truth, is the only way to remain unmoved at the sentiments of others. The fear of man brings a snare; by halting in our duty and giving back in the time of trial, our hands grow weaker, our spirits get mingled with the people, our ears grow dull as to hearing the language of the True Shepherd, that when we look at the way of the righteous, it seems as though it was not for us to follow them.   [57]

CHAPTER IV

1757   The 13th day, 2nd month, 1757. Being then in good health and abroad with Friends visiting families, I lodged at a Friend's house in Burlington, and going to bed about the time usual with me, I woke in the night and my meditations as I lay were on the goodness and mercy of the Lord, in a sense whereof my heart was contrite. After this I went to sleep again, and sleeping a short time I awoke. It was yet dark and no appearance of day nor moonshine, and as I opened my eyes I saw a light in my chamber at the apparent distance of five feet, about nine inches diameter, of a clear, easy brightness and near the center the most radiant. As I lay still without any surprise looking upon it, words were spoken to my inward ear which filled my whole inward man. They were not the effect of thought nor any conclusion in relation to the appearance, but as the language of the Holy One spoken in my mind. The words were, "Certain Evidence of Divine Truth," and were again repeated exactly in the same manner, whereupon the light disappeared.

Feeling an exercise in relation to a visit to the southern parts to increase upon me, I acquainted our Monthly Meeting therewith and obtained their certificate. I expecting to go alone, one of my brothers who lived in Philadelphia, having some business in North Carolina, proposed going with me part of the way. But as he had a view of some outward affairs, to accept of him as a companion seemed some difficulty with me, whereupon I had conversation with him at sundry times; and at length feeling easy in my mind, I had conversation with several elderly Friends of Philadelphia on the subject, and he obtaining a certificate suitable to the occasion, we set off [*blank*] day, 5th month, 1757, and fell in at Nottingham Week Day Meeting and lodged at John Churchman's. Here I met with our friend Benjamin Buffington from New England, who was returning from a visit to the southern provinces.

179

QUAKER SPIRITUALITY

Thence we crossed the river Susquehanna and lodged at William Cox's in Maryland; and soon after I entered this province a deep and painful exercise came upon me, which I often had some feeling of since my mind was drawn towards these parts, and with which I had acquainted my brother before we agreed to join as companions.

As the people in this and the southern provinces live much on the labour of slaves, many of whom are used hardly, my concern was that I might attend with singleness of heart to the voice of the True Shepherd and be so supported as to remain unmoved at the faces of men.

As it is common for Friends on a visit to have entertainment free of cost, a difficulty arose in my mind with respect to saving my own money by kindness received which to me appeared to be the gain of oppression. Receiving a gift, considered as a gift, brings the receiver under obligations to the benefactor and has a natural tendency to draw the obliged into a party with the giver. To prevent difficulties of this kind and to preserve the minds of judges from any bias was that divine prohibition, "Thou shalt not receive any gift, for a gift blindeth the eyes of the wise, and perverteth the words of the righteous." —Law of Moses [Ex 23:8].

As the disciples were sent forth without any provision for their journey and our Lord said the workman is worthy of his meat, their labour in the Gospel was considered as a reward for their entertainment, and therefore not received as a gift, yet in regard to my present journey I could not see my way clear in that respect. The odds appeared thus: the entertainment the disciples met with was from such whose hearts God had opened to receive them, from a love to them and the Truth they published; but we, considered as members of the same Society, look upon it as a piece of civility to receive each other in such visits, and such reception at times is partly in regard to reputation, and not from an inward unity of heart and spirit.

Conduct is more convincing than language, and where people by their actions manifest that the slave trade is not so disagreeable to their principles but that it may be encouraged, there is not a sound uniting with some Friends who visit them.

The prospect of so weighty a work, and being so distinguished from many who I esteemed before myself, brought me very low, and such were the conflicts of my soul. [58–60]

# #

Being thus helped to sink down into resignation, I felt a deliverance from that tempest in which I had been sorely exercised, and in calmness of mind went forward, trusting that the Lord, as I faithfully attended to him, would be a counsellor to me in all difficulties, and that by his strength I should be enabled even to leave money with the members of [the] Society where I had entertainment when I found that omitting of it would obstruct that work to which I believed he had called me. And as I copy this after my return, I may here add that oftentimes I did so under a sense of duty.

The way in which I did it was thus: when I expected soon to leave a Friend's house where I had entertainment, if I believed that I should not keep clear from the gain of oppression without leaving money, I spoke to one of the heads of the family privately and desired them to accept of me pieces of silver and give them to such of their Negroes as they believed would make the best use of them; and at other times I gave them to the Negroes myself, as the way looked clearest to me. As I expected this before I came out, I had provided a large number of small pieces, and thus offering them to some who appeared to be wealthy people was a trial to both me and them. But the fear of the Lord so covered me at times that the way was made easier than I expected, and few if any manifested any resentment at the offer, and most of them after some talk accepted of them.

7th day, 5th month, 1757. Lodged at a Friend's house, and the next day being First-day of the week was at Patapsco Meeting, then crossed Patuxent River and lodged at a public house at the head of Severn.

9th. Breakfasted at a Friend's house, who afterward putting us a little on our way, I had conversation with him in the fear of the Lord concerning his slaves, in which my heart was tender; and I used much plainness of speech with him, which he appeared to take kindly. We pursued our journey without appointing meetings, being pressed in my mind to be at the Yearly Meeting in Virginia, and in my travelling on the road I often felt language rise from the center of my mind thus: "Oh Lord, I am a stranger in the earth; hide not thy face from me" [Ps 119:19].

11th day, 5th month. We crossed the rivers Potomac and Rappahannock and lodged at Port Royal. And on the way, we happening in company with a colonel of the militia who appeared to be a thoughtful man, I took occasion to remark on the odds in general betwixt a people used to labour moderately for their living, training up their children in frugality and business, and those who live on the labour of slaves, the former in my view being the most happy life; with which he concurred and mentioned the trouble arising from the untoward, slothful disposition of the Negroes, adding that one of our labourers would do as much in a day as two of their slaves. I replied that free men whose minds were properly on their business found a satisfaction in improving, cultivating, and providing for their families, but Negroes, labouring to support others who claim them as their property and expecting nothing but slavery during life, had not the like inducement to be industrious.

After some further conversation I said that men having power too often misapplied it; that though we made slaves of the Negroes and the Turks made slaves of the Christians, I, however, believed that liberty was the natural right of all men equally, which he did not deny, but said the lives of the Negroes were so wretched in their own country that many of them lived better here than there. I only said, "There's great odds in regard to us on what principle we act." And so the conversation on that subject ended. And I may here add that another person some time afterward mentioned the wretchedness of the Negroes occasioned by their intestine wars as an argument in favour of our fetching them away for slaves, to which I then replied: "If compassion on the Africans in regard to their domestic troubles were the real motives of our purchasing them, that spirit of tenderness being attended to would incite us to use them kindly, that as strangers brought out of affliction their lives might be happy among us; and as they are human creatures, whose souls are as precious as ours and who may receive the same help and comfort from the Holy Scriptures as we do, we could not omit suitable endeavours to instruct them therein. But while we manifest by our conduct that our views in purchasing them are to advance ourselves, and while our buying captives taken in war animates those parties to push on that war and increase desolations amongst them, to say they live unhappy in Africa is far from being an argument in our favour."

And I further said, "The present circumstances of these provinces to me appears difficult, that the slaves look like a burdensome stone to such who burden themselves with them, and that if the white people retain a resolution to prefer their outward prospects of gain to all other considerations and do not act conscientiously toward them as fellow creatures, I believe that burden will grow heavier and heavier till times change in a way disagreeable to us"—at which the person appeared very serious and owned that in considering their condition and the manner of their treatment in these provinces, he had sometimes thought it might be just in the Almighty to so order it. [60–62]

\# \#

14th day, 5th month. Was at Camp Creek Monthly Meeting and then rode to the mountains up James River and had a meeting at a Friend's house, in both which I felt sorrow of heart, and my tears were poured out before the Lord, who was pleased to afford a degree of strength by which way opened to clear my mind amongst Friends in those places. From thence I went to Fork Creek and so to Cedar Creek again, at which place I now had a meeting. Here I found a tender Seed, and as I was preserved in the ministry to keep low with the Truth, the same Truth in their hearts answered it, that it was a time of mutual refreshment from the presence of the Lord. I lodged at James Stanley's, father to William Stanley, one of the young men who suffered imprisonment at Winchester last summer on account of their testimony against fighting, and I had some satisfactory conversation with him concerning it. [63–64]

\# \#

The prospect of a road lying open to the same degeneracy in some parts of this newly settled land of America, in respect to our conduct towards the Negroes, hath deeply bowed my mind in this journey; and though to briefly relate how these people are treated is no agreeable work, yet after often reading over the notes I made as I travelled, I find my mind engaged to preserve them.

Many of the white people in those provinces take little or no care of Negro marriages, and when Negroes marry after their own way, some make so little account of those marriages that with views of outward interest they often part men from their wives by selling them far asunder, which is commom when estates are sold by executors at vendue. Many whose labour is heavy being followed at their business in the field by a man with a whip, hired for that purpose, have in common little else to eat but one peck of Indian corn and salt for one week with some few potatoes. (The potatoes they commonly raise by their labour on the first day of the week.)

The correction ensuing on their disobedience to overseers or slothfulness in business is often very severe and sometimes desperate.

Men and women have many times scarce clothes enough to hide their nakedness, and boys and girls ten and twelve years old are often stark naked amongst their master's children.

Some of our Society and some of the Society called New Lights use some endeavours to instruct those they have in reading, but in common this is not only neglected but disapproved.

These are a people by whose labour the other inhabitants are in a great measure supported, and many of them in the luxuries of life. These are a people who have made no agreement to serve us and who have not forfeited their liberty that we know of. These are souls for whom Christ died, and for our conduct toward them we must answer before that Almighty Being who is no respecter of persons.

They who know the only true God and Jesus Christ whom he hath sent, and are thus acquainted with the merciful, benevolent Gospel Spirit, will therein perceive that the indignation of God is kindled against oppression and cruelty, and in beholding the great distress of so numerous a people will find cause for mourning.

[65–66]

\#　\#

29th day, 5th month. At the house where I lodged was a meeting of ministers and elders at the ninth hour in the morning, at which time I found an engagement to speak freely and plainly to them concerning their slaves, mentioning how they as the first rank in the Society, whose conduct in that case was much noticed by others, were under the stronger obligations to look carefully to themselves, expressing how needful it was for them in that situation to be thoroughly divested of all selfish views, that living in the pure Truth, and acting conscientiously towards those people in their education, and otherwise, they might be instrumental in helping forward a work so exceeding necessary and so much neglected amongst them. At the 12th hour the meeting of worship began, which was a solid meeting.

The 30th, about the 10th hour, Friends met to finish their business, and then the meeting for worship ensued, which to me was a laborious time; but through the goodness of the Lord, Truth I believe gained some ground, and it was a strengthening opportunity to the honest-hearted.

[67]

\#　\#

JOHN WOOLMAN

From an Epistle Written by John Woolman:
To Friends at Their Monthly Meeting at
New Garden and Cane Creek in North Carolina

Where slaves are purchased to do our labour, numerous difficulties attend it. To rational creatures bondage is uneasy and frequently occasions sourness and discontent in them, which affects the family and such who claim the mastery over them, and thus people and their children are many times encompassed with vexations which arise from their applying to wrong methods to get a living.

I have been informed that there are a large number of Friends in your parts who have no slaves, and in tender and most affectionate love I now beseech you to keep clear from purchasing any. Look, my dear Friends, to divine Providence, and follow in simplicity that exercise of body, that plainness and frugality, which true wisdom leads to; so may you be preserved from those dangers which attend such who are aiming at outward ease and greatness.

Treasures, though small, attained on a true principle of virtue are sweet in the possession, and while we walk in the light of the Lord there is true comfort and satisfaction. Here neither the murmurs of an oppressed people, nor throbbing, uneasy conscience, nor anxious thoughts about the event of things hinder the enjoyment of it.   [69]

# #

When I was at Newbegun Creek, a Friend was there who laboured for his living, having no Negroes, and had been a minister many years. He came to me the next day, and as we rode together he signified that he wanted to talk with me concerning a difficulty he had been under and related it near as follows, to wit: that as monies had of late years been raised by a tax to carry on the wars, he had a scruple in his mind in regard to paying it and chose rather to suffer distraint of goods than pay it. And as he was the only person who refused it in those parts and knew not that anyone else was in the like circumstance, he signified that it had been a heavy trial upon him, and the more so for that some of his brethren had been uneasy with his conduct in that case, and added that from a sympathy he felt with me yesterday in meeting, he found a freedom thus to open the matter

185

in the way of querying concerning Friends in our parts; whereupon I told him the state of Friends amongst us as well as I was able, and also that I had for some time been under the like scruple. I believed him to be one who was concerned to walk uprightly before the Lord and esteemed it my duty to preserve this memorandum.

From hence I went back into Virginia and had a meeting near James Copeland's; it was a time of inward suffering, but through the goodness of the Lord I was made content. Then to another meeting where through the renewings of pure love we had a very comfortable meeting.

Travelling up and down of late, I have had renewed evidences that to be faithful to the Lord and content with his will concerning me is a most necessary and useful lesson for me to be learning, looking less at the effects of my labour than at the pure motion and reality of the concern as it arises from heavenly love. In the Lord Jehovah is everlasting strength, and as the mind by a humble resignation is united to him and we utter words from an inward knowledge that they arise from the heavenly spring, though our way may be difficult and require close attention to keep in it, and though the manner in which we may be led may tend to our own abasement, yet if we continue in patience and meekness, heavenly peace is the reward of our labours.   [71–72]

#   #

Thence taking three meetings in my way, I went home under a humbling sense of the gracious dealings of the Lord with me in preserving me through many trials and afflictions in my journey.   [74]

CHAPTER V

1758　　The 4th day, 4th month, 1758, orders came to some officers in Mount Holly to prepare quarters a short time for about one hundred soldiers; and an officer and two other men, all inhabitants of our town, came to my house, and the officer told me that he came to speak with me to provide lodging and entertainment for two soldiers, there being 6 shillings a week per man allowed as pay for it. The case being new and unexpected, I made no answer suddenly but sat a time silent, my mind being inward. I was fully convinced that the proceedings in wars are inconsistent with the purity of the Christian religion, and to be hired to entertain men who were then under pay as soldiers was a difficulty with me. I expected they had legal authority for what they did, and after a short time I said to the officer, "If the men are sent here for entertainment, I believe I shall not refuse to admit them into my house, but the nature of the case is such that I expect I cannot keep them on hire." One of the men intimated that he thought I might do it consistent with my religious principles, to which I made no reply, as believing silence at that time best for me.

　　Though they spake of two, there came only one, who tarried at my house about two weeks and behaved himself civilly. And when the officer came to pay me I told him that I could not take pay for it, having admitted him into my house in a passive obedience to authority. I was on horseback when he spake to me, and as I turned from him he said he was obliged to me, to which I said nothing; but thinking on the expression I grew uneasy, and afterwards being near where he lived I went and told him on what grounds I refused pay for keeping the soldier.　　　　　　　　　　　　　　　[88–89]

# #

　　The Monthly Meeting of Philadelphia having been under a concern on account of some Friends who this summer, 1758, had

187

bought Negro slaves, the said meeting moved it in their Quarterly Meeting to have the minute reconsidered in the Yearly Meeting which was made last on that subject. And the said Quarterly Meeting appointed a committee to consider it and report to their next, which committee having met once and adjourned, and I, going to Philadelphia to meet a committee of the Yearly Meeting, was in town the evening on which the Quarterly Meeting's committee met the second time, and finding an inclination to sit with them, was admitted; and Friends had a weighty conference on the subject. And soon after their next Quarterly Meeting I heard that the case was coming to our Yearly Meeting, which brought a weighty exercise upon me, and under a sense of my own infirmities and the great danger I felt of turning aside from perfect purity, my mind was often drawn to retire alone and put up my prayers to the Lord that he would be graciously pleased to strengthen me, that setting aside all views of self-interest and the friendship of this world, I might stand fully resigned to his holy will.

In this Yearly Meeting several weighty matters were considered, and towards the last, that in relation to dealing with persons who purchase slaves. During the several sittings of the said meeting, my mind was frequently covered with inward prayer, and I could say with David that tears were my meat day and night [Ps 42:3]. The case of slave-keeping lay heavy upon me, nor did I find any engagement to speak directly to any other matter before the meeting. Now when this case was opened, several faithful Friends spake weightily thereto, with which I was comforted, and feeling a concern to cast in my mite, I said in substance as follows:

> In the difficulties attending us in this life, nothing is more precious than the mind of Truth inwardly manifested, and it is my earnest desire that in this weighty matter we may be so truly humbled as to be favoured with a clear understanding of the mind of Truth and follow it; this would be of more advantage to the Society than any mediums which are not in the clearness of divine wisdom. The case is difficult to some who have them, but if such set aside all self-interest and come to be weaned from the desire of getting estates, or even from holding them together when Truth requires the contrary, I believe way will open that they will know how to steer through those difficulties.

JOHN WOOLMAN

Many Friends appeared to be deeply bowed under the weight of the work and manifested much firmness in their love to the cause of truth and universal righteousness in the earth. And though none did openly justify the practice of slave-keeping in general, yet some appeared concerned lest the meeting should go into such measures as might give uneasiness to many brethren, alleging that if Friends patiently continued under the exercise, the Lord in time to come might open a way for the deliverance of these people. And I, finding an engagement to speak, said:

> My mind is often led to consider the purity of the Divine Being and the justice of his judgments, and herein my soul is covered with awfulness. I cannot omit to hint of some cases where people have not been treated with the purity of justice, and the event hath been melancholy.
>
> Many slaves on this continent are oppressed, and their cries have reached the ears of the Most High! Such is the purity and certainty of his judgments that he cannot be partial in our favour. In infinite love and goodness he hath opened our understandings from one time to another concerning our duty toward this people, and it is not a time for delay.
>
> Should we now be sensible of what he requires of us, and through a respect to the private interest of some persons or through a regard to some friendships which do not stand on an immutable foundation, neglect to do our duty in firmness and constancy, still waiting for some extraordinary means to bring about their deliverance, it may be that by terrible things in righteousness God may answer us in this matter.

Many faithful brethren laboured with great firmness, and the love of Truth in a good degree prevailed. Several Friends who had Negroes expressed their desire that a rule might be made to deal with such Friends as offenders who bought slaves in future. To this it was answered that the root of this evil would never be effectually struck at until a thorough search was made into the circumstances of such Friends who kept Negroes, in regard to the righteousness of their motives in keeping them, that impartial justice might be administered throughout.

Several Friends expressed their desire that a visit might be made to such Friends who kept slaves, and many Friends declared that they believed liberty was the Negro's right, to which at length no opposition was made publicly, so that a minute was made more full on that subject than any heretofore and the names of several Friends entered who were free to join in a visit to such who kept slaves.   [91–93]

CHAPTER VI

1758–1759   In the beginning of the 12th month, 1758, I joined in company with my friends John Sykes and Daniel Stanton in visiting such who had slaves. Some whose hearts were rightly exercised about them appeared to be glad of our visit. And in some places our way was more difficult, and I often saw the necessity of keeping down to that root from whence our concern proceeded, and have cause in reverent thankfulness humbly to bow down before the Lord, who was near to me and preserved my mind in calmness under some sharp conflicts and begat a spirit of sympathy and tenderness in me toward some who were grievously in the spirit of this world.

In the 1st month, 1759, having found my mind drawn towards a visit to some of the more active members in our Society at Philadelphia, who had slaves, I met my friend John Churchman there by an agreement, and we continued about a week in the city. We visited some sick people and some widows and their families, and the other part of our time was mostly employed in visiting such who had slaves. It was a time of deep exercise, looking often to the Lord for his assistance, who in unspeakable kindness favoured with the influence of that spirit which crucifies to the greatness and showy grandeur of this world and enabled us to go through some heavy labours in which we found peace.

24th day, 3rd month, 1759. I was at our General Spring Meeting at Philadelphia, after which I again joined with John Churchman on a visit to some more who had slaves in Philadelphia, and with thankfulness to our Heavenly Father I may say that divine love and a true sympathizing tenderness of heart prevailed at times in this service.

Having at times perceived a shyness in some Friends of considerable note towards me, I found an engagement in gospel love to pay a visit to one of them, and as I dwelt under the exercise I felt a resignedness in my mind to go; so I went and told him in private I had a desire to have an opportunity with him alone, to which he readily agreed. And then in the fear of the Lord, things relating to that shyness were searched to the bottom, and we had a large conference which I believe was of use to both of us, and am thankful that way was opened for it.

14th day, 6th month, 1759. Having felt drawings in my mind to visit Friends about Salem, and having the agreement of our Monthly Meeting therein, I attended their Quarterly Meeting and was out seven days and at seven meetings in some of which I was chiefly silent; and in others, through the baptizing power of Truth, my heart was enlarged in heavenly love and found a near fellowship with the brethren and sisters in the manifold trials attending their Christian progress through this world.

In 7th month, 1759, I found an increasing concern on my mind to visit some active members in our Society who had slaves, and having no opportunity of the company of such who were named on the minutes of the Yearly Meeting, I went alone to their houses and in the fear of the Lord acquainted them with the exercise I was under; and thus, sometimes by a few words, I found myself discharged from a heavy burden. After this, our friend John Churchman coming into our province with a view to be at some meetings and to join again in the visit to those who had slaves, I bore him company in the said visit to some active members, in which I found inward satisfaction.

At our Yearly Meeting, 1759, we had some weighty meetings where the power of Truth was largely extended to the strengthening of the honest-minded. As Friends read over the epistles to be sent to the Yearly Meetings along this continent, I observed in most of them, both this year and last, it was recommended to Friends to labour against that of buying and keeping slaves, and in some of them closely treated upon. As this practice hath long been a heavy exercise to me, as I have often waded through mortifying labours on that account and at times in some meetings been almost alone therein, now observing the increasing concern in the Society and seeing how the Lord was raising up and qualifying servants for his work, not only in this respect but for promoting the cause of Truth in general, I was humbly bowed in thankfulness before him.

This meeting continued near a week, and for several days in the forepart of it my mind was drawn into a deep inward stillness, and being at times covered with the spirit of supplication my heart was secretly poured out before the Lord. And near the conclusion of the meeting for business way opened that in the pure flowings of divine love I expressed what lay upon me, which as it then arose in my mind was first to show how deep answers to deep in the hearts of the sincere and upright, though in their different growths they may not all have attained to the same clearness in some points relating to our testimony. [95–97]

\# \#

I had conversation at my lodging with my beloved friend Samuel Eastburn, who expressed a concern to join in a visit to some Friends in that county who had Negroes; and as I had felt a draught in my mind to that work in the said county, I came home and put things in order. And on the 11th day, 12th month, I went over the river and on the next day was at Buckingham Meeting, where through the descendings of the heavenly dew my mind was comforted and drawn into a near unity with the flock of Jesus Christ.

Entering upon this visit appeared weighty, and before I left home my mind was often sad, under which exercise I felt at times that Holy Spirit which helps our infirmities, through which in private my prayers at times were put up to God that he would be pleased to so purge me from all selfishness that I might be strengthened to discharge my duty faithfully, how hard soever to the natural part. We proceeded on the visit in a weighty frame of spirit and went to the houses of the most active members through the county who had Negroes, and through the goodness of the Lord my mind was preserved in resignation in times of trial. And though the work was hard to nature, yet through the strength of that love which is stronger than death, tenderness of heart was often felt amongst us in our visits, and we parted with several families with greater satisfaction than we expected.

We visited Joseph White's family, he being in England, had also a family meeting at the house of an elder who bore us company, and was at Makefield on a First-day, at all which times my heart was truly thankful to the Lord, who was graciously pleased to renew his lovingkindness to us, his poor servants, uniting us together in his work. [102]

CHAPTER VII

1760   Having for some time past felt a sympathizing in my mind with Friends eastward, I opened my concern in our Monthly Meeting, and obtaining a certificate, set forward 17th day, 4th month, 1760, joining in company by a previous agreement with my beloved friend Samuel Eastburn.   [106]

# #

We crossed from the east end of Long Island to New London, about thirty miles, in a large open boat. While we were out, the wind rising high, the waves several times beat over us, that to me it appeared dangerous, but my mind was at that time turned to him who made and governs the deep, and my life was resigned [to] him; and as he was mercifully pleased to preserve us, I had fresh occasion to consider every day as a day lent to me and felt a renewed engagement to devote my time, and all I had, to him who gave it.

We had five meetings in Narragansett and thence to Newport. Our gracious Father preserved us in a humble dependence on him, through deep exercises that were mortifying to the creaturely will. In several families in the country where we lodged, I felt an engagement on my mind to have a conference with them in private concerning their slaves, and through divine aid I was favoured to give up thereto. Though in this thing I appear singular from many whose service in travelling I believe is greater than mine, I do not think hard of them for omitting it. I do not repine at having so unpleasant a task assigned me, but look with awfulness to him who appoints to his servants their respective employments and is good to all who serve him sincerely.

We got to Newport in the evening, and on the next day visited two sick persons and had comfortable sittings with them, and in the afternoon attended the burial of a Friend. The next day we were at the meeting at Newport, forenoon and after, where the spring of the ministry was opened and strength given to declare the word of Life to the people.

The next day we went on our journey, but the great number of slaves in these parts and the continuance of that trade from there to Guinea made a deep impression on me, and my cries were often put up to my Father in secret that he would enable me to discharge my duty faithfully in such way as he might be pleased to point out to me.

We took Swansea, Freetown, and Taunton in our way to Boston, where also we had a meeting. Our exercise was deep and the love of Truth prevailed, for which I bless the Lord.   [107–108]

#   #

We visited the meetings in those parts and were measurably baptized into a feeling of the state of the Society, and in bowedness of spirit went to the Yearly Meeting at Newport, where I understood that a large number of slaves were imported from Africa and then on sale by a member of our Society. At this meeting we met with John Storer from England, Elizabeth Shipley, Ann Gaunt, Hannah Foster, and Mercy Redman from our parts, all ministers of the Gospel, of whose company I was glad. At this time I had a feeling of the condition of Habakkuk as thus expressed: "When I heard, my belly trembled, my lips quivered, my appetite failed, and I grew outwardly weak. I trembled in myself that I might rest in the day of trouble" [Hb 3:16]. I had many cogitations and was sorely distressed.

I was desirous that Friends might petition the Legislature to use their endeavours to discourage the future importation of them, for I saw that this trade was a great evil and tended to multiply troubles and bring distresses on the people in those parts, for whose welfare my heart was deeply concerned at this time. But I perceived several difficulties in regard to petitioning, and such was the exercise of my mind that I had thought of endeavouring to get an opportunity to speak a few words in the House of Assembly, they being then sitting in town. This exercise came upon me in the afternoon on the second day of the Yearly Meeting, and going to bed I got no sleep till my mind was wholly resigned therein; and in the morning I inquired of a Friend how long the Assembly were likely to continue sitting, who told me they were expected to be prorogued that day or the next.

As I was desirous to attend the business of the meeting and perceived the Assembly were likely to depart before the business was over, after considerable exercise, humbly seeking to the Lord for instruction, my mind settled to attend on the business of the meeting, on the last day of which I had prepared a short essay of a petition to be presented to the Legislature if way opened. And having understood there were men in authority in cases relating to the Society, I opened my mind to several of them and showed them the essay I had made, and afterward opened the case in the meeting for business, in substance as follows:

> I have been under a concern for some time on account of the great number of slaves which are imported into this colony. I am aware that it is a tender point to speak to, but apprehend I am not clear in the sight of heaven without speaking to it, I have prepared an essay of a petition proposed, if way open, to be presented to the Legislature, and what I have to propose to this meeting is that some Friends may be named to walk aside and look over it, and report whether they believe it suitable to be read in this meeting. If they should think well of reading it, it will remain for the meeting, after hearing it, to consider whether to take any further notice of it as a meeting or not.

After a short conference some Friends went out and, looking over it, expressed their willingness to have it read, which being done, many expressed their unity with the proposal, and some signified that to have the subjects of the petition enlarged upon and to be signed out of meeting by such who were free would be more suitable than to do it there. Though I expected at first that if it was done, it would be in that way, yet such was the exercise of my mind that to move it in the hearing of Friends when assembled appeared to me as a duty, for my heart yearned towards the inhabitants of these parts, believing that by this trade there had been an increase of unquietness amongst them and the way made easy for the spreading of a spirit opposite to that meekness and humility which is a sure resting place for the soul, and that the continuance of this trade would not only render their healing more difficult but increase their malady. Having thus far proceeded, I felt easy to leave the essay amongst Friends, for them to proceed in it as they believed best.   [108–110]

#   #

JOHN WOOLMAN

The Yearly Meeting being now over, there yet remained on my mind a secret, though heavy, exercise in regard to some leading active members about Newport being in the practice of slave-keeping. This mentioned to two ancient Friends who came out of the country, and proposed to them, if way opened, to have some conversation with those Friends; and thereupon one of those country Friends and I consulted one of the most noted elders who had them, and he in a respectful manner encouraged me to proceed to clear myself of what lay upon me. Now I had near the beginning of the Yearly Meeting a private conference with this said elder and his wife concerning theirs, so that the way seemed clear to me to advise with him about the way of proceeding. I told him I was free to have a conference with them all together in a private house, or if he believed they would take it unkind to be asked to come together and to be spoke with one in the hearing of another, I was free to spend some time among them and visit them all in their own houses. He expressed his liking to the first proposal, not doubting their willingness to come together, and as I proposed a visit to only ministers, elders, and overseers, he named some others whom he desired might be present also; and as a careful messenger was wanted to acquaint them in a proper manner, he offered to go to all their houses to open the matter to them, and did so.

About the eighth hour the next morning we met in the meeting-house chamber, and the last-mentioned country Friend, also my companion and John Storer with us. Then after a short time of retirement, I acquainted them with the steps I had taken in procuring that meeting and opened the concern I was under, and so we proceeded to a free conference upon the subject. My exercise was heavy and I was deeply bowed in spirit before the Lord, who was pleased to favour with the seasoning virtue of Truth, which wrought a tenderness amongst us, and the subject was mutually handled in a calm and peaceable spirit. And at length feeling my mind released from that burden which I had been under, I took my leave of them in a good degree of satisfaction, and by the tenderness they manifested in regard to the practice and the concern several of them expressed in relation to disposing of them after their decease, I believed that a good exercise was spreading amongst them; and I am humbly thankful to God, who supported my mind and preserved me in a good degree of resignation through these trials.

QUAKER SPIRITUALITY

Thou who sometimes travels in the work of the ministry and art made very welcome by thy friends seest many tokens of their satisfaction in having thee for their guest. It's good for thee to dwell deep, that thou mayest feel and understand the spirits of people. If we believe Truth points towards a conference on some subjects in a private way, it's needful for us to take heed that their kindness, their freedom, and affability do not hinder us from the Lord's work. I have seen that in the midst of kindness and smooth conduct to speak close and home to them who entertain us, on points that relate to their outward interest, is hard labour; and sometimes when I have felt Truth lead toward it, I have found myself disqualified by a superficial friendship, and as the sense thereof hath abased me and my cries have been to the Lord, so I have been humbled and made content to appear weak or as a fool for his sake, and thus a door hath opened to enter upon it.

To attempt to do the Lord's work in our own way and to speak of that which is the burden of the Word in a way easy to the natural part does not reach the bottom of the disorder. To see the failings of our friends and think hard of them, without opening that which we ought to open, and still carry a face of friendship—this tends to undermine the foundation of true unity. The office of a minister of Christ is weighty, and they who now go forth as watchmen had need to be steadily on their guard against the snares of prosperity and an outside friendship. [111–112]

\#   \#

Being two days going to Nantucket and having been once before, I observed many shoals in their bay, which makes sailing more dangerous, especially in stormy nights. I observed also a great shoal which enclosed their harbor and prevents their going in with sloops except when the tide is up. Waiting without this shoal for the rising of the tide is sometimes hazardous in storms, and waiting within they sometimes miss a fair wind. I took notice that on that small island are a great number of inhabitants and the soil not very fertile, the timber so gone that for vessels, fences, and firewood they depend chiefly on buying from the main, the cost whereof, with most of their other expenses, they depend principally upon the whale fishery to answer. I considered that if towns grew larger and lands near navigable waters more cleared, timber and wood would require more labour to get it. I understood that the whales, being much hunted, and sometimes wounded and not killed, grew more shy and difficult to come at.

I considered that the formation of the earth, the seas, the islands, bays, and rivers, the motions of the winds and great waters, which cause bars and shoals in particular places, were all the works of him who is perfect wisdom and goodness; and as people attend to his heavenly instruction and put their trust in him, he provides for them in all parts where he gives them a being.

And as in this visit to these people I felt a strong desire for their firm establishment on the sure foundation, besides what was said more publicly I was concerned to speak with the women Friends in their Monthly Meeting of business, many being present, and in the fresh spring of pure love to open before them the advantage, both inward and outward, of attending singly to the pure guidance of the Holy Spirit, and therein to educate their children in true humility and the disuse of all superfluities, reminding them of the difficulties their husbands and sons were frequently exposed to at sea, and that the more plain and simple their way of living was, the less need of running great hazards to support them in it—encouraging the young women in their neat, decent way of attending themselves on the affairs of the house, showing, as the way opened, that where people were truly humble, used themselves to business, and were content with a plain way of life, that it had ever been attended with more true peace and calmness of mind than those have had who, aspiring to greatness and outward show, have grasped hard for an income to support themselves in it. And as I observed they had few or no slaves amongst them, I had to encourage them to be content without them, making mention of the numerous troubles and vexations which frequently attend the minds of people who depend on slaves to do their labour. [114–115]

\#   \#

That poverty of spirit and inward weakness with which I was much tried the forepart of this journey has of late appeared to me as a dispensation of kindness. Appointing meetings never appeared more weighty to me, and I was led into a deep search whether in all things my mind was resigned to the will of God, often querying with myself what should be the cause of such inward poverty, and greatly desired that no secret reserve in my heart might hinder my access to the Divine Fountain. In these humbling times I was made watchful and excited to attend the secret movings of the Heavenly Principle in my mind, which prepared the way to some duties that in more easy and prosperous times as to the outward I believe I should have been in danger of omitting.   [115]

CHAPTER VIII

1761–1763   Having felt my mind drawn towards a visit to a few
meetings in Pennsylvania, I was very desirous to be rightly instructed
as to the time of setting off, and on 10th day, 5th month, 1761, being
the first day of the week, I went to Haddonfield Meeting, concluding
in my mind to seek for heavenly instruction and come home or go on,
as I might then believe best for me; and there through the springing
up of pure love I felt encouragement and so crossed the river. In this
visit I was at two Quarterly and three Monthly Meetings and in the
love of Truth felt my way open to labour with some noted Friends
who kept Negroes. And as I was favoured to keep to the root and
endeavoured to discharge what I believed was required of me, I found
inward peace therein, from time to time, and thankfulness of heart of
the Lord, who was graciously pleased to be a guide to me.

In the 8th month, 1761, having felt drawings in my mind to visit
Friends in and about Shrewsbury, I went there and was at their
Monthly Meeting and their First-day meeting and had a meeting at
Squan and another in Squankum, and as way opened had conversa-
tion with some noted Friends concerning their slaves, and returned
home in a thankful sense of the goodness of the Lord.

From a care I felt growing in me for some years, I wrote
Considerations on Keeping Negroes, Part Second, which were printed this
year, 1762. When the Overseers of the Press had done with it, they
offered to get a number printed, to be paid for out of the Yearly
Meeting stock and to be given away; but I being most easy to publish
them at my own expense, and offering my reasons, they appeared
satisfied.

This stock is the contribution of the members of our religious
Society in general, amongst whom are some who keep Negroes, and
being inclined to continue them in slavery, are not likely to be
satisfied with those books being spread amongst a people where many
of the slaves are learned to read, and especially not at their expense;

and such, often receiving them as a gift, conceal them. But as they who make a purchase generally buy that which they have a mind for, I believed it best to sell them, expecting by that means they would more generally be read with attention. Advertisements being signed by order of the Overseers of the Press, directed to be read in Monthly Meetings of business within our own Yearly Meeting, informing where the books were and that the price was no more than the cost of printing and binding them, many were taken off in our parts. Some I sent to Virginia, some to York, and some to Newport to my acquaintance there; and some I kept, expecting to give part of them away where there appeared a prospect of doing it to advantage.

In my youth I was used to hard labour, and though I was middling healthy, yet my nature was not fitted to endure so much as many others, that being often weary, I was prepared to sympathize with those whose circumstance in life as freemen required constant labour to answer the demands of their creditors, and with others under oppression. In the uneasiness of body which I have many times felt by too much labour, not as a forced but a voluntary oppression, I have often been excited to think on the original cause of that oppression which is imposed on many in the world. And the latter part of the time wherein I laboured on our plantation, my heart through the fresh visitations of heavenly love being often tender and my leisure time frequently spent in reading the life and doctrines of our blessed Redeemer, the account of the sufferings of martyrs, and the history of the first rise of our Society, a belief was gradually settled in my mind that if such who had great estates generally lived in that humility and plainness which belongs to a Christian life, and laid much easier rents and interests on their lands and moneys and thus led the way to a right use of things, so great a number of people might be employed in things useful that labour both for men and other creatures would need to be no more than an agreeable employ, and divers branches of business which serve chiefly to please the natural inclinations of our minds, and which at present seem necessary to circulate that wealth which some gather, might in this way of pure wisdom be discontinued. And as I have thus considered these things, a query at times hath arisen: Do I in all my proceedings keep to that use of things which is agreeable to universal righteousness? And then there hath some degree of sadness at times come over me, for that I accustomed myself to some things which occasioned more labour than I believed divine wisdom intends for us. [117–119]

JOHN WOOLMAN

\#   \#

In visiting people of note in the Society who had slaves and labouring with them in brotherly love on that account, I have seen, and the sight has affected me, that a conformity to some customs distinguishable from pure wisdom has entangled many, and the desire of gain to support these customs greatly opposed the work of Truth. And sometimes when the prospect of the work before me has been such that in bowedness of spirit I have been drawn into retired places, and besought the Lord with tears that he would take me wholly under his direction and show me the way in which I ought to walk, it hath revived with strength of conviction that if I would be his faithful servant I must in all things attend to his wisdom and be teachable, and so cease from all customs contrary thereto, however used amongst religious people.   [119]

\#   \#

And on the 31st day, fifth month, 1761, I was taken ill of a fever, and after having it near a week I was in great distress of body. And one day there was a cry raised in me that I might understand the cause why I was afflicted and improve under it, and my conformity to some customs which I believed were not right were brought to my remembrance. And in the continuation of the exercise I felt all the powers in me yield themselves up into the hands of him who gave me being and was made thankful that he had taken hold of me by his chastisement, feeling the necessity of further purifying. There was now no desire in me for health until the design of my correction was answered, and thus I lay in abasement and brokenness of spirit. And as I felt a sinking down into a calm resignation, so I felt, as in an instant, an inward healing in my nature, and from that time forward I grew better.

Though I was thus settled in mind in relation to hurtful dyes, I felt easy to wear my garments heretofore made, and so continued about nine months. Then I thought of getting a hat the natural colour of the fur, but apprehension of being looked upon as one affecting singularity felt uneasy to me. And here I had occasion to consider that things, though small in themselves, being clearly enjoined by divine authority became great things to us, and I trusted the Lord would support me in the trials that might attend singularity while that singularity was only for his sake. On this account I was under close exercise of mind in the time of our General Spring Meeting, 1762, greatly desiring to be rightly directed. And at a time when one of my dear brethren was concerned in humble supplication, I, being then deeply bowed in spirit before the Lord, was made willing, in case I got safe home, to speak for a hat the natural colour of the fur, and did so.

In attending meetings this singularity was a trial upon me, and more especially at this time, as being in use among some who were fond of following the changeable modes of dress; and as some Friends who knew not on what motives I wore it carried shy of me, I felt my way for a time shut up in the ministry. And in this condition, my mind being turned toward my Heavenly Father with fervent cries that I might be preserved to walk before him in the meekness of wisdom, my heart was often tender in meetings, and I felt an inward consolation, which to me was very precious under those difficulties.

I had several dyed garments fit for use, which I believed it best to wear till I had occasion of new ones, and some Friends were apprehensive that my wearing such a hat savored of an affected singularity, and such who spoke with me in a friendly way I generally informed in a few words that I believed my wearing it was not in my own will. I had at times been sensible that a superficial friendship had been dangerous to me, and many Friends being now uneasy with me I found to be a providential kindness. And though I had an inclination to acquaint some valuable Friends with the manner of my being led into these things, yet upon a deeper thought I was for a time most easy to omit it, believing the present dispensation was profitable and trusting that if I kept my place the Lord in his own time would open the hearts of Friends towards me, since which I've had cause to admire his goodness and loving-kindness in leading about and in-structing, and opening and enlarging my heart in some of our meetings. [120–122]

\#   \#

Having many years felt love in my heart towards the natives of this land who dwell far back in the wilderness, whose ancestors were the owners and possessors of the land where we dwell, and who for a very small consideration assigned their inheritance to us, and being at Philadelphia in the 8th month, 1761, on a visit to some Friends who had slaves, I fell in company with some of those natives who lived on the east branch of the river Susquehanna at an Indian town called

Wyalusing, about two hundred miles from Philadelphia. And in conversation with them by an interpreter, as also by observations on their countenance and conduct, I believed some of them were measurably acquainted with that divine power which subjects the rough and froward will of the creature; and at times I felt inward drawings towards a visit to that place, of which I told none except my dear wife until it came to some ripeness.

And then in the winter, 1762, I laid it before Friends at our Monthly and Quarterly and then at our General Spring Meeting, and having the unity of Friends and being thoughtful about an Indian pilot, there came a man and three women from a little beyond that town to Philadelphia on business; and I, being informed thereof by letter, met them in town on the 5th month, 1763. And after some conversation finding they were sober people, I, by the concurrence of Friends in that place, agreed to join them as companions in their return; and the 7th day, 6th month, following we appointed to meet at Samuel Foulke's at Richland. Now as this visit felt weighty and was performed at a time when travelling appeared perilous, so the dispensations of divine Providence in preparing my mind for it have been memorable, and I believe it good for me to give some hints thereof.

After I had given up to go, the thoughts of the journey were often attended with an unusual sadness, in which times my heart was frequently turned to the Lord with inward breathings for his heavenly support, that I might not fail to follow him wheresoever he might lead me.   [122–123]

#   #

And thus in true love and tenderness I parted from Friends, expecting the next morning to proceed on my journey, and being weary went early to bed.

And after I had been asleep a short time, I was awaked by a man calling at my door, and arising was invited to meet some Friends at a public house in our town who came from Philadelphia so late that Friends were generally gone to bed. These Friends informed me that an express arrived the last morning from Pittsburgh and brought news that the Indians had taken a fort from the English westward and slain and scalped English people in divers places, some near the said Pittsburgh, and that some elderly Friends in Philadelphia, knowing the time of my expecting to set off, had conferred together and thought good to inform me of these things before I left home, that I might consider them and proceed as I believed best. So I, going again to bed, told not my wife till morning. My heart was turned to the Lord for his heavenly instruction, and it was a humbling time to me.

When I told my dear wife she appeared to be deeply concerned about it, but in a few hours time my mind became settled in a belief that it was my duty to proceed on my journey, and she bore it with a good degree of resignation. In this conflict of spirit there were great searchings of heart and strong cries to the Lord that no motion might be in the least degree attended to but that of the pure spirit of Truth.

The subjects before-mentioned, on which I had so lately spake in public, were now very fresh before me, and I was brought inwardly to commit myself to the Lord to be disposed of as he saw good. So I took leave of my family and neighbours in much bowedness of spirit and went to our Monthly Meeting at Burlington. And after taking leave of Friends there I crossed the river, accompanied by my friends Israel and John Pemberton; and parting the next morning with Israel, John bore me company to Samuel Foulke's, where I met the before-mentioned Indians, and we were glad to see each other.

Here my friend Benjamin Parvin met me and proposed joining as a companion, we having passed some letters before on the subject. And now on his account I had a sharp trial, for as the journey appeared perilous, I thought if he went chiefly to bear me company and we should be taken captive, my having been the means of drawing him into these difficulties would add to my own afflictions. So I told him my mind freely and let him know that I was resigned to go alone, but after all, if he really believed it to be his duty to go on, I believed his company would be very comfortable to me. It was indeed a time of deep exercise, and Banjamin appeared to be so fastened to the visit that he could not be easy to leave me; so we went on, accompanied by our friends John Pemberton, and William Lightfoot of Pikeland, and lodged at Bethlehem.

And there parting with John, William and we went forward on the 9th day, 6th month, and got lodging on the floor at a house about five miles from Fort Allen. Here we parted with William, and at this place we met with an Indian trader lately come from Wyoming, and in conversation with him I perceived that many white people do often sell rum to the Indians, which I believe is a great evil. First, they being thereby deprived of the use of their reason and their spirits violently agitated, quarrels often arise which end in mischief, and the bitterness and resentment occasioned hereby are frequently of long continuance. Again, their skins and furs, gotten through much fatigue and hard travels in hunting, with which they intended to buy clothing, these when they begin to be intoxicated they often sell at a low rate for more rum; and afterward when they suffer for want of the necessaries of life, [they] are angry with those who for the sake of gain took the advantage of their weakness. Of this their chiefs have often complained at their treaties with the English.

Where cunning people pass counterfeits and impose that on others which is only good for nothing, it is considered as a wickedness, but to sell that to people which we know does them harm and which often works their ruin, for the sake of gain, manifests a hardened and corrupt heart and is an evil which demands the care of all true lovers of virtue to suppress. And while my mind this evening was thus employed, I also remembered that the people on the frontier, among whom this evil is too common, are often poor people, who venture to the outside of a colony that they may live more independent on such who are wealthy, who often set high rents on their land, being renewedly confirmed in a belief that if all our inhabitants lived according to sound wisdom, labouring to promote universal love and righteousness, and ceased from every inordinate desire after wealth and from all customs which are tinctured with luxury, the way would be easy for our inhabitants, though much more numerous than at present, to live comfortably on honest employments, without having that temptation they are often under of being drawn into schemes to make settlements on lands which have not been purchased of the Indians, or of applying to that wicked practice of selling rum to them.   [124–126]

#   #

Near our tent, on the sides of large trees peeled for that purpose were various representations of men going to and returning from the wars, and of some killed in battle, this being a path heretofore used by warriors. And as I walked about viewing those Indian histories, which were painted mostly in red but some with black, and thinking on the innumerable afflictions which the proud, fierce spirit produceth in the world—thinking on the toils and fatigues of warriors travelling over mountains and deserts, thinking on their miseries and distresses when wounded far from home by their enemies, and of their bruises and great weariness in chasing one another over the rocks and mountains, and of their restless, unquiet state of mind who live in this spirit, and of the hatred which mutually grows up in the minds of the children of those nations engaged in war with each other—during these meditations the desire to cherish the spirit of love and peace amongst these people arose very fresh in me.

This was the first night that we lodged in the woods, and being wet with travelling in the rain, the ground and our tent wet, and the bushes wet which we purposed [to] lay under our blankets, all looked discouraging. But I believed that it was the Lord who had thus far brought me forward and that he would dispose of me as he saw good, and therein I felt easy. So we kindled a fire with our tent door open to it; and with some bushes next the ground, and then our blankets, we made our bed, and lying down got some sleep. And in the morning feeling a little unwell, I went into the river all over. The water was cold, and soon after I felt fresh and well.

11th day, 6th month. The bushes being wet we tarried in our tent till about eight o'clock, then going on crossed a high mountain supposed to be upward of four miles wide, and the steepness on the north side exceeded all the others. We also crossed two swamps, and it raining near night, we pitched our tent and lodged.

About noon on our way we were overtaken by one of the Moravian brethren going to Wyalusing, and an Indian man with him who could talk English; and we, being together while our horses ate grass, had some friendly conversation; then they, travelling faster than we, soon left us. This Moravian, I understood, had spent some time this spring at Wyalusing and was by some of them invited to come again.

12th day, 6th month, and first of the week. It being a rainy day we continued in our tent, and here I was led to think on the nature of the exercise which hath attended me. Love was the first motion, and then a concern arose to spend some time with the Indians, that I might feel and understand their life and the spirit they live in, if haply I might receive some instruction from them, or they be in any degree helped forward by my following the leadings of Truth amongst them. And as it pleased the Lord to make way for my going at a time when the troubles of war were increasing, and when by reason of much wet weather travelling was more difficult than usual at that season, I looked upon it as a more favourable opportunity to season my mind and bring me into a nearer sympathy with them. And as mine eye was to the great Father of Mercies, humbly desiring

to learn what his will was concerning me, I was made quiet and
content. [126–128]

# #

I was led into a close, laborious inquiry whether I, as an individual, kept clear from all things which tended to stir up or were
connected with wars, either in this land or Africa, and my heart was
deeply concerned that in future I might in all things keep steadily to
the pure Truth and live and walk in the plainness and simplicity of a
sincere follower of Christ.

And in this lonely journey I did this day greatly bewail the
spreading of a wrong spirit, believing that the prosperous, convenient
situation of the English requires a constant attention to divine love
and wisdom, to guide and support us in a way answerable to the will
of that good, gracious, and almighty Being who hath an equal regard
to all mankind. And here luxury and covetousness, with the numerous oppressions and other evils attending them, appeared very afflict-
ing to me, and I felt in that which is immutable that the seeds of great
calamity and desolation are sown and growing fast on this continent.
Nor have I words sufficient to set forth that longing I then felt that
we who are placed along the coast, and have tasted the love and
goodness of God, might arise in his strength and like faithful messengers labour to check the growth of these seeds, that they may not
ripen to the ruin of our posterity.

We reached the Indian settlement at Wyoming, and here we were
told that an Indian runner had been at that place a day or two before
us and brought news of the Indians taking an English fort westward
and destroying the people, and that they were endeavouring to take
another—and also that another Indian runner came there about midnight the night next before we got there, who came from a town
about ten miles above Wyalusing and brought news that some Indian
warriors from distant parts came to that town with two English
scalps and told the people that it was war with the English.

Our pilots took us to the house of a very ancient man, and soon
after we had put in our baggage, there came a man from another
Indian house some distance off. And I, perceiving there was a man
near the door, went out; and he having a tomahawk wrapped under
his match-coat out of sight, as I approached him he took it in his hand.
I, however, went forward, and speaking to him in a friendly way
perceived he understood some English. My companion then coming

out, we had some talk with him concerning the nature of our visit in these parts; and then he, going into the house with us and talking with our pilots, soon appeared friendly and sat down and smoked his pipe. Though his taking his hatchet in his hand at the instant I drew near him had a disagreeable appearance, I believe he had no other intent than to be in readiness in case any violence was offered to him.

Hearing the news brought by these Indian runners, and being told by the Indians where we lodged that what Indians were about Wyoming expected in a few days to move to some larger towns, I thought that to all outward appearance it was dangerous travelling at this time, and was after a hard day's journey brought into a painful exercise at night, in which I had to trace back and feel over the steps I had taken from my first moving in the visit. And though I had to bewail some weakness which at times had attended me, yet I could not find that I had ever given way to a wilful disobedience. And then as I believed I had under a sense of duty come thus far, I was now earnest in spirit beseeching the Lord to show me what I ought to do.

In this great distress I grew jealous of myself, lest the desire of reputation as a man firmly settled to persevere through dangers, or the fear of disgrace arising on my returning without performing the visit, might have some place in me. Thus I lay full of thoughts a great part of the night, while my beloved companion lay and slept by me, till the Lord my gracious Father, who saw the conflicts of my soul, was pleased to give quietness. Then was I again strengthened to commit my life and all things relating thereto into his heavenly hands; and getting a little sleep toward day, when morning came we arose.

And then on the 14th day, 6th month, we sought out and visited all the Indians hereabouts that we could meet with, they being chiefly in one place about a mile from where we lodged, in all perhaps twenty. Here I expressed the care I had on my mind for their good and told them that true love had made me willing thus to leave my family to come and see the Indians and speak with them in their houses. Some of them appeared kind and friendly. [129–131]

#   #

We went on and reached Wyalusing about the middle of the afternoon, and the first Indian that we saw was a woman of a modest countenance, with a babe, who first spake to our pilot and then with a harmonious voice expressed her gladness at seeing us, having before heard of our coming. Then by the direction of our pilot we sat down on a log, and he went to the town to tell the people that we were come. My companion and I sitting thus together in a deep inward stillness, the poor woman came and sat near us; and great awfulness coming over us, we rejoiced in a sense of God's love manifested to our poor souls.

After a while we heard a conch shell blow several times, and then came John Curtis and another Indian man who kindly invited us into a house near the town, where we found I suppose about sixty people sitting in silence. And after sitting a short time, I stood up and in some tenderness of spirit acquainted them with the nature of my visit and that a concern for their good had made me willing to come thus far to see them—all in a few short sentences, which some of them, understanding, interpreted to the others; and there appeared gladness amongst them. Then I showed them my certificate, which was explained to them; and the Moravian who overtook us on the way, being now here, bid me welcome.

18th day, 6th month. We rested ourselves this forenoon, and the Indians, knowing that the Moravian and I were of different religious Societies, and as some of their people had encouraged him to come and stay awhile with them, were, I believe, concerned that no jarring or discord might be in their meetings; and they, I suppose having conferred together, acquainted me that the people at my request would at any time come together and hold meetings, and also told me that they expected the Moravian would speak in their settled meetings, which are commonly held morning and near evening. So I found liberty in my heart to speak to the Moravian and told him of the care I felt on my mind for the good of these people, and that I believed no ill effects would follow it if I sometimes spake in their meetings when love engaged me thereto, without calling them together at times when they did not meet of course; whereupon he expressed his good will toward my speaking at any time all that I found in my heart to say.

So near evening I was at their meeting, where the pure Gospel love was felt, to the tendering some of our hearts. And the interpreters, endeavouring to acquaint the people with what I said, in short sentences, found some difficulty, as none of them were quite perfect in the English and Delaware tongue. So they helped one another and we laboured along, divine love attending. And afterwards feeling my mind covered with the spirit of prayer, I told the interpreters that I found it in my heart to pray to God and believed if I prayed right he would hear me, and expressed my willingness for them to omit interpreting; so our meeting ended with a degree of divine love. And before the people went out I observed Papunehang (the man who had been zealous in labouring for a reformation in that town, being then very tender) spoke to one of the interpreters, and I was afterward told that he said in substance as follows: "I love to feel where words come from."

19th day, 6th month, and first of the week. This morning in the meeting the Indian who came with the Moravian spake a short time to the people. And in the afternoon, they coming together and my heart being filled with a heavenly care for their good, I spake to them awhile by interpreters, but none of them being perfect in the work. And I, feeling the current of love run strong, told the interpreters that I believed some of the people would understand me, and so proceeded, in which exercise I believe the Holy Ghost wrought on some hearts to edification, where all the words were not understood. [132–133]

\# \#

I now, feeling my mind at liberty to return, took my leave of them in general at the conclusion of what I said in meeting, and so we prepared to go homeward. But some of their most active men told us that when we were ready to move, the people would choose to come and shake hands with us, which those who usually came to meeting did. And from a secret draught in my mind, I went amongst some who did not use to go to meeting and took my leave of them also. And the Moravian and his Indian interpreter appeared respectful to us at parting. [135]

\# \#

We expected only two Indians to be our company, but when we were ready to go, we found many of them were going to Bethlehem with skins and furs, who chose to go in company with us. So they loaded two canoes which they desired us to go in, telling us that the waters were so raised with the rains that the horses should be taken by such who were better acquainted with the fording places. So we, with several Indians, went in the canoes, and others went on horses, there being seven besides ours. And we meeting with the horsemen once on the way by appointment, and then near night a little below a branch called Tunkhannock, we lodged there; and some of the young

men, going out a little before dusk with their guns, brought in a
deer.   [135]

# #

25th day, 6th month. We reached Bethlehem, taking care on the
way to keep foremost and to acquaint people on and near the road
who these Indians were. This we found very needful, for that the
frontier inhabitants were often alarmed at the report of English being
killed by Indians westward.

Amongst our company were some who I did not remember to
have seen at meeting, and some of these at first were very reserved,
but we being several days together and behaving friendly toward
them and making them suitable returns for the services they did us,
they became more free and sociable.

26th day, 6th month, and first of the week. Having carefully
endeavoured to settle all affairs with the Indians relative to our
journey, we took leave of them, and I thought they generally parted
with us affectionately. So we, getting to Richland, had a very comfortable meeting amongst our friends. Here I parted with my kind
friend and companion Benjamin Parvin, and accompanied by my
friend Samuel Foulke we rode to John Cadwalader's, from whence I
reached home the next day, where I found my family middling well.
And they and my friends all along appeared glad to see me return
from a journey which they apprehended dangerous. But my mind
while I was out had been so employed in striving for a perfect
resignation, and I had so often been confirmed in a belief that
whatever the Lord might be pleased to allot for me would work for
good [that] I was careful lest I should admit any degree of selfishness
in being glad overmuch, and laboured to improve by those trials in
such a manner as my gracious Father and Protector intends for me.

Between the English inhabitants and Wyalusing we had only a
narrow path, which in many places is much grown up with bushes
and interrupted by abundance of trees lying across it, which together
with the mountains, swamps and rough stones, it is a difficult road to
travel, and the more so for that rattlesnakes abound there, of which
we killed four—that people who have never been in such places have
but an imperfect idea of them. But I was not only taught patience but
also made thankful to God, who thus led me about and instructed me
that I might have a quick and lively feeling of the afflictions of my
fellow creatures whose situation in life is difficult.   [136–137]

CHAPTER IX

1763–1769   Notes at our Yearly Meeting at Philadelphia, 9th month, 1764. First John Smith of Marlborough, aged upward of eighty years, a faithful minister though not eloquent, in our meeting of ministers and elders on the 25th stood up and, appearing to be under a great exercise of spirit, informed Friends in substance as follows, to wit: that he had been a member of the Society upward of sixty years and well remembered that in those early times Friends were a plain, lowly-minded people, and that there was much tenderness and contrition in their meetings; that at the end of twenty years from that time, the Society increasing in wealth and in some degree conforming to the fashions of the world, true humility was less apparent and their meetings in general not so lively and edifying; that at the end of forty years many of them were grown very rich—that wearing of fine costly garments and using of silver (and other) watches became customary with them, their sons, and their daughters, and many of the Society made a specious appearance in the world, which marks of outward wealth and greatness appeared on many in our meetings of ministers and elders, and as these things became more prevalent, so the powerful overshadowings of the Holy Ghost were less manifest in the Society, that there had been a continued increase of these ways of life even until now, and that the weakness which hath now overspread the Society and the barrenness manifest amongst us is matter of much sorrow.

He then mentioned the uncertainty of his attending these meetings in future, expecting his dissolution was now near, and signified that he had seen in the true light that the Lord would bring back his people from these things into which they were thus degenerated but that his faithful servants must first go through great and heavy exercises therein.

29th day, 9th month, 1764. The committee appointed by the

JOHN WOOLMAN

Yearly Meeting some time since now made report in writing of their proceedings in that service, in which they signified that in the course of their proceedings they had been apprehensive that some persons holding offices in government inconsistent with our principles and others who kept slaves—these remaining active members in our meetings of discipline—had been one means of weakness more and more prevailing in the management thereof in some places.

After this report was read, an exercise revived on my mind which at times had attended me several years, and inward cries to the Lord were raised in me that the fear of man might not prevent me from doing what he required of me; and standing up I spake in substance as follows:

> I've felt a tenderness in my mind toward persons in two circumstances mentioned in that report—that is, toward such active members who keep slaves and such who hold offices in civil government—and have desired that Friends in all their conduct may be kindly affectioned one toward another. Many Friends who keep slaves are under some exercise on that account and at times think about trying them with freedom, but find many things in their way. And the way of living and annual expenses of some of them are such that it is impracticable for them to set their slaves free without changing their own way of life. It has been my lot to be often abroad, and I have observed in some places, at Quarterly and Yearly Meetings and at some stages where travelling Friends and their horses are often entertained, that the yearly expense of individuals therein is very considerable. And Friends in some places crowding much on persons in these circumstances for entertainment hath often rested as a burden on my mind for some years past, and I now express it in the fear of the Lord, greatly desiring that Friends now present may duly consider it.

In fifty pounds are four hundred half crowns. If a slave be valued at fifty pounds and I with my horse put his owner to half a crown expense, and I with many others for a course of years repeat these expense [sic] four hundred times, then on a fair computation this slave may be accounted a slave to the public under the direction of the man he calls master.

[19th day, 10th] month, 1764. I, having hired a man to work, perceived in conversation that he had been a soldier in the late war on this continent. And in the evening, giving a narrative of his captivity amongst the Indians, he informed me that he saw two of his fellow captives tortured to death, one of which, being tied to a tree, had abundance of pine splinters run into his body and then set on fire, and that this was continued by intervals near two days before he expired, that they opened the belly of the other and fastened a part of his bowels to a tree, and then whipped the poor creature till by his running round the tree his bowels were drawn out of his body.

This relation affected me with sadness, under which I went to bed, and the next morning soon after I awoke a fresh and living sense of divine love was spread over my mind, in which I had a renewed prospect of the nature of that wisdom from above which leads to a right use of all gifts both spiritual and temporal, and gives content therein. Under a feeling thereof I wrote as follows:

Hath he who gave me a being attended with many wants unknown to brute creatures given me a capacity superior to theirs?—and shown me that a moderate application to business is proper to my present condition, and that this, attended with his blessing, may supply all outward wants while they remain within the bounds he hath fixed, and no imaginary wants proceeding from an evil spirit have any place in me? Attend then—O my soul!—to this pure wisdom, as thy sure conductor through the manifold dangers in this world.

Does pride lead to vanity? Does vanity form imaginary wants? Do these wants prompt men to exert their power in requiring that of others which themselves would rather be excused from, was the same required of them?

Do those proceedings beget hard thoughts? Does hard thought when ripe become malice? Does malice when ripe become revengeful, and in the end inflict terrible pains on their fellow creatures and spread desolations in the world?

Does mankind walking in uprightness delight in each other's happiness? And do these creatures, capable of this attainment, by giving way to an evil spirit employ their wit and strength to afflict and destroy one another? Remember then—O my soul!—the quietude of those in whom Christ governs, and in all thy proceedings feel after it.

Does he condescend to bless thee with his presence? To move and influence to action? To dwell in thee and walk in thee? Remember then thy station as a being sacred to God, accept of the strength freely offered thee, and take heed that no weakness in conforming to expensive, unwise, and hard-hearted customs, gendering to discord and strife, be given way to. Does he claim my body as his temple and graciously grant that I may be sacred to him? Oh! that I may prize this favour and that my whole life may be conformable to this character.

Remember, O my soul, that the Prince of Peace is thy Lord, that he communicates his unmixed wisdom to his family, that they, living in perfect simplicity, may give no just cause of offense to any creature, but may walk as he walked.

An exercise having at times for several years attended me in regard to paying a religious visit to Friends on the eastern shore of Maryland, such was the nature of this exercise that I believed the Lord moved me to travel on foot amongst them, that by so travelling I might have a more lively feeling of the condition of the oppressed slaves, set an example of lowliness before the eyes of their masters, and be more out of the way of temptation to unprofitable familiarities. The time now drawing near in which I believed it my duty to lay my concern before our Monthly Meeting, I perceived in conversation with my beloved friend John Sleeper that he was under a concern to travel the same way, and also to travel on foot in the form of a servant amongst them, as he expressed it. This he told me before he knew aught of my exercise.

We, being thus drawn the same way, laid our exercise and the nature of it before Friends, and obtaining certificates we set off the 6th day, 5th month, 1766. [139–15]

# #

. . . . I crossed Susquehanna, and coming amongst people who lived in outward ease and greatness, chiefly on the labour of slaves, my heart was much affected, and in awful retiredness my mind was gathered inward to the Lord, being humbly engaged that in true resignation I might receive instruction from him respecting my duty amongst this people.

Though travelling on foot was wearisome to my body, yet thus travelling was agreeable to the state of my mind. I went gently on, being weakly, and was covered with sorrow and heaviness on account of the spreading, prevailing spirit of this world, introducing customs grievous and oppressive on one hand, and cherishing pride and wantonness on the other. In this lonely walk and state of abasement and humiliation, the state of the church in these parts was opened before me, and I may truly say with the prophet, "I was bowed down at the hearing of it; I was dismayed at the seeing of it" [Is 21:3]. Under this exercise I attended the Quarterly Meeting at Gunpowder, and in bowedness of spirit I had to open with much plainness what I felt respecting Friends living in fullness on the labours of the poor oppressed Negroes. And that promise of the Most High was now revived, "I will gather all nations and tongues, and they shall come and see my glory" [Is 66:18].   [149–150]

#   #

From thence I went on and was at meetings at Concord, Middletown, Providence, and Haddonfield, and so home, where I found my family well. A sense of the Lord's merciful preservation in this my journey incites reverent thankfulness to him.

#   #

On the 5th, 5th month, 1768, I left home under the humbling hand of the Lord, having obtained a certificate in order to visit some meetings in Maryland; and to proceed without a horse looked clearest to me. I was at Quarterly Meetings at Philadelphia and Concord and then went on to Chester River, and crossing the bay with Friends, was at the Yearly Meetings at West River. Thence back to Chester River and, taking a few meetings in my way, proceeded home.

It was a journey of much inward waiting, and as my eye was to the Lord, way was several times opened to my humbling admiration when things had appeared very difficult. In my return I felt a relief of mind very comfortable to me, having through divine help laboured in much plainness, both with Friends selected and in the more public meetings, so that I trust the pure witness in many minds was reached.

11th day, 6th month, 1769. Sundry cases have happened of late years within the limits of our Monthly Meeting respecting that of exercising pure righteousness towards the Negroes, in which I have lived under a labour of heart that equity might be steadily kept to. On this account I have had some close exercises amongst Friends, in which way I may thankfully say I find peace. And as my meditations have been on universal love, my own conduct in time past became of late very grievous to me.

As persons setting Negroes free in our province are bound by law to maintain them in case they have need of relief, some who scrupled keeping slaves for term of life (in the time of my youth) were wont to detain their young Negroes in their service till thirty years of age, without wages, on that account. And with this custom I so far agreed that I, as companion to another Friend in executing the will of a deceased Friend, once sold a Negro lad till he might attain the age of thirty years and applied the money to use of the estate.

With abasement of heart I may now say that sometimes as I have sat in a meeting with my heart exercised towards that awful Being who respecteth not persons nor colours, and have looked upon this lad, I have felt that all was not clear in my mind respecting him. And as I have attended to this exercise and fervently sought the Lord, it hath appeared to me that I should make some restitution, but in what way I saw not till lately, when being under some concern that I may be resigned to go on a visit to some part of the West Indies,[30] and was under close engagement of spirit, seeking to the Lord for counsel herein, that of joining in the sale aforesaid came heavily upon me, and my mind for a time was covered with darkness and sorrow. And under this sore affliction my heart was softened to receive instruction, and here I first saw that as I had been one of the two executors who had sold this lad nine years longer than is common for our own children to serve, so I should now offer a part of my substance to redeem the last half of that nine years; but as the time was not yet come, I executed a bond, binding me and my executors to pay to the man he was sold to what to candid men might appear equitable for the last four years and a half of his time, in case the said youth was then living and in a condition likely to provide comfortably for himself.   [151–153]

---

30. Between "Indies" and "and was," MS. P (duplicating an erased portion in MS. A) adds: "and have obtained a certificate from Friends, but the time of leaving my family hath not appeared clear to me."

CHAPTER X

1769–1770   While I was under this bodily weakness, my mind being at times exercised for the good of my fellow creatures in the West Indies, I grew jealous over myself lest the disagreeableness of the prospect should hinder me from obediently attending thereto; for though I knew not that the Lord required me to go there, yet I believed that resignation was now called for in that respect, and feeling a danger of not being wholly devoted to him, I was frequently engaged to watch unto prayer that I might be preserved. And upward of a year having passed, I walked one day in a solitary wood; my mind being covered with awfulness, cries were raised in me to my merciful Father that he would graciously keep me in faithfulness, and it then settled on my mind as a duty to open my condition to Friends at our Monthly Meeting, which I did soon after as follows: "An exercise hath attended me for some time past and of late been more weighty upon me, under which I believe it is required of me to be resigned to go on a visit to some part of the West Indies." And in the Quarterly and General Spring Meeting [I] found no clearness to express anything further than that I believed resignation herein was required of me. And having obtained certificates from all said meetings, I felt like a sojourner at my outward habitation, kept free from worldly encumbrance, and was often bowed in spirit before the Lord, with inward breathings to him that I might be rightly directed.

And I may here note that being, when young, joined as executor with another Friend, we two, in executing the will of the deceased, sold a Negro lad till he might attain the age of thirty, on which account I had now great sorrow, as before related; and having settled matters relating to this youth, I soon after provided a sea-store and bed and things fitting for a voyage. And hearing of a vessel likely to sail from Philadelphia for Barbados, I spake with one of the owners at

Burlington, and soon after went on purpose to Philadelphia and spake with him again, at which time he told me there was a Friend in town who was part owner of the said vessel. But I felt no inclination at that time to speak with him, but returned home. And awhile after, I took leave of my family, and going to Philadelphia, had some weighty conversation with the first-mentioned owner and showed him a writing as follows:

25th day, 11th month, 1769. As an exercise with respect to a visit to Barbados hath been weighty on my mind, I may express some of the trials which have attended me. Under these trials I have at times rejoiced, in that I have felt my own self-will subjected.

I once, some years ago, retailed rum, sugar, and molasses, the fruits of the labour of slaves, but then had not much concern about them save only that the rum might be used in moderation; nor was this concern so weightily attended to as I now believe it ought to have been. But of late years being further informed respecting the oppressions too generally exercised in these islands, and thinking often on the degrees that there are in connections of interest and fellowship with the works of darkness (Eph 5:11), and feeling an increasing concern to be wholly given up to the leadings of the Holy Spirit, it hath appeared that the small gain I got by this branch of trade should be applied in promoting righteousness in the earth. And near the first motion toward a visit to Barbados, I believed the outward substance I possess should be applied in paying my passage, if I go, and providing things in a lowly way for my subsistence. But when the time drew near in which I believed it required of me to be in readiness, a difficulty arose which hath been a continued trial for some months past, under which I have with abasement of mind from day to day sought the Lord for instruction, and often had a feeling of the condition of one formerly who bewailed himself for that the Lord hid his face from him.

During these exercises my heart hath been often contrite, and I have had a tender feeling of the temptations of my fellow creatures labouring under those expensive customs distinguishable from "the simplicity that there is in

Christ" (2 Cor 11:3), and sometimes in the renewings of Gospel love have been helped to minister to others.

That which hath so closely engaged my mind in seeking to the Lord for instruction is whether, after so full information of the oppression the slaves in the West Indies lie under who raise the West India produce, as I had in reading *A Caution and Warning to Great Britain and Her Colonies*, wrote by Anthony Benezet, it is right for me to take passage in a vessel employed in the West India trade.

To trade freely with oppressors and, without labouring to dissuade from such unkind treatment, seek for gain by such traffic tends, I believe, to make them more easy respecting their conduct than they would be if the cause of universal righteousness was humbly and firmly attended to by those in general with whom they have commerce; and that complaint of the Lord by his prophet, "They have strengthened the hands of the wicked" [Ez 13:22], hath very often revived in my mind. [155–157]

# #

At length one of them asked me if I would go and see the vessel, but I had not clearness in my mind to go, but went to my lodgings and retired in private.

I was now under great exercise of mind, and my tears were poured out before the Lord with inward cries that he would graciously help me under these trials. In this case I believe my mind was resigned, but did not feel clearness to proceed; and my own weakness and the necessity of divine instruction was impressed upon me.

I was for a time as one who knew not what to do and was tossed as in a tempest, under which affliction the doctrine of Christ, "Take no thought for the morrow" [Mt 6:34], arose livingly before me. I remembered it was some days before they expected the vessel to sail and was favoured to get into a good degree of stillness, and having been near two days in town, I believed my obedience to my Heavenly Father consisted in returning homeward. And then I went over amongst Friends on the Jersey shore and tarried till the morning on which they had appointed to sail. And as I lay in bed the latter part of that night my mind was comforted and I felt what I esteemed a fresh confirmation that it was the Lord's will that I should pass through some further exercises near home.

JOHN WOOLMAN

So I went home and still felt like a sojourner with my family, and in the fresh spring of pure love had some labours in a private way amongst Friends on a subject relating to Truth's testimony, under which I had frequently been exercised in heart for some years. I remember as I walked on the road under this exercise, that passage in Ezekiel came fresh before me, "Whithersoever their faces were turned, thither they went." And I was graciously helped to discharge my duty in the fear and dread of the Almighty. [158–159]

CHAPTER XI

1772   Having been some time under a religious concern to prepare for crossing the seas, in order to visit Friends in the northern parts of England, and more particularly Yorkshire, after consideration I thought it expedient to inform Friends of it at our Monthly Meeting at Burlington, who, having unity with me therein, gave me a certificate. I afterwards communicated the same to our Quarterly Meeting and they likewise certified their concurrence. Sometime after, at the General Spring Meeting of ministers and elders, I thought it my duty to acquaint them with the religious exercise which attended my mind; and they likewise signified their unity therewith by a certificate, dated the 24th of third month, 1772, directed to Friends in Great Britain.

In the fourth month I thought the time was come to make some inquiry for a suitable conveyance.[31]

#   #

Memorandum of My Proceedings to Take a Passage
for England on a Religious Visit
My beloved friend Samuel Emlen, Jr., having taken a passage for himself in the cabin of the ship called *Mary and Elizabeth*, James Sparks master, and John Head of the city of Philadelphia the owner, and I feeling a draft in my mind towards the steerage of the same ship, went first of all and opened to Samuel the feeling I had concerning it.

My beloved friend wept when I spake to him and appeared glad that I had thoughts of going in the vessel with him, though my prospect was towards the steerage, and he offering

---

31. This insertion taken from Par. 1, Chapter 11, p. 237, of Whittier edition of *The Journal of John Woolman.*

to go with me, we two went on board, first into the cabin, a commodious room, and then into the steerage, where we sat down on a chest, the sailors being busy about us. Then the owner of the ship, a member of our Society, came and sat down with us.

Here my mind was turned toward Christ the heavenly Counsellor, and I feeling at this time my own will subjected, my heart was contrite before him. [163]

\#   \#

A motion was made by the owner to go and sit in the cabin as a place more retired; but I felt easy to leave the ship and made no agreement as to a passage in her, but told the owner if I took a passage in the ship I believed it would be in the steerage, but did not say much as to my exercise in that case.

After I went to my lodgings and the case was a little known in town, a friend laid before me the great inconvenience attending that steerage, which for a time appeared very discouraging to me. I soon after went to bed, and my mind was under a deep exercise before the Lord, whose helping hand was manifested to me as I slept that night, and his love strengthened my heart. And in the morning I went with two friends on board the vessel again; and after a short time spent therein, I went with Samuel Emlen to the house of the owner, to whom in the hearing of Samuel only I opened my exercise in substance as follows, in relation to a scruple I felt with regard to a passage in the steerage.

\#   \#

As my mind was now opened, I told the owner that I had at several times in my travels seen great oppressions on this continent, at which my heart had been much affected and brought often into a feeling of the state of the sufferers. And having many times been engaged, in the fear and love of God, to labour with those under whom the oppressed have been borne down and afflicted, I have often perceived that a view to get riches and provide estates for children, to live conformable to customs which stand in that spirit wherein men have regard to the honours of this world—that in the pursuit of these things I had seen many entangled in the spirit of oppression, and the exercise of my soul been such that I could not find peace in joying in anything which I saw was against that wisdom which is pure.

QUAKER SPIRITUALITY

After this I agreed for a passage in the steerage, and hearing in town that Joseph White had a mind to see me, I felt the reviving of a desire to see him and went then to his house and next day home, where I tarried two nights. And then early in the morning I parted with my family under a sense of the humbling hand of God upon me, and going to Philadelphia had opportunity with several of my beloved friends, who appeared to be concerned for me on account of the unpleasant situation of that part of the vessel where I was likely to lodge.

In these opportunities my mind through the mercies of the Lord was kept low, in an inward waiting for his help; and friends, having expressed their desire that I might have a place more convenient than the steerage, did not urge but appeared disposed to leave me to the Lord.

Having stayed two nights in Philadelphia, I went the next day to Darby Monthly Meeting, where through the strength of divine love my heart was enlarged toward the youth then present, under which I was helped to labour in some tenderness of spirit.

Then lodging at William Horne's, I with one friend went to Chester, where meeting with Samuel Emlen we went on board 1st day, 5th month, 1772; and as I sat down alone on a seat on the deck, I felt a satisfactory evidence that my proceedings were not in my own will but under the power of the Cross of Christ.

\# \#

As my lodgings in the steerage, now near a week, hath afforded me sundry opportunities of seeing, hearing, and feeling with respect to the life and spirit of many poor sailors, an inward exercise of soul hath attended me in regard to placing out children and youth where they may be likely to be exampled and instructed in the pure fear of the Lord. And I, being much amongst the seamen, have from a motion of love sundry times taken opportunities with one alone and in a free conversation laboured to turn their minds towards the fear of the Lord; and this day we had a meeting in the cabin, where my heart was contrite under a feeling of divine love.   [166]

\# \#

Five lads training up for the seas were now on board this ship, two of them brought up amongst our Society, one of which hath a right amongst Friends, by name James Nayler, to whom James

226

Nayler mentioned in Sewel's history appears to have been uncle to his father. I often feel a tenderness of heart toward these poor lads and at times look at them as though they were my children according to the flesh. [167]

\# \#

Desires were now renewed in me to embrace every opportunity of being inwardly acquainted with the hardships and difficulties of my fellow creatures and to labour in his love for the spreading of pure universal righteousness in the earth.

The frequent opportunities of hearing conversation amongst the sailors in respect to the voyages to Africa and the manner of bringing the deeply oppressed slaves into our islands, the thoughts of their condition, frequently in chains and fetters, on board the vessels, with hearts loaded with grief under the apprehension of miserable slavery—as my mind was frequently opened to meditate on these things, my own lodging, now in the steerage, with the advantage of walking the deck when I would, appeared a commodious situation compared with theirs.

17th day, 5th month, and first of the week. Had a meeting in the cabin, to which the seamen generally came. My spirit was contrite before the Lord, whose love at this time affected my heart.

This afternoon felt a tender sympathy of soul with my poor wife and family left behind, in which state my heart was enlarged in desires that they may walk in that humble obedience wherein the everlasting Father may be their guide and support through all the difficulties in this world; and a sense of that gracious assistance through which my mind hath been strengthened to take up the Cross and leave them, to travel in the love of Truth, hath begotten thankfulness in my heart to our great Helper. [172–173]

\# \#

This afternoon, saw that part of England called the Lizard. Some dunghill fowls yet remained of those the passengers took for eating. I believe about fourteen perished in the storms at sea by the waves breaking over the quarter deck, and a considerable number with sickness at different times. I observed the cocks crew doming down [the] Delaware and while we were near the land, but afterward I think I did not hear one of them crow till we came near the land in England, when they again crowed a few times.

QUAKER SPIRITUALITY

In observing their dull appearance at sea and the pining sickness of some of them, I often remembered the Fountain of Goodness, who gave being to all creatures, and whose love extends to that of caring for the sparrows; and I believe where the love of God is verily perfected and the true spirit of government watchfully attended to, a tenderness toward all creatures made subject to us will be experienced, and a care felt in us that we do not lessen that sweetness of life in the animal creation which the great Creator intends for them under our government.   [178–179]

#   #

Had a head wind up the Thames; lay sometimes at anchor; saw many ships passing and some anchor near; and had large opportunity of feeling the spirit in which the poor bewildered sailors too generally live. That lamentable degeneracy which so much prevails on the people employed on the seas so affected my heart that I may not easily convey the feeling I have had to another.   [179–180]

CHAPTER XII

1772   8th day, 6th month, 1772. Landed at London and went straightway to the Yearly Meeting of Ministers and Elders which had been gathered about (I suppose) half an hour. In this meeting my mind was humbly contrite. Afternoon meeting of business opened, which by adjournments held near a week. In these meetings I often felt a living concern for the establishment of Friends in the pure life of Truth, and my heart was enlarged in the meeting of ministers, meeting of business, and in several meetings for public worship, and I felt my mind united in true love in the faithful labourers now gathered from the several parts of this Yearly Meeting.   [181]

# #

The Whittier edition[32] of John Woolman's Journal *contains a long footnote to his probable hasty toilet in a crowded steerage and Woolman's entry late into the Yearly Meeting of Ministry and Elders in London.*

There is a story told of his first appearance in England which I have from my friend William J. Allison, editor of the Friends' Review, and which he assures me is well authenticated. The vessel reached London on the morning of the fifth day of the week, and John Woolman, knowing that the meeting was then in session, lost no time in reaching it. Coming in late and unannounced, his peculiar dress and manner excited attention and apprehension that he was an itinerant enthusiast. He presented the certificate from Friends in America, but the dissatisfaction still remained,

---

32. Ibid., pp. 257–59.

*and someone remarked that perhaps the stranger Friend
might feel that his dedication of himself to this apprehended
service was accepted, without further labor, and that he
might now feel that he was free to return to his home. John
Woolman sat silent for a space, seeking the unerring counsel
of Divine Wisdom. He was profoundly affected by the unfa-
vorable reception he met with, and his tears flowed freely.
In the love of Christ and his fellow-men he had, at a painful
sacrifice, taken his life in his hands, and left behind the peace
and endearments of home. That love still flowed out towards
the people of England; must it henceforth be pent up in his
own heart? He rose at last and stated that he could not feel
himself released from his prospect of labor in England. Yet
he could not travel in the ministry without the unity of
Friends; and while that was withheld he could not feel easy
to be of any cost to them. He could not go back as had been
suggested; but he was acquainted with a mechanical trade,
and while the impediment to his services continued he
hoped that Friends would be kindly willing to employ him
in such business as he was capable of, that he might not be
chargeable to any.*

*A deep silence prevailed over the assembly, many of
whom were touched by the wise simplicity of the stranger's
words and manner. After a season of waiting, John Woolman felt that words were given him as a minister of Christ.
The spirit of his Master bore witness to them in the hearts of
his hearers. When he closed, the Friend who had advised
against his further service rose up and humbly confessed his
error, and avowed his full unity with the stranger. All doubt
was removed; there was a general expression of unity and
sympathy, and John Woolman, owned by his brethren
passed on to his work.*

\#   \#

15th, 6th month. Left London and went to Quarterly Meeting at
Hertford.

1st day, 7th month, 1772. Have been at Quarterly Meetings at
Sherrington, at Northampton, at Banbury, at Shipston, and had
sundry meetings between. My mind hath been bowed under a sense
of divine goodness manifested amongst us. My heart hath often been

enlarged in true love amongst ministers and elders and in public meetings, that through the Lord's goodness I believe it hath been a fresh visitation to many, in particular to the youth.

17th day, 7th month. Was this day at Birmingham. Have been at Coventry, at Warwick, and have been at meetings in Oxfordshire and sundry places. Have felt the humbling hand of the Lord upon me and through his tender mercies find peace in the labours I have went through.

26th day, 7th month, 1772. Have continued travelling northward, visiting meetings. Was this day at Nottingham, which in the forenoon especially was through divine love a heart-tendering season. Next day had a meeting in a Friend's house with Friends' children and some Friends. This through the strengthening arm of the Lord was a time to be thankfully remembered.

2nd day, 8th month, first of week. Was this day at Sheffield, a large inland town. Have been at sundry meetings last week and feel inward thankfulness for that divine support which hath been graciously extended to me.

9th day, 8th month, first of week. Was at Rushworth. Have lately passed through some painful labour but have been comforted under a sense of that divine visitation which I feel extended toward many young people.

16th, 8th month, and first of week. Was at Settle. It hath of late been a time of inward poverty, under which my mind hath been preserved in a watchful, tender state, feeling for the mind of the Holy Leader, and find peace in the labours I have passed through.

On inquiry in many places I find the price of rye about 5 shillings; wheat about 8 shillings; oatmeal 12 shillings for 120 pound; mutton from 3 pence to 5 pence per pound; bacon from 7 pence to 9 pence; cheese from 4 pence to 6 pence; butter from 8 pence to 10 pence, house rent for a poor man from 25 shillings to 40 shillings per year, to be paid weekly; wood for fire very scarce and dear; coal in some places 2 shillings 6 pence per hundredweight, but near the pits not a quarter so much. Oh, may the wealthy consider the poor!

The wages of labouring men in several counties toward London, 10 pence per day in common business; the employer finds small beer and the labourer finds his own food; but in harvest and hay time, wages about 1 shilling and the labourer have all his diet. In some parts of the north of England poor labouring men have their food where they work and appear in common to do rather better than nearer London. Industrious women who spin in the factories get some 4 pence, some 5 pence, and so on; 6, 7, 8, 9 pence, or 10 pence, and find their own house-room and diet. Great numbers of poor people live chiefly on bread and water in the southern parts of England and some in the northern parts, and many poor children learn not to read. May those who have plenty lay these things to heart!

Stagecoaches frequently go upwards of a hundred miles in 24 hours, and I have heard Friends say in several places that it is common for horses to be killed with hard driving, and many others driven till they grow blind. These coaches running chief part of the night do often run over foot people in the dark.

Postboys pursue their business, each one to his stage, all night through the winter. Some boys who ride long stages suffer greatly in winter nights, and at several places I have heard of their being froze to death. So great is the hurry in the spirit of this world that in aiming to do business quick and to gain wealth the creation at this day doth loudly groan!

As my journey hath been without a horse, I have had several offers of being assisted on my way in these stages, but have not been in them, nor have I had freedom to send letters by these posts in the present way of their riding, the stages being so fixed and one boy dependent on another as to time, that they commonly go upward of 100 miles in 24 hours, and in the cold long winter nights the poor boys suffer much.

I heard in America of the way of these posts and cautioned Friends in the General Meeting of Ministers and Elders at Philadelphia and in the Yearly Meeting of Ministers and Elders at London not to send letters to me on any common occasion by post. And though on this account I may be likely to hear seldomer from the family I left behind, yet for righteousness sake I am through divine favour made content.

I have felt great distress of mind since I came on this island, on account of the members of our Society being mixed with the world in various sorts of business and traffic carried on in impure channels. Great is the trade to Africa for slaves! And in loading these ships abundance of people are employed in the factories, amongst whom are many of our Society! Friends in early times refused on a religious principle to make or trade in superfluities, of which we have many large testimonies on record, but for want of faithfulness some gave way, even some whose examples were of note in Society, and from thence others took more liberty. Members of our Society worked in superfluities and bought and sold them, and thus dimness of sight came over many. At length Friends got into the use of some superfluities in dress and in the furniture of their houses, and this hath spread from less to more, till superfluity of some kinds is common amongst us.

In this declining state many look at the example one of another and too much neglect the pure feeling of Truth. Of late years a deep exercise hath attended my mind that Friends may dig deep, may carefully cast forth the loose matter and get down to the rock, the sure foundation, and there hearken to that divine voice which gives a clear and certain sound, and I have felt in that which doth not deceive that if Friends who have known the Truth keep in that tenderness of heart where all views of outward gain are given up, and their trust is only on the Lord, he will graciously lead some to be patterns of deep self-denial in things relating to trade and handicraft labour, and that some who have plenty of the treasures of this world will example in a plain frugal life and pay wages to such whom they may hire, more liberally than is now customary in some places.

23rd, 8th month. Was this day at Preston Patrick. Here I dreamed of mother. Had a comfortable meeting. I have several times been entertained in the houses of Friends who had sundry things about them which had the appearance of outward greatness, and as I have kept inward, way hath opened for conversation in private, in which divine goodness hath favoured us together with heart-tendering times.

A deviation amongst us as a Society from that simplicity that there is in Christ becoming so general, and the trade from this island to Africa for slaves, and other trades carried on through oppressive channels, and abundance of the inhabitants being employed in factories to support a trade in which there is unrighteousness, and some growing outwardly great by gain of this sort: the weight of this degeneracy hath lain so heavy upon me, the depth of this revolt been so evident, and desires in my heart been so ardent for a reformation, so ardent that we might come to that right use of things where, living on a little, we might inhabit that holy mountain on which they neither *hurt nor destroy*! and may not only stand clear from oppressing our fellow creatures, but may be so disentangled from connections in interest with known oppressors, that in us may be fulfilled that prophecy: "Thou shalt be far from oppression" [Is 54:14]. Under the weight of this exercise the sight of innocent birds in the branches and sheep in the pastures, who act according to the will of their Creator, hath at times tended to mitigate my trouble.

26th day, 8th month, 1772. Being now at George Crosfield's, in Westmoreland County in England, I feel a concern to commit to writing that which to me hath been a case uncommon. In a time of sickness with the pleurisy a little upward of two years and a half ago, I was brought so near the gates of death that I forgot my name. Being then desirous to know who I was, I saw a mass of matter of a dull gloomy colour, between the south and the east, and was informed that this mass was human beings in as great misery as they could be and live, and that I was mixed in with them and henceforth might not consider myself as a distinct or separate being. In this state I remained several hours. I then heard a soft, melodious voice, more pure and harmonious than any voice I had heard with my ears before, and I believed it was the voice of an angel who spake to other angels. The words were, "*John Woolman is dead.*" I soon remembered that I once was John Woolman, and being assured that I was alive in the body, I greatly wondered what that heavenly voice could mean. I believed beyond doubting that it was the voice of an holy angel, but as yet it was a mystery to me.

I was then carried in spirit to the mines, where poor oppressed people were digging rich treasures for those called Christians, and heard them blaspheme the name of Christ, at which I was grieved, for his name to me was precious. Then I was informed that these heathens were told that those who oppressed them were the followers of Christ, and they said amongst themselves: "If Christ directed them to use us in this sort, then Christ is a cruel tyrant."

All this time the song of the angel remained a mystery, and in the morning my dear wife and some others coming to my bedside, I asked them if they knew who I was; and they, telling me I was John Woolman, thought I was only light-headed, for I told them not what the angel said, nor was I disposed to talk much to anyone, but was very desirous to get so deep that I might understand this mystery.

My tongue was often so dry that I could not speak till I had moved it about and gathered some moisture, and as I lay still for a time, at length I felt divine power prepare my mouth that I could speak, and then I said: "I am crucified with Christ, nevertheless I live; yet not I, but Christ that liveth in me, and the life I now live in the flesh is by faith in the Son of God, who loved me and gave himself for me" [Gal 2:20]. Then the mystery was opened, and I perceived there was joy in heaven over a sinner who had repented and that that language *John Woolman is dead* meant no more than the death of my own will.

Soon after this I coughed and raised much bloody matter, which I had not during this vision, and now my natural understanding returned as before. Here I saw that people getting silver vessels to set off their tables at entertainments was often stained with worldly glory, and that in the present state of things, I should take heed how I fed myself from out of silver vessels.

Soon after my recovery I, going to our Monthly Meeting, dined at a Friend's house, where drink was brought in silver vessels and not in any other. And I, wanting some drink, told him my case with weeping, and he ordered some drink for me in another vessel.

The like I went through in several Friends' houses in America and have also in England since I came here, and have cause with humble reverence to acknowledge the loving-kindness of my Heavenly Father, who hath preserved me in such a tender frame of mind that none, I believe, have ever been offended at what I have said on that occasion.

After this sickness I spake not in public meetings for worship for near one year, but my mind was very often in company with the oppressed slaves as I sat in meetings, and though under this dispensation I was shut up from speaking, yet the spring of the Gospel ministry was many times livingly opened in me and the divine gift operated by abundance of weeping in feeling the oppression of this people.

It being now so long since I passed through this dispensation and the matter remaining fresh and livingly on my mind, I believe it safest for me to write it.   [181–187]

# #

I rested a few days in body and mind with our Friend Jane Crosfield, who was once in America. Was on the sixth day of the week at Kendal in Westmorland.

I have known poverty of late and been graciously supported to keep in the patience and am thankful under a sense of the goodness of the Lord towards those that are of a contrite spirit.   [188]

# #

13th day, 9th month. Was this day at Richmond, a small meeting, but the townspeople coming in, the house was crowded. It was a time of heavy labor and I believe was a profitable meeting.

At this place I heard that my kinsman, William Hunt from Carolina, who was on a religious visit to Friends in England, departed from this life the 9th day, 9th month, 1772, at Newcastle, of the smallpox. He appeared in public testimony when he was a youth. His ministry was in the pure love and life of Truth, and his conduct in general agreeable thereto. [189]

\# \#

9th month, 28, '72. Being now at the house of my friend Thomas Priestman in the city of York, so weak in body that I know not how my sickness may end, I am concerned to leave in writing a case the remembrance whereof hath often affected me. An honest-hearted Friend in America, who departed this life a little less than a year ago, some months before his departure, he told me in substance as follows:

That he saw in a dream or night vision a great pond of blood from which a fog rose up. Some distance from him he saw this fog spread round about and great numbers of people walking backwards and forwards in it, the garments of whom had a tincture of blood in 'em. I perceived he apprehended that by the pool of blood was represented the state of those hardhearted men through whose means much blood is shed in Africa and many lives destroyed through insupportable stench and other hardships in crossing the sea, and through extreme oppression bring many slaves to an untimely end, and that the fog in which the people were walking represented the gain arising on merchandise or traffic which many were taking hold of and, at the same time, knew that the gain was the gain of oppression.

This Friend, in his last sickness having several days had an inclination to see me, at length sent a messenger and I without delay went. He asked to be with me in private, which was granted; he then told me some matters in particular in regard to the gain of oppression, which he felt not easy to leave the world without [opening to me. All this time] he appeared calm [and quiet], and the family coming in by his consent, death in about one hour appeared evidently upon him, and I believe in about five hours from my going in he quietly breathed his last; and as I believe he left no memorandum in writing of that dream or vision of the night, at this time I believe it seasonable for me to do it. John Woolman.[33]

> *The sickness referred to in this final* Journal *entry was a virulent case of smallpox. Woolman bore all of its rigors with his quiet acceptance knowing inwardly the truth of William Penn's words, "We can fall no deeper than God's arms can reach, however deep we fall." Doctors and apothecaries did what they could to save his life and William Tuke and his wife Esther gave him the most loving and sensitive care. In ten days he was dead. In what is believed to be Priestman's report of Woolman's last days that were spent in his house in York the final paragraph reads: "Thus the patient and faithful servant of the Lord finished a life of deep exercise and many sorrows, at the house of his friend, Robert Priestman, the 7th day of the 10th month, 1772, and was interred in Friends burying ground the 9th of the same, after a large and solid meeting held on the occasion in the great meeting house."*
>
> *According to a letter written by William Tuke to Reuben Haines on October 26, 1772, during the final illness Woolman told Tuke "that he was not willing to have the coffin of oak because it is a wood more useful than ash for some other purposes." He then dictated the following to Tuke, which Woolman then signed:*

> > *York, 29th of 9th month, 1772. An ash coffin made plain without any manner of superfluities—the corpse to be wrapped in cheap flannel, the expense of which I leave my wearing clothes to defray, as also the digging of the grave; and I desire that William Tuke may take my clothes after my decease and apply them accordingly.*

> *John Woolman* [306]

---

33. This entry for September 28 appears to have been dictated by Woolman and written by someone else, probably Thomas Priestman. Some revisions have been made in the manuscript; since it cannot be determined which of them may have been suggested by Woolman at the time, the present editor has had to decide rather arbitrarily which readings to transcribe. The problem involves only minor changes of phrase, which do not materially affect the meaning. The signature, in very shaky handwriting, appears to be Woolman's own.

SELECTIONS FROM

QUAKER STRONGHOLDS
by Caroline Stephen

CAROLINE STEPHEN
(*1834–1909*)

Precisely a century after John Woolman's death at York (1772), Caroline Stephen was taken to her first Friends Meeting for Worship where she at last discovered herself to be spiritually at home. She belonged to a most distinguished British family. Her father, Sir James Stephen, had been Regius Professor of History at Cambridge. Her brother, Sir Leslie Stephen, was a brilliant writer of his time and his daughter, Caroline's niece, was Virginia Woolf.

Caroline Stephen became a Friend by convincement and blessed the Quakers with a highly articulate account of what she had personally found to be authentic in their witness. Her Quaker Strongholds, which appeared in 1890 and has gone through several printings, is a Quaker classic and the selections that are made here are all, with one exception, taken from it. Two years after her death, Thomas Hodgkin wrote a brief memoir,[34] Caroline Stephen and the Society of Friends. An introductory paragraph summing up her Quaker insights is so telling that I have included it in this foreword:

The fundamental truth which underlay all the teaching of George Fox and the Early Friends was this: God, who spoke of old to His people by the mouth of prophets and apostles, and who gave the fullest revelation of Himself in the person of Jesus Christ, still speaks; and we may every one of us, if we will, hear that Divine Voice in the secret of our hearts. "Both before and since His blessed manifestation in the

---

34. Thomas Hodgkin, *The Vision of Faith*, (Cambridge: Heffer and Son, 1911), pp. xxxv–xxxvi.

flesh, Christ has been the light and life, the rock and strength, of all that ever feared God; present with them in their temptations, He follows them in their travels and afflictions, supports and carries them through and over the difficulties that have attended them in their earthly pilgrimage." Or, as George Fox says of one of his meetings, "My message unto them from the Lord was, that they should all come together again and wait to feel the Lord's power and spirit in themselves, to gather them together to Christ, that they might be taught of Him who says, 'Learn of Me.'" This is, of course, Mysticism, but it is also the setting forth of a truth not formally denied by any section of the Christian Church, though few have felt it so intensely or preached it so persistently as the Early Friends. In their advocacy of this doctrine, and in their obedience to what they conceived to be its practical consequences, they suffered bitter persecution both from Roundhead and Cavalier, did many noble deeds, and spoke some unwise and unmeasured words, but displayed a new and much needed type of Christianity to the world.

QUAKER STRONGHOLDS

T HE NOTORIOUS disinclination of Friends to any attempts at proselytizing, and perhaps some lingering effects of persecution, probably account for the very common impression that Friends' meetings are essentially private—mysterious gatherings into which it would be intrusive to seek admission. [1–2]

# #

Some such vague impression floated, I believe, over my own mind, when, some seventeen years ago, I first found myself within reach of a Friends' meeting, and, somewhat to my surprise, cordially made welcome to attend it. The invitation came at a moment of need, for I was beginning to feel with dismay that I might not much longer be able conscientiously to continue to join in the Church of England service. [2]

# #

At any rate, it was fast leading me to dread the moment when I should be unable either to find the help I needed, or to offer my tribute of devotion in any place of worship amongst my fellow Christians. When lo, on one never-to-be-forgotten Sunday morning, I found myself one of a small company of silent worshipers, who were content to sit down together without words, that each one might feel after and draw near to the divine Presence, unhindered at least, if not helped, by any human utterance. Utterance I knew was free, should the words be given; and before the meeting was over, a sentence or two were uttered in great simplicity by an old and apparently un-taught man, rising in this place amongst the rest of us. I did not pay much attention to the words he spoke, and I have no recollection of their purport. My whole soul was filled with the unutterable peace of the undisturbed opportunity for communion with God, with the sense that at last I had found a place where I might, without the faintest suspicion of insincerity, join with others in simply seeking his presence. To sit down in silence could at the least pledge me to nothing; it might open to me (as it did that morning) the very gate of heaven. And since that day, now more than seventeen years ago, Friends' meetings have indeed been to me the greatest of outward helps to a fuller and fuller entrance into the spirit from which they have sprung; the place of the most soul-subduing, faith-restoring, strengthening, and peaceful communion, in feeding upon the bread of life, that I have ever known. I cannot but believe that what has helped me so unspeakably might be helpful to multitudes in this day of shaking of all that can be shaken, and of restless inquiry after spiritual good. It is in the hope of making more widely known the true source and nature of such spiritual help that I am about to attempt to describe what I have called our strongholds—those principles which cannot fail, whatever may be the future of the Society which for more than two hundred years has taken its stand upon them. I wish to trace, as far as my experience as a "convinced Friend" enables me to do so, what is the true life and strength of our Society; and the manner in which its principles, as actually embodied in its practice, its organization, and, above all, its manner of worship, are fitted to meet the special needs of an important class in our own day.

[3–5]

# #

Organization: Every congregation meeting habitually for worship on the first day of the week is one of a group of probably four or five Monthly Meetings, which in like manner unite to form a Quarterly Meeting, at whose quarterly sittings matters of larger importance are considered, and the eighteen Quarterly Meetings of Great Britain form in their turn the London Yearly Meeting. It may in a certain sense be said, indeed, that it is the Society of Friends of Great Britain, for every Friend is a member of the Monthly, Quarterly, and Yearly Meetings to which he or she belongs, and is entitled to a voice in all their deliberations.

[7]

# #

CAROLINE STEPHEN

Certain "queries" have from the earliest times been appointed by the authority of the Yearly Meeting, to be read and considered at certain seasons in the subordinate meetings . . .[35]   [11]

\#   \#

The business of the elders is to watch over the [recorded] ministers in the exercise of their gift; that of the overseers to see to the relief of the poorer members, the care of the sick, and other such matters; to watch over the members generally with regard to their Christian conduct, to warn privately any who may be giving cause of offence or scandal, and in case of need to bring the matter before the Monthly Meeting, to be dealt with as it may require.   [13]

\#   \#

The very copious biographical literature of the Society teems with the records of journeys undertaken "under an impression of religious duty," and lasting sometimes for months, or even years, before the Friend could "feel clear" of the work. No limit is ever set beforehand to such work. It is felt to be work in which the daily unfolding of the divine ordering must be watched and waited for.

[15–16]

\#   \#

I have already referred to the peculiarity which lies at the root of all the rest; namely, our views as to the nature of the true Gospel ministry, as a call bestowed on men and women, on old and young, learned and unlearned; bestowed directly from above, and not to be conferred by any human authority, or hired for money; to be exer-

---

35. In the Appendix to *Quaker Strongholds*, a dozen such Queries used at the close of the nineteenth century are quoted. Three of them are: Are you in the practice of private retirement and waiting upon the Lord . . . and do you live in habitual dependence upon the help and guidance of the Holy Spirit?

\#   \#

Are you faithful in maintaining Christian testimony against war, as inconsistent with the precepts and spirit of the Gospel?

\#   \#

Do you maintain strict integrity in all your transactions in trade and in your other outward concerns; and are you careful not to defraud the public revenue?

245

cised under the sole and immediate direction of the one Master, the only Head of the Church, Christ the Lord. As a consequence of this view, Friends have, as is well known, refused as a matter of conscience to pay tithes, or in any way to contribute to the maintenance of a paid ministry, and of the services prescribed by the Established Church.

Closely connected with these views on ministry is our testimony against the observance of any religious rites or ceremonies whatever. Neither baptizing with water, nor the breaking of bread and drinking of wine, are recognized by us as divinely ordained institutions of permanent obligation, and neither of these ceremonies is practised by us. [16–17]

\#   \#

The one corner-stone of belief upon which the Society of Friends is built is the conviction that God does indeed communicate with each one of the spirits he has made, in a direct and living inbreathing of some measure of the breath of his own life; that he never leaves himself without a witness in the heart as well as in the surroundings of man; and that in order clearly to hear the divine voice thus speaking to us we need to be still; to be alone with him in the secret place of his presence; that all flesh should keep silence before him.

[20]

\#   \#

The history of the sudden gathering of the Society, of its rapid formation into a strongly organized body, and of the extraordinary constancy, zeal, and integrity displayed by its original members, is a most impressive proof of the trueness of their aim.[36] [21]

\#   \#

When questioned as to the reality and nature of the inner light, the early Friends were accustomed in return to ask the questions whether they did not sometimes feel something within them that showed them their sins; and to assure them that this same power,

---

36. "In 1656 Fox computed that there were seldom less than 1000 in prison; and it has been asserted that, between 1661 and 1697, 13,562 Quakers were imprisoned, 152 were transported, and 338 died in prison or of their wounds" (*Encyclopaedia Britannica*, s.v. "Quakers").

which *made manifest*, and therefore was truly light, would also, if yielded to, lead them out of sin. This assurance, that the light which revealed was also the power which would heal sin, was George Fox's gospel. The power itself was described by him in many ways. Christ within, the hope of glory; the light, life, Spirit, and grace of Christ; the Seed, the new birth, the power of God unto salvation, and many other such expressions, flow forth in abundant streams to heartfelt eloquence. To "turn people to the light within," to "direct them to Christ, their free Teacher," was his daily business.   [21–22]

# #

The perennial justification of Quakerism lies in its energetic assertion that the kingdom of heaven is within us; that we are not made dependent upon any outward organization for our spiritual welfare. Its perennial difficulty lies in the inveterate disposition of human beings to look to each other for spiritual help, in the feebleness of their perception of that divine voice which speaks to each one in a language no other ear can hear, and in the apathy which is content to go through life without the attempt at any true individual communion with God.   [24]

# #

I believe the doctrine of Fox and Barclay (i.e., briefly, that the "Word of God" is Christ, not the Bible, and that the Scriptures are profitable in proportion as they are read in the same spirit which gave them forth) to have been a most valuable equipoise to the tendency of other Protestant sects to transfer the idea of infallibility from the Church to the Bible. Nothing, I believe, can really teach us the nature and meaning of inspiration but personal experience of it. That we may all have such experience if we will but attend to the divine influences in our own hearts, is the cardinal doctrine of Quakerism. Whether this belief, honestly acted on, will manifest itself in the homespun and solid, but only too sober morality of the typical everyday Quaker, or whether it will land us in the mystical fervours of an Isaac Penington, or the apostolic labours of a John Woolman or a Stephen Grellet, must depend chiefly upon our natural temperament and special gifts.   [28–29]

# #

QUAKER SPIRITUALITY

Here we are confronted with the real "peculiarity" of Quakerism —its relation to mysticism. There is no doubt that George Fox himself and the other fathers of the Society were of a strongly mystical turn of mind, though not in the sense in which the word is often used by the worshipers of "common sense," as a mild term of reproach, to convey a general vague dreaminess. Nothing, certainly could be less applicable to the early Friends that any such reproach as this. They were fiery, dogmatic, pugnacious, and intensely practical and soberminded. But they were assuredly mystics in what I take to be the more accurate sense of that word—people, that is, with a vivid consciousness of the inwardness of the light of truth.   [30–31]

\#   \#

A true mystic believes that all men have, as he himself is conscious of having, an inward life, into which as into a secret chamber, he can retreat at will.[37] In this inner chamber he finds a refuge from the ever-changing aspects of outward existence; from the multitude of cares and pleasures and agitations which belong to the life of the senses and the affections; from human judgments; from all change, and chance, and turmoil, and distraction. He finds there, first repose, then an awful guidance; a light which burns and purifies; a voice which subdues; he finds himself in the presence of his God.   [32–33]

\#   \#

Believing in God, and worshiping him with one's whole heart, trusting him absolutely and loving him supremely, seem to me to be but various stages in the growth of one Seed.   [40]

\#   \#

That individual and immediate guidance, in which we recognize that "the finger of God is come unto us," seems to come in, as it were, to complete and perfect the work rough-hewn by morality and conscience. We may liken the laws of our country to the cliffs of our island, over which we rarely feel ourselves in any danger of falling;

---

37. Let me not be understood to mean that the process of "keeping the mind" (in Quaker phrase) "retired to the Lord" is an easy one. On the contrary, it may need strenuous effort. But the *effort* can be made at will and even the mere effort thus to retire from the surface to the depths of life is sure to bring help and strengthening—is in itself a strengthening, steadying process.

248

the moral standard of our social circle to the beaten highway road which we can hardly miss. Our own conscience would then be represented by a fence, by which some parts of the country are enclosed for each one, the road itself at times barred or narrowed. And that divine guidance of which I am speaking could be typified only by the pressure of a hand upon ours, leading us gently to step to the right or the left, to pause or to go forward, in a manner intended for and understood by ourselves alone. [43-44]

\# \#

The divine guidance is away from self-indulgence, often away from outward success; through humiliation and failure, and many snares and temptations; over rough roads and against opposing forces —always uphill. Its evidence of success is in the inmost, deepest, most spiritual part of our existence. [49]

\# \#

It seems to me that nothing but silence can heal the wounds made by disputations in the region of the unseen. No external help, at any rate, has ever in my own experience proved so penetratingly efficacious as the habit of joining in a public worship based upon silence. Its primary attraction for me was in the fact that it pledged me to nothing, and left me altogether undisturbed to seek for help in my own way. But before long I began to be aware that the united and prolonged silences had a far more direct and powerful effect than this. They soon began to exercise a strangely subduing and softening effect upon my mind. There used, after a while, to come upon me a deep sense of awe, as we sat together and waited—for what? In my heart of hearts I knew in whose name we were met together, and who was truly in the midst of us. Never before had his influence revealed itself to me with so much power as in those quiet assemblies.

And another result of the practice of silent waiting for the unseen presence proved to be a singularly effectual preparation of mind for the willing reception of any words which might be offered "in the name of a disciple." The words spoken were indeed often feeble, and always inadequate (as all words must be in relation to divine things), sometimes even entirely irrelevant to my own individual needs, though at other times profoundly impressive and helpful; but, coming as they did after the long silences which had fallen like dew upon the thirsty soil, they went far deeper, and were received into a much less thorny region than had ever been the case with the words I had listened to from the pulpit.

In Friends' meetings also, from the fact that every one is free to speak, one hears harmonies and correspondences between very various utterances such as are scarcely to be met with elsewhere. It is sometimes as part-singing compared with unison. The free admission of the ministry of women, of course, greatly enriches this harmony. I have often wondered whether some of the motherly counsels I have listened to in our meeting would not reach some hearts that might be closed to the masculine preacher. [54–56]

\# \#

But it is not only the momentary effect of silence as a help in public worship that constitutes its importance in Quaker estimation. The silence we value is not the mere outward silence of the lips. It is a deep quietness of heart and mind, a laying aside of all preoccupation with passing things—yes, even with the workings of our own minds; a resolute fixing of the heart upon that which is unchangeable and eternal. This "silence of all flesh" appears to us to be the essential preparation for any act of true worship. It is also, we believe, the essential condition at all times of inward illumination. "Stand still in the light," says George Fox again and again, and then strength comes—and peace and victory and deliverance, and all other good things. "Be still, and know that I am God." It is the experience, I believe, of all those who have been most deeply conscious of his revelations of himself, that they are made emphatically to the "waiting" soul—to the spirit which is most fully conscious of its own inability to do more than wait in silence before him. [56–57]

\# \#

What Friends undoubtedly believe and maintain is that to the listening heart God does speak intelligibly; and further, that some amongst his worshipers are gifted with a special openness to receive, and power to transmit in words, actual messages from himself. Is this more than is necessarily implied in the belief that real communion with him is not only possible, but is freely open to all?

We do not regard those who have the gift of "ministry" as infallible, or even as necessarily closer to God than many of the silent worshipers who form the great majority in every congregation. We feel that the gift is from above, and that on all of us lies the responsibility of being open to it, willing to receive it, should it be bestowed, and to use it faithfully while entrusted with it. But we fully recognize that to do this perfectly requires a continual submission of the will, and an unceasing watchfulness. [59–60]

\# \#

As I have already said, I do not feel that ours is the only lawful manner of worship; I do not even think it at all clear that it would be for all people and at all times the most helpful. But I do believe it to be the purest conceivable. I am jealous for its preservation from any admixture of adventitious "aids to devotion." I believe that its absolute freedom and flexibility, its unrivalled simplicity and gravity, make it a vessel of honour prepared in an especial manner for the conveyance of the pure water of life to many in these days who are hindered from satisfying their souls' thirst by questionable additions to the essence of divine worship. [63]

\# \#

Let no one go to Friends' meetings with the expectation of finding everything to his taste. [64]

\# \#

Criticism fades away abashed in the presence of what is felt to be a real, however faltering, endeavour to open actual communication with the Father of spirits, and with each other as in his presence and in his name. To my own mind, any living utterance of a human voice pleading for itself and for the objects of its love in words fresh from the heart, has a power and a pathos infinitely beyond that of the most perfect expression of devotion read or recited according to an appointed order. [64]

\# \#

Hitherto I have been speaking of our meetings for public worship. But, as Friends love to say, our worship does not begin when we sit down together in our public assemblies, nor end when we leave them. The worship in spirit and in truth is in no way limited by time and place. The same ideas of a waiting "in the silence of all flesh" to hear the voice of the Lord speaking within us, characterizes the

Friends' private times of worship; or, as the more cautious expression is, of "religious retirement."   [66–67]

\#   \#

And not only in name, but in method, are these times marked with the same peculiar character as our public meetings. In Friends' families of the old-fashioned type (which are more numerous still, I fancy, than many people suspect) the family meeting consists simply of the reading of a portion of Scripture, and then a pause of silence, which may or may not be broken by words of prayer or of testimony.

[67]

\#   \#

A silent pause before meals is the Friends' equivalent for "saying grace"—a practice which I own I think has much to recommend it. Here, again, there is, of course, the opportunity for words, should words spontaneously rise to the lips of any of those present.   [67–68]

\#   \#

The word "prayer" may, it is true, be used in the restricted sense of making requests; but in that case let it be distinctly understood and kept in mind that it is but a part—the lowest and least essential part—of worship or communion with God. It is of prayer in the larger sense—not request, but communion—that we may rightly and wisely speak as the very breath of our spiritual life; as the power by which life is transfigured; as that to which all things are possible. But this distinction between request and communion is *not* habitually kept in mind by those who write and speak of prayer, nor even by all those who practise it. It seems to me as if many even deeply experienced Christians were using all their energy to encourage and stimulate above all that part of prayer which has surely the most of the merely human and carnal in it, rather than to show forth that nobler part to which this should be but the innocent and natural prelude.

[73–74]

\#   \#

Surely we may with reverence say that, in a true and a deep sense, God himself is the answer to prayer.   [90]

\#   \#

CAROLINE STEPHEN

Our ministry may be said to be free in several distinct senses.
1. It is open to all.
2. Its exercise is not subject to any prearrangement.
3. It is not paid. [91]

\# \#

Other Christian bodies have from very early times recognized a distinction between clergy and laity, and have regarded at least two sacraments as having been instituted by Christ himself, and as being in some sense or other "necessary to salvation"; and the greater number, or at any rate the largest, of these bodies have habitually adopted the use of liturgical forms of public worship.

At the root of this abstinence from all generally accepted practices, there lies the one conviction of the all-sufficiency of individual and immediate communication with the Father of our spirits; and a profound belief that by his coming in the flesh of our Lord Jesus Christ did, in fact, open a new and living access to God. [93]

\# \#

It was a bold thing indeed for the early Friends to break loose at once from the whole ecclesiastical system, with its venerable and long-established claim to be the divinely ordained channel of spiritual nutriment. In doing so, they no doubt took up an attitude of hostility towards the "hireling priests," and their "steeple-houses" and "so-called ordinances," which, however comparatively intelligible it may have been at the time, was yet not only highly obnoxious, but would even seem to have led them into some degree of injustice.

After sixty or seventy years of severe persecution, however, borne with extraordinary patience as well as constancy, their right to carry out their own manner of worship was fully allowed; and by a strange result of changes, partly within the Society itself and partly in the surrounding mental atmosphere, Friends, from being regarded as peculiarly pestilent heretics, came to be looked on as the most harmless and least obnoxious of Nonconformists. I believe, however, that this can be the case only as long as we are content to acquiesce in a purely passive and dwindling state. Any attempt to promulgate our peculiar views must necessarily give offence. We may, perhaps, no longer think it a duty to denounce the institution of a separate clergy, and the observance of "so-called ordinances," as positively unlawful or sinful. But to say plainly that we consider them as superfluous, requires hardly less boldness, and is scarcely likely to be more palatable. [94–95]

\# \#

It is, however, a great help in doing so to be able to point to the very remarkable fact of the existence during more than two centuries of a body of people whose lives bear abundant witness to the reality of their Christian profession, amongst whom these "ordinances" have been altogether disused.

I am far from venturing to claim that the Society of Friends does actually exhibit a perfect living instance of what has been called "primitive Christianity revived," but I do believe its ideal to be the true, and the only true one; that of a Church, or "gathered people," living with the one object of obeying the teaching of Christ himself to the very uttermost—his own teaching, not that of those who have spoken in his name, even though they be apostles, except insofar as they speak in accordance with it. To *live* the Sermon on the Mount, and the rest of the Gospel teaching, and in all things to listen for the living voice of the good Shepherd, watching constantly that no human tradition divert our attention from it,—this is our acknowledged aim and bond of union as a Society. Our conviction of its sufficiency is the ground of our existence as a separate body. [95–96]

\# \#

I have said that our corner-stone and foundation is our belief that God does indeed communicate with each one of the spirits he has made in a direct and living inbreathing of some measure of the breath of his own life. That belief is not peculiar to us. What is peculiar to us is our testimony to the freedom and sufficiency of this immediate divine communication to each one. The ground of our existence as a separate body is our witness to the independence of the true Gospel ministry of all forms and ceremonies, and of all humanly imposed limitations and conditions. We desire to guard this supreme function of the human spirit from all disturbing influences as jealously as the mariner guards his compass from anything which might deflect the needle from the pole; and for the same reason—that we believe the direct influence of the divine mind upon our own to be our one unerring Guide in the voyage of life, and that the faculty by which we discern it is but too easily drawn aside by human influences. There is surely, a very deep significance and value in the Protestant instinct of independence in this deepest region. The Quaker tradition of "non-resistance" has attracted a degree of popular attention which is, I think, out of all proportion to that bestowed on the profound and stubborn independence of Quakerism—its resolute vindication of each man's individual responsibility to his Maker, and to him alone. The supreme value assigned by Friends to consistency of conduct—to strict veracity and integrity, and other plain moral duties—has, I believe, an intimate connection with their abandonment of all reliance upon outward observances, or official support and absolution.

[114–115]

\#   \#

It is only through deep experience, both of inward exercises and of outward sorrows, that any one can become fully qualified to hold forth the word of life to others, as signified by the familiar Quaker expression, "a deeply baptized minister." So strongly have some Friends felt this necessity that they have come to distrust, if not to condemn, whatever appears to them "superficial" or easily produced in ministry. A holy awe, deepening at times, I believe, into even too anxious a restraint, has ever surrounded the exercise of our emphatically "free" ministry—free from all human and outward moulding, precisely in order that it may be the more sacredly reserved to the divine and inward moulding and restraining as well as impelling power.

[115–116]

\#   \#

The nearest approach to a description of what we hold to be a high ministry would seem to be—words spoken during, and arising from, actual communion with God.

[117]

\#   \#

The idea of "testimony," or practical witness-bearing to a stricter obedience to the teaching of Jesus Christ than is thought necessary by the mass of those who are called by his name, has been strongly impressed upon Friends from the very outset, and the persecution which it brought upon them did but burn it irrevocably into the Quaker mind.

[118]

\#   \#

QUAKER SPIRITUALITY

The Yearly Meeting, which was not constituted till 1672 (or twenty-four years from the date of George Fox's beginning to preach), finding the "testimonies" against war, oaths, and superfluities already in full practice, expressly recognized them as belonging to "our Christian profession," and directed inquiry as to the faithfulness of Friends in maintaining them to be made in certain queries addressed from time to time to all the subordinate meetings.   [122]

\# \#

Friends have ever maintained and acted upon the belief that war and strife of all kinds are opposed to the spirit and the teaching of Christ, and have felt themselves, as his disciples, precluded from engaging in them. They have steadfastly refused to take up arms at the bidding of any human authority, or in the presence of any danger. This course of conduct has, of course, brought them into frequent collision with the civil power, and needs for its justification, as Friends are the first to acknowledge, the warrant of a higher than any national authority.   [129]

\# \#

To yield one's self unreservedly to divine guidance; resolutely, and at whatever cost, to refuse to participate in that which one's own conscience has been taught to condemn;—this is the ancient and inestimable Quaker ideal.   [136]

\# \#

As a body, Friends have always recognized "the just authority of the civil magistracy," and have, I believe, never disputed the lawfulness of the use of "the sword" (whatever may be meant by that expression) in maintaining that authority. George Fox himself repeatedly reminded magistrates that they should not "bear the sword in vain," but that they should use it for the punishment of evil-doers, not of those who did well.   [137–138]

\# \#

It is, indeed, not easy to define the precise kind or amount of luxury which is incompatible with Christian simplicity; or rather it must of necessity vary. But the principle is, I think, clear. In life, as in art, whatever does not help, hinders. All that is superfluous to the main object of life must be cleared away, if that object is to be fully at-

256

tained. In all kinds of effort, whether moral, intellectual, or physical, the essential condition of vigour is a severe pruning away of redundance. Is it likely that the highest life, the life of the Christian body, can be carried on upon easier terms? [144]

\# \#

The idea of a scrupulous guard over the lips, which is so strongly characteristic of all Friends at all worthy of the name, culminates in their united testimony against oaths. This has, indeed, been always regarded by Friends as a matter of simple obedience to a plain command of Jesus Christ; and I think that nothing but long habit could reconcile any sincere disciple to the ordinary interpretation of his words as intended to forbid "profane swearing" only. Many others besides Friends have felt this scruple; but to our Society belongs the indisputable credit of having, through a long and severe course of suffering for their "testimony," obtained a distinct recognition of the sufficiency in their case of a plain affirmation, thereby vindicating a principle which is beginning to be generally recognized—the principle of having but one rule for all cases, that of plain truth; of being as much bound by one's word as one's bond. [150–151]

\# \#

The refusal to pay tithes is a testimony against a paid ministry, and I need here only say that in all these cases of resistance to the demands of authority, for military service, for oaths, or for tithes, the idea has been that of witnessing at one's own cost against unjust or unrighteous demands. It is, I think, fair to claim that it is at one's own cost that one refuses a demand even for money when it is made by those who have the power to take the money or its equivalent by force, and when no resistance is ever offered to their doing so. Friends have again and again submitted patiently to the levying of much larger sums than those originally claimed, as well as to severe and sometimes lifelong imprisonments, and other penalties, rather than by any act of their own give consent to exactions which they believed to be unrighteous in their origin or purpose. [151–152]

\# \#

Quakerism is an honest endeavour to carry out this principle in the Christian life; to weigh "in the balance of the sanctuary" the meat that endureth against the meat that perisheth; to cleave to the eternal at the sacrifice, if necessary, of all that is temporal. [154]

\# \#

The Society of Friends has always refused to require adhesion to any formularies as an express or even implied condition of membership; and surely it has done wisely.[38] It has frankly and steadily accepted the Bible as the one common standard and storehouse of written doctrine, but it has always had the courage to trust unreservedly to the immediate teaching of "the Spirit which gave forth the Scriptures" for their interpretation, and for the leading of each one "into all truth"; it has hitherto been true to its belief in the living Guide. [186–187]

---

38. When any person applies for membership, the Monthly Meeting appoints one or more Friends to visit the applicant, and to report to the meeting the result of the interview, before a reply is given. The precise conditions to be fulfilled in such cases are nowhere laid down, but the object is understood, in a general way, to be to ascertain that the applicant is fully "convinced of Friends' principles." The test is thus a purely personal and individual one, and partakes of the elasticity which characterizes all our arrangements, and which is felt to favor the fullest dependence upon divine guidance.

SELECTIONS FROM

THE WRITINGS OF RUFUS M. JONES

RUFUS M. JONES
(*1863–1948*)

It is hard to see how there could be any serious disagreement that in the first half of the twentieth century the weightiest voice that interpreted Quakerism both in its history and in outlining its present and future course was that of Rufus M. Jones. The monumental task of editing and helping to write the six-volume history of the Religious Society of Friends; the large share that he had in founding and guiding the American Friends Service Committee; the quality of his own spiritual life; the stream of books and articles that came from his pen; the power of his ministry and his public service as an interpreter of the spiritual life in that generation, all undergird this assessment of the impact of his life and service. In addition, he taught philosophy at Haverford College for forty years and has left his stamp upon the college and its graduates.

The passages from his writings that have been selected here have been taken principally from Finding the Trail of Life; The Luminous Trail; *the six important prefaces that he wrote for the volumes of the Quaker History Series; and his classic* The Faith and Practice of the Quakers.

FINDING THE TRAIL OF LIFE

I AM CONVINCED by my own life and by wide observation of children that mystical experience is much more common than is usually supposed. Children are not so absorbed as we are with things and with problems. They are not so completely organized for dealing with the outside world as we older persons are. They do not live by cut-and-dried theories. They have more room for surprise and wonder. They are more sensitive to intimations, flashes, openings. The invisible impinges on their souls and they *feel* its reality as something quite natural. Wordsworth was no doubt a rare and unusual child, but many a boy, who was never to be a poet, has felt as he did. "I was often unable," he says, in the preface to his great "Ode," "to think of external things as having external existence, and I communed with all that I saw as something not apart from, but inherent in, my own immaterial nature. Many times while going to school have I grasped at a wall or tree to recall myself from this abyss of idealism to the reality." The world within is just as real as the world without until events force us to become mainly occupied with the outside one.

[10–11]

\# \#

My roots for many generations were deep in Quaker subsoil. There were, however, some features connected with my arrival which might naturally discourage a newcomer. The house to which I came was most plainly furnished. It was many miles from any city; a cold, bleak winter was at its height—January 25th, 1863—and there seemed to be almost no conveniences for comfort and few preparations for what we usually call culture. But these matters troubled me not a bit. It never occurred to me that this was a world of inequalities and I had no prevision of the struggle by which one wins what he gets.

RUFUS M. JONES

The only real fact I can relate about these first hours is one which shows what the highest ambition of my family was and it will also illustrate a characteristic trait in the member of my family who did very much to shape my life in those years when I was plastic to the touch. As soon as I came into the arms of my Aunt Peace, my father's oldest sister who lived with us—one of God's saints—she had an "opening" such as often came to her, for she was gifted with prophetic vision, "This child," she said, "will one day bear the message of the Gospel to distant lands and to peoples across the sea." It was spoken solemnly and with a calm assurance as though she saw the little thing suddenly rising out of her lap to go. That prophecy may seem like a simple word but it expressed the highest ideal of that devoted woman, and her faith in the fulfillment never slackened, even when the growing boy showed signs of doing anything else rather than realizing that hope. If the neighbors, in the period of my youth, had been told of this prophecy it would, I am afraid, almost have shaken their faith in the forevision of this remarkable woman whom they all loved and whose insight they implicitly trusted.

While I was too young to have any religion of my own, I had come to a home where religion kept its fires always burning. We had very few "things," but we were rich in invisible wealth. I was not "christened" in a church, but I was sprinkled from morning till night with the dew of religion. We never ate a meal which did not begin with a hush of thanksgiving; we never began a day without "a family gathering" at which mother read a chapter of the Bible, after which there would follow a weighty silence. These silences, during which all the children of our family were hushed with a kind of awe, were very important features of my spiritual development. There was work inside and outside the house waiting to be done, and yet we sat there hushed and quiet, doing nothing. I very quickly discovered that something *real* was taking place. We were feeling our way down to that place from which living words come and very often they did come. Some one would bow and talk with God so simply and quietly that he never seemed far away. The words helped to explain the silence. We were now finding what we had been searching for. When I first began to think of God I did not think of him as very far off. At meeting some of the Friends who prayed shouted loud and strong when they called upon him, but at home he always heard easily and he seemed to be there with us in the living silence. My first steps in religion were thus *acted*. It was a religion which we *did* together.

QUAKER SPIRITUALITY

Almost nothing was *said* in the way of instructing me. We all joined together to listen for God and then one of us talked to him for the others. In these simple ways my religious disposition was being-unconsciously formed and the roots of my faith in unseen realities were reaching down far below my crude and childish surface thinking. [18–22]

\# \#

One of the earliest home memories out of the dim period of "first years" is the return of my Aunt Peace—the aunt of the prophecy—from an extensive religious visit through the Quaker meetings of Ohio and Iowa. I was, of course, most impressed with the things she brought me. They were as wonderful to me as the dark-skinned natives, which Columbus carried back, were to the people who crowded about his returning ship. Iowa was farther off then than the Philippines are now. But the next impression was made by the marvelous stories of special providences and strange leadings which had been experienced on the journey. I listened as though one of the Argonauts was telling of his adventures in search of the Golden Fleece. Every place where there was a Quaker meetinghouse had its peculiar episode which I had told over and over to me. Every little boy whom she had seen and talked with in that far-flung world was described to me and called by name. This was the first event which made me realize that the world was so big. Before this, it seemed to me that it came to an end where the sky touched the hills. But now my aunt had been out beyond the place where the sky came down, and she had found the earth still going on out there! But after all, the most wonderful thing was the way in which God took care of her and told her what to do and to say in every place where she went. It seemed exactly like the things they read to me out of the life of Joseph and Samuel and David, and I supposed that everybody who was good had their lives cared for and guided in this wonderful way. I made up my mind to be good and to be one of the guided kind! [28–29]

\# \#

The thing which had the most to do, however, with my deliverance from fear was my childlike discovery that God was with me and that *I belonged to him.* I say "discovery," but it was a discovery slowly made and in the main gathered from the atmosphere of our home. God, as I have said, was as *real* to everybody in our family as was our

264

house or our farm. I soon realized that Aunt Peace *knew* him and that grandmother had lived more than eighty years in intimate relation with him. I caught their simple faith and soon had one of my own. I gradually came to feel assured that whatever might be there in the dark of my bedroom, God anyhow was certainly there, stronger than everything else combined. I learned to whisper to him as soon as I got into bed—I never learned to pray kneeling by the bedside. I never saw anybody do that until I went away to boarding school. I "committed" everything to him. I told him that I couldn't take care of myself and asked him to guard and keep the little boy who needed him. And then, I believed that he would do it. I knew that Aunt Peace never doubted and I tried to follow her plan of life. There were times in my childhood when the God I loved was more real than the things I feared and I am convinced that all children would be genuinely religious if they had someone to lead them rightly to God, to whom they belong. [38–39]

# #

Everybody at home, as well as many of our visitors, believed implicitly in immediate divine guidance. Those who went out from our meeting to do extended religious service—and there were many such visits undertaken—always seemed as directly selected for these momentous missions as were the prophets of an earlier time. As far back as I can remember, I can see Friends sitting talking with my grandmother of some "concern" which was heavy upon them, and the whole matter seemed as important as though they had been called by an earthly king to carry on the affairs of an empire. It was partly these cases of divine selection and the constant impression that God was using these persons whom I knew to be his messengers that made me so sure of the fact that we were his chosen people. At any rate I grew up with this idea firmly fixed, and the events which will be told in a later chapter deepened the feeling. [47–48]

# #

When I was ten came one of the crises of my life. It was a great misfortune, which turned out to be a blessing, as is usually the case, if one has eyes to see it. It was the injury to my foot which nearly cost me my leg and seriously threatened my life. Through all the pain and suffering I discovered what a mother's love was. [60]

# #

265

QUAKER SPIRITUALITY

For nine months I never took a step, and for the first week of my suffering, mother sat by me every night, and I felt her love sweep over me. As soon as I was through the racking pain, something had to be done to entertain me—to make the long hours pass, for everybody in our household was occupied with their own tasks. Grandmother, who was eighty-eight years old, had plenty of leisure, and so it was arranged for us to entertain each other. I decided to read the Bible through out loud to her. She could knit mechanically with flying needles, giving no more attention to her fingers than she did to the movement of the hands on the clock. [61]

# #

Before I began the New Testament I was well enough to go out, so that my reading stopped, and it was not until much later that I got deeply hold of that message which came from the Master. The Old Testament was the book of my boyhood. My heroes and heroines were there. It gave me my first poetry and my first history, and I got my growing ideas of God from it. The idea of choice, the fact that God chose a people and that he chose individuals for his missions, was rooted in my thought. [65]

# #

But greatly as I loved the Bible and devoutly as I believed in my first years that it was to be taken in literal fashion, I am thankful to say that I very early caught the faith and insight, which George Fox and other Quaker leaders had taught, that God is always revealing himself, and that truth is not something finished, but something unfolding as life goes forward. In spite of the fact that I lived in a backwoods community into which modern ideas had not penetrated and belonged to an intensely evangelical family, I nevertheless grew up with an attitude of breadth toward Scripture. I searched it, I loved it, I believed it, but I did not think that God stopped speaking to the human race when "the beloved disciple" finished his last book in the New Testament. The very fact that the spirit of God could impress his thought and will upon holy men of old and had done it made me feel confident that he could continue to do that, and consequently that more light and truth could break through men in our times and in those to come. I cannot be too thankful that that little group of believers who made the Bible my living book and who helped me to find and to love its treasures also had spiritual depth enough to give me the key to a larger freedom that enabled me in later years to keep the Bible still as my book, without at the same time preventing me from making use of all that science and history have revealed or can reveal of God's creative work and of his dealing with men.   [65–66]

#   #

Among the many influences which went to form and determine my early life—and so in a measure my whole life—I should give a large place to the visits of itinerant Friends who came to us from far and near. It was a novel custom, this constant interchange of gifted ministers. Something like it apparently prevailed in the early Church, as *The Teaching of the Apostles* indicates, and some of the small religious sects at various periods have maintained an extensive intervisitation, but Friends in the first half of the nineteenth century had developed a form of itinerant ministry which was almost without parallel. It was an admirable method, especially for our rural neighborhoods. We were isolated, and without this contact with the great world we should have had a narrow ingrowing life, but through this splendid spiritual cross-fertilization, we had a chance to increase and improve the quality of our life and thought. The ends of the earth came to our humble door. We got into living contact with Quaker faith and thought in every land where "our religious Society," as we called it, had members. These visitors brought us fresh messages, but, what was not less important, they were themselves unique personalities and were full of incidents and traveler's lore, and thus they formed an excellent substitute for the books which we lacked. They spoke with a prestige and influence which home people seldom have and they brought a contribution into my life which I can hardly overestimate.

Our little local group also had its outgoing stream of itinerant ministry and I was almost as much interested in hearing the story of experiences related by our returning members as I was in listening to the strangers who came among us from afar. My great-uncle drove in his carriage at least twice from Maine to Ohio and Indiana on religious visits, visiting families and attending meetings as he went and living much of the time on his journey in his own carriage. My Aunt Peace made many journeys to remote regions in America and brought back vast stores of information and wisdom. Uncle Eli and Aunt Sybil, who in my youth were among the foremost living Quakers in gift and power of ministry, went back and forth like spiritual shuttles, now weaving their strands of truth into our lives and now again weaving in some far away spot of the earth. It was a very common and ordinary matter for New England Friends to drive to "the Provinces," especially to Nova Scotia, on religious visits, and, as soon as the railroads made travel easy and rapid, there was an almost unbroken stream of circulating ministry. [74–76]

# #

I felt a certain awe because they always came with "a concern," which means that they had left their homes and had undertaken the long journey because they had received an unmistakable and irresistible call to go out and preach what was given them. This was no ordinary visit. Here was a man under our roof who had come because God sent him. I supposed that he had something inside which had told him to go and where to go. [78]

# #

These itinerant ministers told us of life and work in far-off lands. They interested us with their narratives, and in our narrow life they performed somewhat the service of the wandering minstrel in the days of the old castles. They gave us new experiences, a touch of wider life and farther-reaching associations, and for me, at least, they made the connection with God more real. I got from them a clearer sense of what I might be. [83]

# #

Very often in these meetings for worship, which held usually for nearly two hours, there were long periods of silence, for we never had singing to fill the gaps. I do not think anybody ever told me what the silence was for. It does not seem necessary to explain Quaker silence to children. They *feel* what it means. They do not know how to use very long periods of hush, but there is something in short, living, throbbing times of silence which *finds* the child's submerged life and stirs it to nobler living and holier aspiration. I doubt if there is any method of worship which works with a subtler power or which brings into operation in the interior life a more effective moral and spiritual culture. Sometimes a real spiritual wave would sweep over the meeting in these silent hushes, which made me feel very solemn and which carried me—careless boy though I was—down into something which was deeper than my own thoughts, and gave me a momentary sense of that Spirit who has been the life and light of men in all ages and in all lands. Nobody in this group had ever heard the word "mystical," and no one would have known what it meant if it had been applied to this form of worship, but in the best sense of the word this was a mystical religion, and all unconsciously I was being prepared to appreciate and at a later time to interpret the experience and the life of the mystics. [89–90]

# #

In our business meetings, by the world's method, all our business could have been transacted in twenty minutes. We often spent two hours at it, because every affair had to be soaked in a spiritual atmosphere until the dew of religion settled on it! Above in the "high seats" sat two men at a table fastened by hinges to the minister's rail. This table was swung up and held by a perpendicular stick beneath. On it lay the old record-book, a copy of the "discipline," and papers of all sorts. The "clerk," the main man of the two at the desk, was another of those marvelous beings who seemed to me to know every-thing by means of something unseen working inside him! How could he tell what "Friends" wanted done? —and yet he always knew. No votes were cast. Everybody said something in his own peculiar way. A moment of silence would come, and the clerk would rise and say, "It appears that it is the sense of the meeting" to do thus and so. Spontaneously from all parts of the house would come from various-ly-pitched voices—"I unite with that," "So do I," "That is my mind," "I should be easy to have it so." And so we passed to the next subject. [96–97]

# #

There were two transactions which were always exciting, and I used each time to live in hope that they would come off. One was "the declaration of intentions of marriage." When such an event occurred the man and woman came in and sat down together, facing the meeting in the completest possible hush. It was an ordeal which made the couple hesitate to rush into marriage until they felt pretty sure that the match was made in heaven. Solemnly they rose, and in-formed us that they purposed taking each other in marriage, and the parents announced their consent. The meeting "united" and permis-sion was given "to proceed." The marriage itself came off at an even more solemn meeting, when the man and woman took each other "until death should separate." I remember one of these occasions, when the frightened groom took the bride "to be his husband," which made the meeting less solemn than usual.

The other interesting event was the liberation of ministers for religious service "in other parts." If the minister were a woman Friend, as often happened in our meeting, she came in with "a companion." They walked up the aisle and sat down with bowed heads. Slowly the bonnet strings were untied, the bonnet handed to the companion, and the ministering woman rose to say that for a long time the Lord had been calling her to a service in a distant Yearly Meeting; that she had put it off, not feeling that she could undertake so important a work, but that her mind could not get any peace; and now she had come to ask Friends to release her for this service. One after another the Friends would "concur in this concern," and the blessing of the Lord would be invoked upon the messenger who was going forth.

Some of these occasions were of a heavenly sort, and the voices of strong men choked in tears as a beloved brother or sister was equipped and set free. From this little meeting heralds went out to almost every part of the world, and the act of liberation was something never to be forgotten, and only to be surpassed by the deep rejoicing which stirred the same company when the journey was over and "the minutes were returned." [98–100]

# #

The turning point, though by no means the attainment, came for me in a very simple incident—of blessed memory. I had gone a step further than usual, and had done something which grieved everybody at home, and I expected a severe punishment, which was administered with extreme infrequency in our home. To my surprise my mother took me by the hand and led me to my room; then she solemnly kneeled down by me, and offered a prayer which reached the very inmost soul of me, and reached also the real Helper. No holy of holies would ever have seemed to the pious Jew more awful with the presence of God than that chamber seemed to me. It was one thing to hear prayer in the meetinghouse, or in the assembled family, but quite another thing to hear my own case laid before God in words which made me see just what I was, and no less clearly what I ought to be, and what with his help I might be. I learned that day what a mother was for! And though I was still far from won, I was at least where I could more distinctly feel the thread between my soul and the Father, quiver and draw me.   [109–110]

#   #

I think that my Uncle Eli more than anybody else helped me to realize—not by what he said, but by what he did—that this goodness of character which I was after is not something miraculous that drops into a soul out of the skies, but is rather something which is formed within as one faithfully does his set tasks, and goes to work with an enthusiastic passion to help make other people good. I saw him growing white and bent with the advance of years, but no touch of age in the slightest degree weakened his efforts to make our neighborhood better. He preached the Gospel on the first day of the week, and the next day worked at a scheme for building up a town library. One day he was trying to do something to destroy the saloon and advance the cause of temperance, and the next he would be raising money to endow an educational institution. Now he would be busy organizing a local missionary society and the next day he might be advocating a better system of taxation for the town. If he drove by he might be on his way to the station to start off for an extended religious visit, or he might be going down the road to visit a sick neighbour. In all his work for the betterment of man at home and abroad, I never saw him discouraged or in doubt about the final issue. He was always full of hope and courage, and radiantly happy to be able to work at human problems.

But the thing which impressed me most, as a thoughtful boy, was that in all this perplexing and wearying work, he was becoming more and more like my ideal of a saint. His face was sunny; his smile was always ready to break out. We were all happier when he came, and he himself seemed to have a kind of inward peace which was very much like what I supposed the heavenly beings had. It had been his preaching which had so influenced my very early life; but it was much more his victorious life, which spoke with an unanswerable power like that of a sunset or the starry sky, that influenced me now in this critical time. I felt that the way to become good was to go to work in the power of God to help make others good, and to help solve the problems of those among whom we live.

I got a further impression of this truth from an event which came at first as a calamity. I went out one morning in early winter to feed our cattle and horses in the barn, and found to my horror that a fearful storm in the night had blown the barn down with almost everything we possessed in it. It was such a wreck as I had never seen. I can remember now the way I felt as I ran through the neighbourhood to call the men together to see if we could save anything. The news went fast, and before the day was over men from near and far gathered in our yard. They were all hard-working people like ourselves, with little wealth beyond their own strong hands. But before they separated they had decided to go to work at once and replace what the storm had destroyed. The entire neighbourhood went to work, and a new structure rose where the ruin had been.

It was a simple deed, which perhaps many towns could parallel, but it affected me in a strange way. I saw, as I had not seen before, that the religion of these men was not merely an affair of the meeting-house; not merely a way to get to heaven. It was something which made them thoughtful of others and ready to sacrifice for others. I saw how it worked itself out in practical deeds of kindness and righteousness. During those days that I worked in the cold of a Maine winter, among those men with their rough clothes and hard hands, I was helping build more than a barn; I was forming a wider view of the religion which such men as these were living by. [120–123]

THE LUMINOUS TRAIL

In the final chapter of Rufus Jones's book The Luminous Trail, *which appeared the year before his death in 1948, he tells of the life and death of his son. He had been married in 1888 to his wife, Sarah Coutant. Their son was born in 1892 and his wife died of tuberculosis seven years later, leaving him to care for his little son. His daughter says of him, "He, and Lowell even more, needed her love, help and care. Now the father had to be mother as well for his little son. Utterly devoted to each other, he and Lowell started life over again in their home in Haverford."*[39]

THE BOY that I am writing about here . . . left me when he was only eleven years old. . . . The birth of this son in midwinter of 1892 was one of the supreme events of my life. He was named Lowell after my beloved poet. I took him in my arms from the doctor—which would not be allowed now in a modern hospital—and felt an unutterable emotion of joy and wonder. . . . I never got away from this divine miracle. There was light on this child's face which I did not put there. There were marks of heavenly origin too plain to miss. Poets admit that the child trails "clouds of glory from God who is our home," but they spoil it all by predicting that the glory will quickly "fade into the light of common day." It was not so with this child. A child looking at a beautiful object was told that it would soon be gone. "Never mind," he said, "there'll be something else beautiful tomorrow." The "light" kept growing plainer and more real through the eleven years he lived here on earth with me. It never became "common day." [153–155]

---

39. *Quakerism: a Spiritual Movement,* (Philadelphia: Phila. Y. M. Friends, 1963), p. 19.

QUAKER SPIRITUALITY

# #

The time came all too soon when I had to be both father and mother to this dear boy, and then the depth of fusion became even greater, and our lives grew together from within in a way that does not often happen. What I did for him cannot be known, but I live to say no human being could have done more to teach me the way of life than he did. He helped me to become simple and childlike, gentle and loving, confident and trustful. [159]

# #

All too soon this boy, "by the vision splendid on his way attended," came to an end here on earth where I could see him. He had diptheria in the spring of 1903. He was given anti-toxin and recovered, as far as we could see, completely. In July I went to England to lecture at the Quaker Summer School, which was to be the opening of the Woodbrooke Settlement at Selly Oak, near Birmingham. Lowell was to stay at his grandmother's home in Ardonia, New York, with a companion. He was always happy at Ardonia. . . . But the night before landing in Liverpool I awoke in my berth with a strange sense of trouble and sadness. As I lay wondering what it meant, I felt myself invaded by a Presence and held by the Everlasting Arms. It was the most extraordinary experience I had ever had. But I had no intimation that anything was happening to Lowell. When we landed in Liverpool a cable informed me that he was desperately ill, and a second cable in answer to one from me brought the dreadful news that he was gone. [162–163]

# #

When my sorrow was at its most acute stage I was walking along a great city highway [Birmingham], when suddenly I saw a little child come out of a great gate, which swung to and fastened behind her. She wanted to go to her home behind the gate, but it would not open. She pounded in vain with her little fist. She rattled the gate. Then she wailed as though her heart would break. The cry brought the mother. She caught the child in her arms and kissed away the tears. "Didn't you know I would come? It is all right now." All of a sudden I saw with my spirit that there was love behind my shut gate. Yes, "where there is so much love, *there must be* more." [165]

THE FAITH AND PRACTICE
OF THE QUAKERS

T HE QUAKER SOCIETY is still a small body and it presents a seemingly feeble front for the age-long battle of Armageddon. It is a tiny band of labourers for the task of building a spiritual civilization. But this is a matter in which *numbers* are not the main thing. The vital question, after all, is whether this small religious Society here in the world today is a living organ of the Spirit or not. Is it possessed by a *live* idea? Is it in the way of life? Has it found a forward path toward the new world that is to be built? Is it an expansive, or a waning, power? It has stood scorn and brutality; it has weathered the beatings and buffetings of a hostile world; it has survived its own blunders and stupid divisions. When now the world has become kind and friendly toward it, and is even eager for it to *prove* its divine mission, can it make a significant contribution to the truth and life and power of the Christianity that is to save and redeem the world?

[13]

\#   \#

It exhibits a warm and intimate type of inward religion. It is broad, inclusive and tolerant. It cares intensely for religious experience and discounts those aspects of religion which are argumentative, speculative, and divisive. It has preserved a good degree of evangelical fervour, without becoming seriously entangled in the network of theology that often goes with the doctrinal word "evangelical." It has kept pretty close to the central meaning of the Incarnation, the definite breaking in of God into the course of history, the coming of eternity into the midst of time, in the form of a living, visible, human-divine Person, through whom all life on its highest levels is to be interpreted. But it discovers no temporal *end* to that life here in the

275

world. The Christ who was a visible presence in Galilee and Judea is just as certainly alive and present now.

> The healing of His seamless dress
> Is by our beds of pain;
> We touch him in life's throng and press,
> And we are whole again.   [15]

\#   \#

When Fox started forth, in 1647–1648, to be, as he believed, the prophet and apostle of a new and completer reformation, his battle-idea was the continuous revelation of God's will in the soul of man. He had been convinced by his own experience, by the testimony of those whom he met among the spiritual sects, and finally by great texts in Scripture, that there is a direct illumination from God within man's inner being. He met the Calvinistic theory of a congenital seed of sin in the new-born child by the counter claim that *there is a Seed of God in every soul.* This "Seed" or "Light," which he proclaimed, was thought of as a capacity *of response* to divine intimations and openings, a basis of inward communication and correspondence between God and man and a moral searchlight revealing to man the absolute distinction between right and wrong.   [28]

\#   \#

William Penn came in person in 1682 to found Philadelphia and to launch his Holy Experiment in Government. There were between 50,000 and 60,000 Friends in England when George Fox died, in 1691.
        [35]

\#   \#

These first Friends who *trembled* with a consciousness of God's nearness to them, and who rightly got the name of "Quakers," were in no doubt about the main fact. There was One nearer to them than breathing who "spoke to their condition." They felt the healing of God drop upon their souls. The whole creation had a new smell. They were "moved" to their tasks. They had dealing not with flesh and blood but with Spirit. They were called out from the plough and shop to enter upon a high commission. *They* at least had no doubt that "something in man" was in direct correspondence with God. They therefore eliminated mediators and seconds, and insisted upon the direct way and that which was first.   [42]

#   #

What the Friends were concerned about, however, with a concern that was absolutely sound, was that the autonomy of the soul should be protected and safeguarded. They had seen enough, and more than enough, of outside compulsion in religious matters. It had been thought of too long as something in the possession and control of a historic institution, something infallibly preserved and held and something to be transmitted ready-made to the new recipient. It was this theory that the Quaker challenged and denied in behalf of the inherent rights of the soul. The soul itself, as even Carthaginian Tertullian admitted, "when it comes to itself, as out of a surfeit, or a sleep, or a sickness and attains something of its natural soundness, speaks of God," and has an experience to tell. This theory of the soul was, of course, not absolutely new. It did, however, run flatly counter to the main current of the Reformation. It was positive heresy in the ears of the followers of Luther and Calvin, and it had no standing with the guardians of orthodoxy anywhere. It seemed out of line with the general prevailing conception of the "fall." It met the pessimism of depravity with a rival optimism about human potentiality. The Puritan saw in man a wreck like that of a ship hopelessly stranded on a reef of jagged rock. The Quaker saw in him a wreck, if wreck at all, like that of the buds in spring, burst from within by the warm sun, after having been tightly sealed all winter against sleet and storm, wrecked indeed, and by the push and power of a deeper, larger life working within and preparing for vast future possibilities.

We have here, then, a type of Christianity which begins with experience rather than with dogma. Luther, again, took this position in his great battle-documents which were written in the years that followed the nailing up of his Theses. His saving *faith* is an inward attitude based upon first-hand experience. It is "an active, powerful thing," "a deliberate confidence in the grace of God," which makes a man "joyous and intrepid" and ready to die for it "a thousand deaths." But as the Reformation proceeded, the old dogma of the Church assumed an ever-increasing importance and in the end doctrine was raised to a status which overpassed anything known in the mediaeval Church. In fact, the acceptance and maintenance of sound doctrines became the essential condition of salvation. *Faith* ceased to be an active, powerful attitude of will; it became synonymous with "belief." The Church was built up around its doctrine and it took on the aspect of a fort or garrison constructed to defend its saving doctrine. This position became an obsession. Christian bodies divided and subdivided over abstruse points of belief. Wars were fought. Nations were wrecked. Humanity was forgotten. The spirit of the divine Founder was ignored in the determination to maintain at all costs the "sacred" decision of some synod. The way of life inaugurated by the Crucified weighed as almost nothing in comparison with the only true theory of the atonement which some man had formulated.

George Fox called all these formulated beliefs "notions." He pointed out that they could all be believed, adopted, held, and defended without cleansing, purifying, or transforming one's heart in the very least. They were thundered from pulpits and received with "amens," but the lives of the affirming congregation seemed to him but little altered thereby. These things appeared to him to occupy a similar position to that which circumcision occupied in St. Paul's mind and which "Works" held in Luther's thought. One could carry all these matters through to the very end and still be the same unchanged person. "Not circumcision, but a new creation," is St. Paul's demand. "Not works, but a discovery by faith that God is for us," is Luther's message. "Not the holding of notions, but an inward transforming experience of God," is George Fox's word of life.

[43–45]

\# \#

If any supposes that Friends have inclined to be "humanists" and to assume that man is so inherently good that he can lift himself by his own belt into a life of consummate truth and beauty, he has not yet caught the deeper note of the Quaker faith. Friends have always exalted Christ. They have been as eager as any Christians to know the facts of the Gospels and to have sound, clear knowledge of the events in the life of the Jesus of history. They have been very desirous to see vividly and effectively that wonderful person who lived and preached and healed, and helped and loved and died and rose again. They have not usually blurred or slighted the outward life lived in the frame of time and space. But, like St. Paul, they are most concerned with the inward Christ. He is the source of their life and power. The Quaker poet John Greenleaf Whittier has finely expressed for the whole fellowship what he means as a living presence:

> Warm, sweet, tender, even yet
> A present help is He;
> And faith has still its Olivet,
> And love its Galilee. [50]

\# \#

The Friends are, to a large extent, weak in symbolizing power. They do not feel the need of the "midway helps." They are arrested and hindered by the visible and tangible symbols. They want to be left to deal directly and immediately with the great realities by which they live. There are times when they do not want *words*, even though they may be very good words. They want to feel the fresh, free currents of life without any sound or voice. They have a fear of stopping with the outward symbol and of not getting beyond it to that deeper reality for which it stands. The result is that throughout their history, they have preferred to seek for the baptism of the Spirit without the use of water, and to experience a communion of soul with the living Christ without the use of bread and wine. [80]

\# \#

The Quaker way of worship is organized to cultivate this deeper and diviner aspect of life. But there are other features of life no less important than worship and occupying a far larger proportion of the day and week. The atmosphere and climate of one's ordinary daily life, the outlook and expectation, the central ambition of the person's real life—those are the things which in the long run largely settle what kind of person one is to be. [89]

\# \#

In all the best generations of Quakerism, the ideal aim and the controlling expectation of the wiser members have been to live *the simple life*. It is, of course, a vague and indefinable term. It is not a magic phrase by which one can do just the opposite of the miracle of Aladdin's lamp, and suddenly leap from the extravagance of palatial living to the quiet Eden of a one-room cottage, with bark dishes and wooden spoons. The simple life does not begin outside, with the house or the spoons. It begins inside, with *the quality of the soul*. It is

279

first and foremost the quality of sincerity, which is the opposite of duplicity or sham. Emerson's famous line, "Your life talks so loudly that I cannot hear the words you say," makes the idea pretty clear. The fountain must be right, if we want the water to be clear. Unclouded honesty at the heart and centre of the man is the true basis of simplicity. The tone of a bell is settled by the quality of the constituent metal, and, if that is wrong in stuff and mixture, you will not get a good bell by putting on a coat of fine paint. [90]

\# \#

Few things are more needed today than this plain, simple note that religion, on its upward-reaching side, is just joyous companionship with God—with God who is nearer than Abraham realized when he talked with him at his tent door, or Jacob dreamed when he saw heaven at the far end of a ladder.

But I pass from simplicity in the inner life and in worship to the "simple life" in the narrower sense. We come now to problems of business, of dress, of recreation, of entertainment, of culture, of luxury, in short to the world-old problem of how to live a Christian life, not in a cloister or an anchorite's cave, but in an eager, busy, complex world of more or less imperfect men and women. The saint of an earlier day tried to cut the knot by withdrawal. He climbed a lonely pillar, or he buried himself in a quiet cell, but even so he could not escape the self which he carried with him. All his problems came back in new fashion, and as far as he succeeded in cutting the bonds which bound him to his fellows he found himself shrinking and shrivelling like a severed branch.

The endeavour to win goodness by withdrawal from society is as vain as the search for the lost fountain or the pursuit of an alchemy which will make gold out of lead. The only possible way to overcome the world is to carry the forces of the spiritual life into the veins of society until peace and love and righteousness prevail there. [92–93]

\# \#

"If I were not a priest", says Tauler, an apostle of the simple life in the fourteenth century, "I should esteem it a gift of the Holy Ghost that I was able to make shoes." And we may add that the latter occupation may be turned to divine service as well as the other. I know a Friend who has served God through his business as much as though he had been ordained bishop of his diocese. His spirit has remained simple and childlike as his business had expanded, and he has made the wheels of his factory turn to man's service. I might just as well have chosen my illustration from the life of a farmer whom I know, who tills his cabbage patch and corn field to the glory of God and the service of man. His acres are broad, his days are crowded, but his home is a home of the simple life. [94]

\# \#

There are, of course, too many Quakers who have neither simplicity nor spaciousness, but where the former quality is attained the latter one is apt to be present. [101]

\# \#

The forerunners of the Quakers had for some centuries before George Fox been opposed to war. The Waldenses were strict and scrupulous in their refusal to fight or to take life in any way. Many of the small heretical sects before the Reformation had similar views on these matters. The Anabaptists were divided in their conclusions about the right of a Christian to bear a sword and they varied in their practice, though there was a large wing of the movement that refused utterly to have any part in war. The influence of Erasmus, the greatest of the humanists, upon the scattered groups of spiritual reformers was very profound. [103–104]

\# \#

George Fox gives us no clue by which we can trace the origin and development of his own position toward war. His outlook and attitude are in every particular similar to the outlook and attitude of these predecessors, but he never quotes them and he supplies no positive evidence of direct correspondence with them. The influences which shaped his mind in this direction were almost certainly subconscious influences, though his constant absorption with the New Testament was without question one of the leading forces that set his thought into antagonism with war. His earliest positive reaction is the famous response which Fox made while in Derby jail to the Commissioners who proposed to make him the captain of a troop of soldiers in the Commonwealth Army. "I told them," he says, "that I lived in the virtue of that life and power that takes away the occasion of all wars. ... I was come into the covenant of peace which was before wars and strifes were." It was a remarkable position for a young man to take and it was oddly enough expressed. The "covenant of peace" into which he had come was almost certainly in his mind the life of the Spirit. He felt that he was raised to the nature and type of the new Adam and was forever done with the ways of the Adam who fell, and it seemed to him that the new and higher life entailed a spirit and method of life which were essentially Christlike. It is a way of life that practises love and forbearance. It seeks to give rather than to get. It conquers by grace and gentleness. It prefers to suffer injustice than in the slightest degree to do it. It wins and triumphs by sacrifice and self-giving. It spreads abroad an atmosphere of trust and confidence and proposes to prepare the way for a new world by creation of a new spirit—which is essentially the spirit of the Cross. If everyone lived thus, there would be "no occasion of war" but "a covenant of peace."

That is the birth of the Quaker "testimony" for peace. Fox laid down no rules for his followers. He formulated no prohibitions. He was easy and lenient towards those who were in the army or the navy and who nevertheless wanted to become "Children of the Light." He always left them free to "follow their Light." He seems to have felt sure that their inward guidance would eventually bring them to "the covenant of peace" which he had found in his own way. There is an interesting tradition that William Penn asked George Fox whether it was right for him to continue his custom of wearing his sword, and that Fox answered, "Wear it as long as thou canst"; i.e., wear it until conscience makes it clear that a sword is not consistent with Christian life and profession. The early Friends in Fox's lifetime did extremely little to clarify and interpret their position any further in this matter. Fox himself frequently uses the phrase, "Our weapons are spiritual, not carnal." That may be taken, I think, as the substance of the Quaker position in the first generation. They were not absolute "non-resisters," but they put their faith and confidence in the gentler forces of the Spirit. On one occasion, when a man rushed at him with a naked rapier, threatening his life, Fox looked at him unmoved and calmly said, "Alack, poor creature, what wouldst thou do with thy carnal weapon? I care no more for it than I would for a straw." There was a certain power in his undisturbed face, a conquering quality in his manner which enabled him to meet rage, brutality, and cruelty and triumph over them. When the Cambridge "scholars" tried to pull him off his horse in their rough, rude sport, he says, "I rid through

them in the Lord's power and they cried, 'He shines, he glistens!'"
An address of the Philadelphia Yearly Meeting in 1774 very well
expresses the ground and attitude of Friends in this first stage.
"Through the influence of the love of Christ in their minds," it says,
"they ceased from conferring with flesh and blood and became obedient to the heavenly vision, in which they clearly saw that all wars and
fightings proceeded from the spirit of this world which is at enmity
with God, and that they must manifest themselves to be the followers
of the Prince of Peace by meekness, humility, and patient suffering."

The greatest single event of the early period in the line of peace
was the launching of the "Holy Experiment" in Pennsylvania by
William Penn. "For the matters of liberty and privilege," Penn wrote
to a friend, "I purpose that which is extraordinary, and leave myself
and succession no power of doing mischief, that the will of one man
may not hinder the good of a whole country." He guaranteed absolute freedom of conscience, declared that governments exist for the
people, laid down the principle that the aim in judicial punishment
should be the reformation of the criminal, and he did everything in
his power to build a great colony on the foundations of truth, justice,
honour, righteousness, and peace. Ideals are seldom realized in their
full glory of conception and there are flaws in the execution of this
noble design, but the Holy Experiment, nevertheless, marks an ep-
och. Penn also contributed a famous essay towards a peaceable solu-
tion of the distracted state of Europe near the end of the seventeenth
century. It was called "An essay toward the Present and Future Peace
of Europe, by the Establishment of an European Dyet, Parliament, or
Estates." An incident occurred in Penn's Colony almost a hundred
years after it was founded which shows very well how the peace
spirit works. In a little settlement on one of the branches of the
Monongahela River in Western Pennsylvania shortly before the Revolutionary War, there was a tiny group of Quakers who had migrated
from Virginia. Among them was a Friend named Henry Beeson who
lived with his family in a cabin in the woods. The Indians were
fiercely hostile to the settlers, as these Indians were in sympathetic
alliance with the French. A group of Indians surged about the cabin
in the night and the family seemed to be doomed unless a miracle
occurred. They overheard on old chief explaining to the Indians that
this family belonged to "the broad brims," who were "William
Penn's people," and that they must not be molested. The Indians

quickly withdrew without doing any harm. It was a fine instance of the ancient "miracle" that love and kindness beget love and kindness, even in the hearts of so-called savage men.

Throughout the eighteenth century—a century replete with wars and fightings—Friends were finding their position and slowly defining their attitude. They were also discovering what it costs in blood and suffering to break with the settled habits of centuries and to stand out against the organized and basic requirements of strong, proud nations. Not in great matters were they tested, but in small matters, such as decorating houses and illuminating on occasions of victory, they were called upon to show their mettle. In a paper of "Tender Advice and Caution" drawn up by the Meeting for Sufferings and the London Morning Meeting in 1760, Friends were advised that they should not only "cease from outward hostility, but that their conversation and conduct must be consistent and *of a piece throughout.* As they should not join with others in shedding the blood of their fellow creatures, neither could they be one with them in rejoicing for the advantages obtained by such bloodshed; as they could not fight with the fighters, neither could they triumph with the conquerors; and therefore they were not to be prevailed upon to make a show of conformity by placing lights in any part of the fronts of their houses; but patiently suffer whatever violences or abuses were committed against them, for the sake of their peaceable *Christian* Testimony." [104–109]

# #

In this spirit, and with even deeper and tenderer spirit, John Woolman had called Friends all over the American Colonies to a way of life consistent with love and brotherhood. [110]

# #

John Woolman wrote, "May we look upon our treasures, the furniture of our houses, and our garments, and try whether the seeds of war have nourishment in these our possessions." [111]

# #

"It requires," he says, "much self-denial and resignation of ourselves to God to attain that state wherein we can freely cease from fighting when wrongfully invaded, if, by our fighting there were a probability of overcoming the Invaders. Whoever rightly attains to it, does in some degree feel that Spirit in which our Redeemer gave His life for us." [111]

# #

But a still more important positive note began to emerge by the middle of the nineteenth century, a note which has not died out and please God never will die out in the hearts of the Quakers. They began to see that it was not enough to stand out for the personal privilege of renouncing war and of living a peaceful life as an individual. They passed over from the mere claim of a privilege to the sense of a weighty obligation. They awoke to the discovery that no man can either live or die unto himself. They came to realize how closely tied into the social fabric we all are. Our noble word "obligation" means just that. Taken out of Latin and turned over into English it becomes "tied-in-ness." Anyone who is intending to claim his own right to walk the path of peace must take also his share of the heavy burden of trying to build a world in which the gentler forces of kindness, love, sympathy, and co-operation are put into function.

John Woolman had seen that "the seeds of war have nourishment" in the daily lives of men insofar as they encourage luxury and unnecessary worldliness. The spirit of love, therefore, if it is to be effective, must operate not only in war-time, but in those important peace-stretches between wars as well. In short, those who propose to hold aloof from fighting and claim the privileges of peace must become devoted *peace-makers*. This is not to be construed to apply alone to those who bring wars to an end, to diplomats and treaty-makers, nor does it mean in any exclusive sense those who make public peace addresses or who sign petitions or who "post o'er land and ocean without rest" to attend peace conferences and conventions. It applies rather to a deeper and more continuous service of living an everyday life which is "in the covenant of peace." It means a home-life which exhibits the sway and dominion of love practised in the domain of the family life. It means a neighbourhood life which makes love prevail between man and man, and between woman and woman. It means a business life which translates and interprets, as much at least as one individual can do it, the principles which underlie the sway and kingdom of God. The Friend had tended to live apart. He went his own way, maintained his standing as one of a "peculiar people," worshiped in isolation from the rest of the community and showed little readiness to share with others his life experience, or his ideals. If society was "in a mess" it was not his fault. If men stupidly went to war and wasted their substance and had their heads blown off, it was something for which he was not responsible. Gradually, however, this deeper sense of corporate life and responsibility began to dawn upon the more sensitive of the Quakers. A new spirit was born. Other things came to seem more important than hat-brims and bonnets, the problems of garb and speech, the height of gravestones, and the *patois* of this little Zion. They came out of their quietism and their petty concerns to face the issues of the larger world. They awoke to their responsibilities as citizens, as heads of business, as Christian men. They became magistrates, they stood for Parliament, they went to work to make their operatives comfortable and happy. They did the work of peace-makers in a multitude of ways which were much more important than holding peace meetings. They widened out their vision and began to think in international terms.

Joseph Sturge and John Bright in England led the way, and in America John G. Whittier was a pioneer of the new idea with many Friends of lesser fame following close behind him.   [113–115]

#   #

During the Franco-Prussian War in 1870–1871, and after the terrible siege of Paris and the devastating work of the Commune, a band of English Friends went about in the midst of the catastrophe relieving suffering, saving life, reorganizing life, restoring confidence, interpreting in practical and constructive ways and showing to war-victims the deeper rebuilding forces of the spirit. The sum of £200,000 ($1,000,000) was raised for this mission of love, but the spiritual effect was far greater than can be expressed in economic or financial terms.

This service of love amid the horrors and devastations of war prepared the way for the vastly greater work of relief during the years of the Great War and its aftermath.   [116]

SELECTIONS FROM

THE WRITINGS OF THOMAS R. KELLY

THOMAS R. KELLY
(1893–1941)

Thomas R. Kelly has been spoken of as a Brother Lawrence of our time: one who brought the presence of God into the commonest acts of daily life. He grew up as a Quaker boy in Ohio. His Quaker mother, widowed when he was only four years old, had moved into the Quaker college town of Wilmington. There by dint of her tireless labor and Tom's own vigilance at self-support, he ultimately studied and graduated. After graduate study at Haverford College and a Ph.D. in philosophy from Hartford Theological Seminary, he taught philosophy at Earlham College and from 1936 until his early death in 1941, at Haverford College.

Following a crushing disappointment in the late autumn of 1937, Thomas Kelly was swept by an experience of the "Presence" where, in his own words, he tells us that he was literally "melted down by the Love of God." During the next three years, in a series of messages that were eventually printed in various Quaker publications, he poured out the prophetic insights that he had experienced and did so with an unmistakable authenticity. A few months after his death in January 1941, I edited and published a selection of these messages, calling the book A Testament of Devotion. *Twenty-five years later, his son, Richard Kelly, published another small volume of additional papers with the apt title* The Eternal Promise. *The selections that follow are taken from both of these collections.*

TESTAMENT OF DEVOTION

M EISTER ECKHART wrote, "As thou art in church or cell, that same frame of mind carry out into the world, into its turmoil and its fitfulness." Deep within us all there is an amazing inner sanctuary of the soul, a holy place, a Divine Center, a speaking Voice, to which we may continuously return. Eternity is at our hearts, pressing upon our time-torn lives, warming us with intimations of an astounding destiny, calling us home unto Itself.   [29]

\#   \#

But the Living Christ within us is the initiator and we are the responders. God the Lover, the accuser, the revealer of light and darkness presses within us. "Behold I stand at the door and knock." And all our apparent initiative is already a response, a testimonial to his secret presence and working within us.   [30]

\#   \#

But the light fades, the will weakens, the humdrum returns. Can we stay this fading? No, nor should we try, for we must learn the disciplines of his will, and pass beyond this first lesson of his grace. But the Eternal Inward Light does not die when ecstasy dies, nor exist only intermittently, with the flickering of our psychic states. Continuously renewed immediacy, not receding memory of the Divine Touch, lies at the base of religious living.   [30–31]

\#   \#

What is here urged are internal practices and habits of the mind. What is here urged are secret habits of unceasing orientation of the deeps of our being about the Inward Light, ways of conducting our inward life so that we are perpetually bowed in worship, while we are also very busy in the world of daily affairs. . . . Yield yourself to

290

him who is a far better teacher than these outward words, and you will have found the Instructor himself, of whom these words are a faint and broken echo.   [31–32]

\#   \#

There is a way of ordering our mental life on more than one level at once. On one level we may be thinking, discussing, seeing, calculating, meeting all the demands of external affairs. But deep within, behind the scenes, at a profounder level, we may also be in prayer and adoration, song and worship, and a gentle receptiveness to divine breathings.

The secular world of today values and cultivates only the first level, assured that *there* is where the real business of mankind is done, and scorns, or smiles in tolerant amusement, at the cultivation of the second level—a luxury enterprise, a vestige of superstition, an occupation for special temperaments. But in a deeply religious culture men know that the deep level of prayer and of divine attendance is the most important thing in the world. It is at this deep level that the real business of life is determined. The secular mind is an abbreviated, fragmentary mind, building only upon a part of man's nature and neglecting a part—the most glorious part—of man's nature, powers, and resources. The religious mind involves the whole of man, embraces his relations with time within their true ground and setting in the Eternal Lover.   [35–36]

\#   \#

Between the two levels is fruitful interplay, but ever the accent must be upon the deeper level, where the soul ever dwells in the presence of the Holy One. For the religious man is forever bringing all affairs of the first level down into the Light, holding them there in the Presence, reseeing them and the whole of the world of men and things in a new and overturning way, and responding to them in spontaneous, incisive, and simple ways of love and faith.   [36]

\#   \#

How, then, shall we lay hold of that life and power, and live the life of prayer without ceasing? By quiet, persistent practice in turning of all our being, day and night, in prayer and inward worship and surrender, toward him who calls in the deeps of our souls. Mental habits of inward orientation must be established. An inner, secret turning to God can be made fairly steady, after weeks and months and years of practice and lapses and failures and returns. It is as simple an art as Brother Lawrence found it, but it may be long before we achieve any steadiness in the process. Begin now, as you read these words, as you sit in your chair, to offer your whole selves, utterly and in joyful abandon, in quiet, glad surrender to him who is within. In secret ejaculations of praise, turn in humble wonder to the Light, faint though it may be. Keep contact with the outer world of sense and meanings. Here is no discipline in absent-mindedness. Walk and talk and work and laugh with your friends. But behind the scenes, keep up the life of simple prayer and inward worship. Keep it up throughout the day. Let inward prayer be your last act before you fall asleep and the first act when you awake. And in time you will find, as did Brother Lawrence, that "those who have the gale of the Holy Spirit go forward even in sleep."

The first days and weeks and months are awkward and painful, but enormously rewarding. Awkward, because it takes constant vigilance and effort and reassertions of the will, at the first level. Painful, because our lapses are so frequent, the intervals when we forget him so long. Rewarding, because we have begun to live. But these weeks and months and perhaps even years must be passed through before he gives us greater and easier stayedness upon himself.

Lapses and forgettings are so frequent. Our surroundings grow so exciting. Our occupations are so exacting. But when you catch yourself again, lose no time in self-recriminations, but breathe a silent prayer for forgiveness and begin again, just where you are. Offer *this* broken worship up to him and say: "This is what I am except thou aid me." Admit no discouragement, but ever return quietly to him and wait in his Presence.

At first the practice of inward prayer is a process of alternation of attention between outer things and the Inner Light. Preoccupation with either brings the loss of the other. Yet what is sought is not alternation, but simultaneity, worship undergirding every moment, living prayer, the continuous current and background of all moments of life. Long practice indeed is needed before alternation yields to concurrent immersion in both levels at once.

The "plateaus in the learning curve" are so long, and many falter and give up, assenting to alternation as the best that they can do. And no doubt in his graciousness God gives us his gifts, even in intermittent communion, and touches us into flame, far beyond our achievements and deserts. But the hunger of the committed one is for unbroken communion and adoration, and we may be sure he longs for us to find it and supplements our weakness. For our quest is of his initiation, and is carried forward in his tender power and completed by his grace. [38–40]

\# \#

There is then no need for fret when faithfully turning to him, if he leads us but slowly into his secret chambers. If he gives us increasing steadiness in the deeper sense of his Presence, we can only quietly thank him. If he holds us in the stage of alternation we can thank him for his loving wisdom, and wait upon his guidance through the stages for which we are prepared. For we cannot take him by storm. The strong man must become the little child, not understanding but trusting the Father.

But to some at least he gives an amazing stayedness in him, a well-nigh unbroken life of humble quiet adoration in his Presence, in the depths of our being. Day and night, winter and summer, sunshine and shadow. He is here, the great Champion. And we are with him, held in his tenderness, quickened into quietness and peace, children in paradise before the Fall, walking with him in the garden in the heat as well as the cool of the day. Here is not ecstasy but serenity, unshakableness, firmness of life-orientation. We are become what Fox calls "established men." [42]

\# \#

There is no new technique for entrance upon this stage where the soul in its deeper levels is continuously at home in him. The processes of inward prayer do not grow more complex, but more simple. In the early weeks we begin with simple, whispered words. Formulate them spontaneously, "Thine only. Thine only." Or seize upon a fragment of the Psalms: "so panteth my soul after Thee, O God." Repeat them inwardly, over and over again. For the conscious cooperation of the surface level is needed at first, before prayer sinks into the second level as habitual divine orientation. Change the phrases, as you feel led, from hour to hour or from forenoon to afternoon. If you wander, return and begin again. [43–44]

\# \#

Voluntary or stated times of prayer merely join into and enhance the steady undercurrent of quiet worship that underlies the hours.

QUAKER SPIRITUALITY

Behind the foreground of the words continues the background of heavenly orientation, as all the currents of our being set toward him. Through the shimmering light of divine Presence we look out upon the world, and in its turmoil and its fitfulness, we may be given to respond, in some increased measure, in ways dimly suggestive of the Son of Man.   [44]

#   #

There come times when prayer pours forth in volumes and originality such as we cannot create. It rolls through us like a mighty tide. Our prayers are mingled with a vaster word, a word that at one time was made flesh. We pray, and yet it is not we who pray, but a Greater who prays in us. Something of our punctiform selfhood is weakened, but never lost. All we can say is, prayer is taking place, and I am given to be in the orbit. In holy hush we bow in Eternity, and know the divine Concern tenderly enwrapping us and all things within his persuading love. Here all human initiative has passed into acquiescence, and he works and prays and seeks his own through us, in exquisite, energizing life. Here the autonomy of the inner life becomes complete and we are joyfully *prayed through*, by a Seeking Life that flows through us into the world of men. Sometimes this prayer is particularized, and we are impelled to pray for particular persons or particular situations with a quiet or turbulent energy that, subjectively considered, seems utterly irresistible. Sometimes the prayer and this Life that flows through us reaches out to all souls with kindred vision and upholds them in his tender care. Sometimes it flows out to the world of blinded struggle, and we become cosmic Saviours, seeking all those who are lost.   [45–46]

#   #

Guidance of life by the Light within is not exhausted as is too frequently supposed, in special leadings towards particular tasks. It begins first of all in a mass revision of our total reaction to the world. Worshiping in the light we become new creatures, making wholly new and astonishing responses to the entire outer setting of life. These responses are not reasoned out. They are, in large measure, spontaneous reactions of felt incompatibility between "the world's" judgments of value and the Supreme Value we adore deep in the Center. There is a total instruction as well as specific instructions from the Light within. The dynamic illumination from the deeper

294

level is shed upon the judgments of the surface level, and lo, the "former things are passed away, behold, they are become new."

Paradoxically, this total instruction proceeds in two opposing directions at once. We are torn loose from earthly attachments and ambitions—*contemptus mundi*. And we are quickened to a divine but painful concern for the world—*amor mundi*. He plucks the world out of our hearts, loosening the chains of attachment. And he hurls the world into our hearts, where we and he together carry it in infinitely tender love.

The second half of the paradox is more readily accepted today than the first. For we fear it means world-withdrawal, world-flight. We fear a life of wallowing in ecstasies of spiritual sensuality while cries of a needy world go unheeded. And some pages of history seem to fortify our fears.

But there is a sound and valid *contemptus mundi* which the Inner Light works within the utterly dedicated soul. Positions of prominence, eminences of social recognition which we once meant to attain—how puny and trifling they become! Our old ambitions and heroic dreams—what years we have wasted in feeding our own insatiable self-pride, when only his will truly matters! Our wealth and property, security now and in old age—upon what broken reeds have we leaned, when he is "the rock of our heart, and our portion forever!"   [47–48]

# #

Double-mindedness in this matter is wholly destructive of the spiritual Life. Totalitarian are the claims of Christ. No vestige of reservation of "our" rights can remain. Straddle arrangements and compromises between our allegiances to the surface level and the divine Center cannot endure. Unless the willingness is present to be stripped of our last earthly dignity and hope, and yet still praise him, we have no message in this our day of refugees, bodily and spiritual. Nor have we yielded to the monitions of the Inner Instructor.

But actually completed detachment is vastly harder than intended detachment. Fugitive islands of secret reservations elude us. Rationalizations hide them. Intending absolute honesty, we can only bring ourselves steadfastly into his presence and pray, "Cleanse thou me from secret faults." And in the X-ray light of Eternity we may be given to see the dark spots of life, and divine grace may be given to reinforce our will to complete abandonment in him. For the guidance of the Light is critical, acid, sharper than a two-edged sword. He asks all, but he gives all. [49–50]

# #

Meister Eckhart wrote: "There are plenty to follow our Lord half-way, but not the other half. They will give up possessions, friends, and honors, but it touches them too closely to disown themselves." It is just this astonishing life which is willing to follow him the other half, sincerely to disown itself, this life which intends *complete* obedience, without *any* reservations, that I would propose to you in all humility, in all boldness, in all seriousness. I mean this literally, utterly, completely, and I mean it for you and for me—commit your lives in unreserved obedience to him. [52]

# #

We have plenty of Quakers to follow God the first half of the way. Many of us have become as mildly and as conventionally religious as were the church folk of three centuries ago, against whose mildness and mediocrity and passionlessness George Fox and his followers flung themselves with all the passion of a glorious and a new discovery and with all the energy of dedicated lives. In some, says William James, religion exists as a dull habit, in others as an acute fever. Religion as a dull habit is not that for which Christ lived and died. [53]

# #

Some men come into holy obedience through the gateway of profound mystical experience.

It is an overwhelming experience to fall into the hands of the living God, to be invaded to the depths of one's being by his presence, to be, without warning, wholly uprooted from all earth-born securities and assurances, and to be blown by a tempest of unbelievable power which leaves one's old proud self utterly, utterly defenseless, until one cries, "All Thy waves and thy billows are gone over me" (Ps 42:7). Then is the soul swept into a Loving Center of ineffable sweetness, where calm and unspeakable peace and ravishing joy steal over one. And one knows now why Pascal wrote, in the center of his greatest moment, the single word, "Fire." [56]

# #

THOMAS R. KELLY

Do not mistake me. Our interest just now is in the life of complete obedience to God, not in amazing revelations of his glory graciously granted only to some. Yet the amazing experiences of the mystics leave a permanent residue, a God-subdued, a God-possessed will. States of consciousness are fluctuating. The vision fades. But holy and listening and alert obedience remains, as the core and kernel of a God-intoxicated life, as the abiding pattern of sober, workaday living. And some are led into the state of complete obedience by this well-nigh passive route, wherein God alone seems to be the actor and we seem to be wholly acted upon. And our wills are melted and dissolved and made pliant, being firmly fixed in him, and he wills in us.

But in contrast to this passive route to complete obedience most people must follow what Jean-Nicholas Grou calls the active way, wherein *we* must struggle and, like Jacob of old, wrestle with the angel until the morning dawns, the active way wherein the will must be subjected bit by bit, piecemeal and progressively, to the divine will.

But the first step to the obedience of the second half is the flaming vision of the wonder of such a life, a vision which comes occasionally to us all, through biographies of the saints, through the journals of Fox and early Friends, through a life lived before our eyes, through a haunting verse of the Psalms—"Whom have I in heaven but Thee? And there is none upon earth that I desire besides Thee" (Ps 73:25)—through meditation upon the amazing life and death of Jesus, through a flash of illumination or, in Fox's language, a great opening. But whatever the earthly history of this moment of charm, this vision of an absolutely holy life is, I am convinced, the invading, urging, inviting, persuading work of the Eternal One.   [58–59]

# #

The second step to holy obedience is this: begin where you are. Obey *now*. Use what little obedience you are capable of, even if it be like a grain of mustard seed. Begin where you are. Live this present moment, this present hour as you now sit in your seats, in utter, utter submission and openness toward him. Listen outwardly to these words, but within, behind the scenes, in the deeper levels of your lives where you are all alone with God the Loving Eternal One, keep up a silent prayer, "Open thou my life. Guide my thoughts where I dare not let them go. But Thou darest. Thy will be done." Walk on

297

the streets and chat with your friends. But every moment behind the scenes be in prayer, offering yourselves in continuous obedience.

And the third step in holy obedience, or a counsel, is this: if you slip and stumble and forget God for an hour, and assert your old proud self, and rely upon your own clever wisdom, don't spend too much time in anguished regrets and self-accusations but begin again, just where you are.

Yet a fourth consideration in holy obedience is this: Don't grit your teeth and clench your fists and say, "I will! I will!" Relax. Take hands off. Submit yourself to God. Learn to live in the passive voice—a hard saying for Americans—and let life be willed through you. For "I will" spells not obedience. [60]

\# \#

No average goodness will do, no measuring of our lives by our fellows, but only a relentless, inexorable divine standard. No relatives suffice; only absolutes satisfy the soul committed to holy obedience. Absolute honesty, absolute gentleness, absolute self-control, unwearied patience and thoughtfulness in the midst of the raveling friction of home and office and school and shop. [66]

\# \#

I have in mind something deeper than the simplification of our external programs, our absurdly crowded calendars of appointments through which so many pantingly and frantically gasp. These do become simplified in holy obedience, and the poise and peace we have been missing can really be found. But there is a deeper, an internal simplification of the whole of one's personality, stilled, tranquil, in childlike trust listening ever to Eternity's whisper, walking with a smile into the dark.

This amazing simplification comes when we "center down," when life is lived with singleness of eye, from a holy Center where the breath and stillness of Eternity are heavy upon us and we are wholly yielded to him. Some of you know this holy, recreating Center of eternal peace and joy and live in it day and night. Some of you may see it over the margin and wistfully long to slip into that amazing Center where the soul is at home with God. Be very faithful to that wistful longing. [74]

\# \#

THOMAS R. KELLY

Hasten unto him who calls you in the silences of your heart.

[75]

\#   \#

I am persuaded that in the Quaker experience of Divine Presence there is a serious retention of both time and the timeless, with the final value and significance located in the Eternal, who is the creative root of time itself. For "I saw also that there was an ocean of darkness and death, but an infinite ocean of light and love which flowed over the ocean of darkness."

The possibility of this experience of Divine Presence, as a repeatedly realized and present fact, and its transforming and transfiguring effect upon all life—this is the central message of Friends. Once discover this glorious secret, this new dimension of life, and we no longer live merely in time but we live also in the Eternal. The world of time is no longer the sole reality of which we are aware. A second Reality hovers, quickens, quivers, stirs, energizes us, breaks in upon us and in love embraces us, together with all things, within himself. We live our lives at two levels simultaneously, the level of time and the level of the Timeless.

[91–92]

\#   \#

The experience of Divine Presence changes all this familiar picture. There come times when the Presence *steals upon us*, all unexpected, not the product of agonized effort, as we live in a new dimension of life.

[93]

\#   \#

The sense of Presence! I have spoken of it as stealing on one unaware. It is recorded of John Wilhelm Rowntree that as he left a great physician's office, where he had just been told that his advancing blindness could not be stayed, he stood by some railings for a few moments to collect himself when he "suddenly felt the love of God wrap him about as though a visible presence enfolded him and a joy filled him such as he had never known before." An amazing timeliness of the Invading Love, as the Everlasting stole about him in his sorrow. I cannot report such a timeliness of visitation, but only unpredictable arrivals and fadings-out. But without doubt it is given to many of richer experience to find the comfort of the Eternal is watchfully given at their crises in time.

QUAKER SPIRITUALITY

In the immediate experience of the Presence, the Now is no mere nodal point between the past and the future. It is the seat and region of the Divine Presence itself. [94–95]

# #

Now is the dwelling place of God himself. In the Now we are at home at last. The fretful winds of time are stilled, the nostalgic longings of this heaven-born earth-traveler come to rest. For the one-dimensional ribbon of time has loosed its hold. It has by no means disappeared. We live within time, within the one-dimensional ribbon. But every time-now is found to be a continuance of an Eternal Now, and in the Eternal Now receives a new evaluation. We have not merely rediscovered time; we have found in this holy immediacy of the Now the root and source of time itself. For it is the Eternal who is the mother of our holy Now, nay, *is* our Now, and time is, as Plato said, merely its moving image. [96]

# #

For the Eternal is urgently, actively breaking into time, working through those who are willing *to be laid hold upon*, to surrender *self*-confidence and *self*-centered effort, that is, self-originated effort, and let the Eternal be the dynamic guide in recreating, through us, our time-world.

This is the first fruit of the Spirit—a joy unspeakable and full of glory.

The second is love. It is second not in importance but merely in order of mentioning. For it is true that in the experience of Divine Presence that which flows over the ocean of darkness is an infinite ocean of light and *love*. In the Eternal Now all men become seen in a new way. We enfold them in our love, and we and they are enfolded together within the great Love of God as we know it in Christ. Once walk in the Now and men are changed, in our sight, as we see them from the plateau heights. They aren't just masses of struggling beings, furthering or thwarting our ambitions, or, in far larger numbers, utterly alien to and insulated from us. We become identified with them and suffer when they suffer and rejoice when they rejoice. [99]

# #

In such a sense of Presence there is a vast background of cosmic Love and tender care for all things (plants included, I find for myself), but in the foreground arise special objects of love and concern and tender responsibility. The people we know best, see oftenest, have most to do with, these *are reloved* in a new and a deeper way. Would that we could relove the whole world! But a special fragment is placed before us by the temporal now, which puts a special responsibility for our present upon us. [100]

\# \#

The invading Love of the Eternal Now must break in through us into *this* time-now. [100]

\# \#

But in the sense of Presence some of the past nows of our time-now change their character entirely. Our old failures are so apt to paralyze us. The Eternal Now may counsel: "Undertake this." Our time-now says: "See what a weakling you proved yourself to be in an earlier case. Better not try it now." But the assurance of the Eternal Now is enough, as it should have been for Moses: "Surely I shall be with thee." Submit yourself to the Eternal Now and in peace serene, in the boldness of perfect faith, you can advance into miraculous living. Or, in the opposite direction, our time-now may say: "Do this. You are well prepared for it. Your education and training fit you, perhaps to teach, to preach, to counsel, to guide an enterprise. And if you don't, nobody will." But the Eternal Now in us may say: "Stay. Wait. Don't rely upon yourself. Don't think you can reason yourself into your obligation. Know you not that I can raise up of these stones men better able than you to do this?"

Thus in faith we go forward, with breath-taking boldness, and in faith we stand still, unshaken, with amazing confidence. For the time-nows are rooted in the Eternal Now, which is a steadfast Presence, an infinite ocean of light and love which is flowing over the ocean of darkness and death. [105]

\# \#

Have you experienced this concern for the sparrow's fall? This is not just Jesus' experience. Nor is it *His inference* about God's tender love; it is *the record of his experience in God.* There is a tendering of the soul, toward *everything* in creation, from the sparrow's fall to the slave under the lash. The hard-lined face of a money-bitten financier is as deeply touching to a *tendered* soul as the burned out eyes of a miner's children, remote and unseen victims of his so-called success. There is a sense in which, in this terrible tenderness, we become one with God and bear in our quivering souls the sins and burdens the benighted-ness and the tragedy of the creatures of the whole world, and suffer in their suffering and die in their death. [106–107]

# #

Against this cosmic suffering and cosmic responsibility we must set the special responsibility experienced in a *concern*. For a Quaker concern particularizes this cosmic tenderness. It brings to a definite and effective focus in some concrete task all that experience of love and responsibility which might evaporate, in its broad generality, into vague yearnings for a golden Paradise. [108]

# #

It is a particularization of *my* responsibility also, in a world too vast and a lifetime too short for me to carry all responsibilites. My cosmic love, or the Divine Lover loving within me, cannot accomplish its full intent, *which is universal saviourhood*, within the limits of three score years and ten. But the Loving Presence does not burden us equally with all things, but considerately puts upon each of us just a few central tasks, as emphatic responsibilities. For each of us these special undertakings are our share in the joyous burdens of love.

Thus the state of having a concern has a foreground and a background. In the foreground is the special task, uniquely illuminated, toward which we feel a special yearning and care. This is the concern as we usually talk about it or present it to the Monthly Meeting. But in the background is a second level, or layer, of universal concern for all the multitude of good things that need doing. Toward them all we feel kindly, but we are dismissed from active service in most of them. And we have an easy mind in the presence of desperately real needs which are not our direct responsibility. We cannot die on *every* cross, nor are we expected to. [108–109]

# #

I wish I might emphasize how a life becomes simplified when dominated by faithfulness to a few concerns. Too many of us have too many irons in the fire. We get distracted by the intellectual claim to our interest in a thousand and one good things, and before we know it we are pulled and hauled breathlessly along by an over-burdened program of good committees and good undertakings. I am persuaded that this fevered life of church workers is not wholesome. Undertakings get plastered on from the outside because we can't turn down a friend. Acceptance of service on a weighty committee should really depend upon an answering imperative within us, not merely upon a rational calculation of the factors involved. The concern-oriented life is ordered and organized from within. And we learn to say no as well as yes by attending to the guidance of inner responsibility. Quaker simplicity needs to be expressed not merely in dress and architecture and the height of tombstones but also in the structure of a relatively simplified and co-ordinated life-program of social responsibilities. And I am persuaded that *concerns* introduce that simplification, and along with it that intensification which we need in opposition to the hurried, superficial tendencies of our age.

We have tried to discover the grounds of the social responsibility and the social sensitivity of Friends. It is not in mere obedience to Bible commands. It is not in anything earthly. The social concern of Friends is grounded in an experience—an experience of the love of God and of the impulse to saviourhood inherent in the fresh quickenings of that Life. Social concern is the dynamic Life of God at work in the world, made special and emphatic and unique, particularized in each individual or group who is sensitive and tender in the leading-strings of love. A concern is God-initiated, often surprising, always holy, for the Life of God is breaking through into the world. Its execution is in peace and power and astounding faith and joy, for in unhurried serenity the Eternal is at work in the midst of time, triumphantly bringing all things up unto himself.   [110–111]

# #

Prune and trim we must, but not with ruthless haste and ready pruning knife, until we have reflected upon the tree we trim, the environment it lives in, and the sap of life which feeds it.   [113]

# #

We have seen and known people who seem to have found this deep Center of living, where the fretful calls of life are integrated, where no as well as yes can be said with confidence. We've seen such lives, integrated, unworried by the tangles of close decisions, unhurried, cheery, fresh, positive. These are not people of dallying idleness nor of obviously mooning meditation; they are busy carrying their full load as well as we, but without any chafing of the shoulders with the burden, with quiet joy and springing step. Surrounding the trifles of their daily life is an aura of infinite peace and power and joy. We are so strained and tense, with our burdened lives; they are so poised and at peace.

If the Society of Friends has anything to say, it lies in this region primarily. Life is meant to be lived from a Center, a divine Center. Each of us can live such a life of amazing power and peace and serenity, of integration and confidence and simplified multiplicity, on one condition—that is, *if we really want to.* There is a divine Abyss within us all, a holy Infinite Center, a Heart, a Life who speaks in us and through us to the world. We have all heard this holy Whisper at times. At times we have followed the Whisper, and amazing equilibrium of life, amazing effectiveness of living set in. But too many of us have heeded the Voice only at times. Only at times have we submitted to his holy guidance. We have not counted this Holy Thing within us to be the most precious thing in the world. We have not surrendered *all else,* to attend to it alone. Let me repeat. Most of us, I fear, have not surrendered all else, in order to attend to the Holy Within.

[115–117]

\# \#

Much of our acceptance of multitudes of obligations is due to our inability to say no. We calculated that that task had to be done, and we saw no one ready to undertake it. We calculated the need and then calculated our time, and decided maybe we could squeeze it in somewhere. But the decision was a heady decision, not made within the sanctuary of the soul. When we say yes or no to calls for service on the basis of heady decisions, we have to give reasons, to ourselves and to others. But when we say yes or no to calls, on the basis of inner guidance and whispered promptings of encouragement from the Center of our life, or on the basis of a lack of any inward "rising" of that Life to encourage us in the call, we have no reason to give, except one—the will of God as we discern it. Then we have begun to live in guidance. And I find he never guides us into an intolerable scramble of panting feverishness. The Cosmic Patience becomes, in part, our patience, for after all God is at work in the world. It is not we alone who are at work in the world, frantically finishing a work to be offered to God.

Life from the Center is a life of unhurried peace and power. It is simple. It is serene. It is amazing. It is triumphant. It is radiant. It takes no time, but it occupies all our time. And it makes our life-programs new and overcoming. We need not get frantic. He is at the helm. And when our little day is done we lie down quietly in peace, for all is well. [123–124]

THE ETERNAL PROMISE

THE STRAIGHTEST ROAD to social gospel runs through profound
mystical experience. The paradox of true mysticism is that individual experience leads to social passion, that the nonuseful engen-
ders the greatest utility. If we seek a social gospel, we must find it
most deeply rooted in the mystic way. Love of God and love of
neighbor are not two commandments, but one. It is the highest
experience of the mystic, when the soul of man is known to be one
with God himself, that utility drops off and flutters away, useless, to
earth, that world-shaking consciousness of mankind in need arises in
one and he knows himself to be the channel of Divine Life. The birth
of true mysticism brings with it the birthday of the widest social
gospel. "American" Christianity is in need of this deeper strain of
expression of direct contact with God, as the source, not of world-
flight, but of the most intensely "practical" Christianity that has yet
been known.   [15]

#   #

The Quaker discovery and message has always been that God
still lives and moves, works and guides, in vivid immediacy, within
the hearts of men. For revelation is not static and complete, like a
book, but dynamic and enlarging, as springing from a *Life* and Soul of
all things. This Light and Life is in all men, ready to sweep us into its
floods, illumine us with its blinding, or with its gentle guiding
radiance, send us tendered but strong into the world of need and pain
and blindness. Surrender of self to that indwelling Life is entrance
upon an astounding, an almost miraculous Life. It is to have that
mind in you which was also in Jesus Christ. "Behold, I stand at the
door and knock." In the silence of your hearts hear him knock.
Outward teachers can only lead us to the threshold. But "God himself
has come to lead his people." Such men and women must be raised

306

up, heaven-led souls who are not "seekers" alone, but "finders," finders who have *been found* by the Father of all the world's prodigals.

. . . How different is the experience of Life . . . when the Eternal Presence suffuses it! Suddenly, unexpectedly, we are lifted in a plateau of peace. The dinning clamor of daily events—so real, so urgent they have been!—is framed in a new frame, is seen from a new perspective. The former things are passed away; behold, they have become new. This world, our world, and its problems, does not disappear nor lose its value. It reappears in a new light, upheld in a new and amazingly *quiet* power. Calm replaces strain, peace replaces anxiety. Assurance, relaxation, and integration of life set in. With hushed breath we do our tasks. Reverently we live in the presence of the Holy. . . . Life itself becomes a sacrament wherein sin is blasphemy. A deep longing for personal righteousness and purity sets in. Old tempting weaknesses no longer appeal as they did before. In patience we smile in loving concern for those who rush about with excited desperation. Oh, why can they not see the ocean of light and love which flows completely over the ocean of darkness and death! But all things [are] in his Providence. A little taste of Cosmic Patience, which a Father-heart must have for a wayward world, becomes ours. The world's work is to be done. But it doesn't have to be *finished* by us. We have taken ourselves too seriously. The life of God overarches *all* lifetimes.   [20–21]

# #

The old self, the little self—how weak it is, and how absurdly confident and how absurdly timid it has been! How jealously we guard its strange precious pride! Famished for superiority-feeling, as Alfred Adler pointed out, its defeats must be offset by a dole of petty victories. In religious matters we still thought that we should struggle to present to God a suitable offering of service. We planned, we prayed, we suffered, we carried the burden. The we, the self, how subtly it intrudes itself into religion! And then steals in, so sweetly, so all-replacing, the sense of Presence, the sense of Other, and he plans, and he bears the burdens, and we are a new creature. Prayer becomes not hysterical cries to a distant God, but gentle upliftings and faint whispers, in which it is not easy to say *who* is speaking, we, or an Other through us. Perhaps we can only say: praying is taking place. Power flows through us, from the Eternal into the rivulets of Time. Amazed, yet not amazed, we stride the stride of the tender giant who dwells within us, and wonders are performed. Active as never before, one lives in the passive voice, alert to be used, fearful of nothing, patient to stand and wait.

It is an amazing discovery, at first, to find that a creative Power and Life is at work in the world. God is no longer the object of a belief; He is a Reality, who has continued, within us, his real Presence in the world. God is aggressive. He is an intruder, a lofty lowly conqueror on whom we had counted too little, because we had counted on ourselves. Too long have we supposed that we must carry the banner of religion, that it was *our* concern. But religion is not our concern; it is God's concern. Our task is to call men to "be still, and know that I am God," to hearken to that of God within them, to invite, to unclasp the clenched fists of self-resolution, to be pliant in his firm guidance, sensitive to the inflections of the inner voice.

For there is a life beyond earnestness to be found. It is the life rooted and grounded in the Presence, the Life which has *been found by* the Almighty. Seek it, seek it. Yet it lies beyond seeking. It arises in *being found*. To have come only as far as religious determination is only to have stood in the vestibule. But our confidence in our shrewdness, in our education, in our talents, in some aspect or other of our self-assured self, is our own undoing. So earnestly busy with anxious, fevered efforts for the kingdom of God have we been, that we failed to hear the knock upon the door, and to know that our chief task is to open that door and be entered by the Divine Life.

There is an old, old story that the gateway to deep religion is self-surrender. Dr. Coomaraswamy, writing upon the art of India, says that all developed religions have as their center the experience of becoming unselfed. But falling in love is an old, old story in the history of the world, yet new to each individual when first it comes. Descriptions of the unselfing which comes with the Invading Love are no substitute for the immediacy of the experience of being unselfed by the Eternal Captain of our souls. Nor is there a freedom so joyous as the enslaving bonds of such amazing, persuading Love.

But according to our Christian conception of the unselfing in religion, to become unselfed is to become truly integrated as a richer self. The little, time-worn self about which we fretted—how narrow its boundaries, how unstable its base, how strained its structure. But the experience of discovering that life is rooted and grounded in the actual, active, loving Eternal One is also to experience our own personal life firm-textured and stable.   [23–25]

THOMAS R. KELLY

\# \#

To you I speak with much hesitation about suffering. For I am only in middle years, and for me life has not been hard. But there is an introduction to suffering which comes with the birthpains of Love. And in such suffering one finds for the first time how deep and profound is the nature and meaning of life. And in such suffering one sees, as if one's eye were newly opened upon a blinding light, the very Life of the Eternal God himself. And there too is suffering, but there, above all, is peace and victory.

Another aspect of the same awakening of the soul-tenderness is the new love of the world. Before, we had loved the world because it enriched our lives—we were the receiving centers. But now all is new, even the nature of love itself. Our families, our dear ones, they are reloved. [30]

\# \#

Worship does not consist in achieving a mental state of concentrated isolation from one's fellows. But in the depth of common worship it is as if we found our separate lives were all one life, within whom we live and move and have our being. Communication seems to take place sometimes without words having been spoken. In the silence we received an unexpected commission to bear in loving intentness the spiritual need of another person sitting nearby. And that person goes away, uplifted and refreshed. Sometimes in that beautiful experience of living worship which the Friends have called "the gathered meeting," it is as if we joined hands and hearts, and lifted them together toward the unspeakable glory. Or it is as if that light and warmth dissolved us together into one. Tears are not to be scorned, then, for we stand together in the Holy of Holies. [34]

\# \#

A few weeks ago a man and his wife told me, with light in their eyes, how, three years ago, in the midst of their eighteen-year-old daughter's death had come to them the peace and Presence of the Great Companion, and had rebuilt them into lives of joyful service among young people of their daughter's generation.... From such people time's arrows fall back, like the spear of Klingsor hurled at the heart of Parsifal.

309

QUAKER SPIRITUALITY

For I am persuaded, that neither death, nor life, nor angels,
nor principalities, nor powers, nor things present, nor
things to come, nor height, nor depth, nor any other creature, shall be able to separate us from the love of God, which
is in Christ Jesus our Lord. (Rom 8:38–39)   [34–35]

\#   \#

Secular action is on the increase and religion as an influence is on
the wane. Quakers appeared in history at just such a time as this,
when the experience of deep religion had grown thin. Preachers
lacked personal relationship with God. The Society of Friends arose
to bring back vital apostolic power. The purpose was not to form
another sect and to justify it by a peculiar tenet. Friends came to dig
down to the wellsprings of spiritual immediacy, holding that religion
means that which you know, feel, experience within yourself. Our
task isn't to nurse the dying embers of a dying sect, but to be
missionaries to Christendom; to live in a real Christian fellowship,
not within a definite organization.   [36]

\#   \#

We are men of double personalities. We have slumbering demons
within us. We all have also a dimly-formed Christ within us. We've
been too ready to say that the demonic man within us is the natural
and the real man, and that the Christ-man within us is the unnatural
and the unreal self. But the case is that our surface potentialities are for
selfishness and greed, for tooth and claw. But deep within, in the
whispers of the heart, is the surging call of the Eternal Christ, hidden
within us all. By an inner isthmus we are connected with the main-
land of the Eternal Love. Surface living has brought on the world's
tragedy. Deeper living leads us to the Eternal Christ, hidden in us all.
Absolute loyalty to this inner Christ is the only hope of a new
humanity. In the clamor and din of the day, the press of Eternity's
warm love still whispers in each of us, as our truest selves. Attend to
the Eternal that he may recreate you and sow you deep into the
furrows of the world's suffering.   [40–41]

\#   \#

Each one of us has the Seed of Christ within him. In each of us
the amazing and the dangerous Seed of Christ is present. It is only a
Seed. It is very small, like the grain of mustard seed. The Christ that

is formed in us is small indeed, but he is great with eternity. But if we dare to take this awakened Seed of Christ into the midst of the world's suffering, it will grow. That's why the Quaker work camps are important. Take a young man or young woman in whom Christ is only dimly formed, but one in whom the Seed of Christ is alive. Put him into a distressed area, into a refugee camp, into a poverty region. Let him go into the world's suffering, bearing this Seed with him, and in suffering it will grow, and Christ will be more and more fully formed in him. As the grain of mustard seed grew so large that the birds found shelter in it, so the man who bears an awakened Seed into the world's suffering will grow until he becomes a refuge for many.

[42–43]

\# \#

The early Quakers were founding no sect; they were reforming Christendom, that had slumped into externals and had lost its true sense of the immediate presence and the creative, triumphant power of the living God within us all. They had a message for all, for they had discovered that "the Lord himself had come to lead his people."

And in that same way the Quaker discovery, not of a doctrine, not of a belief, but of a Life, a life filled with God, a life listening, obedient, triumphant, holy—in that same way the Quaker discovery was only a rediscovery of the life and power and fellowship and joy and radiance which moved the early Church. Its rediscovery today is desperately needed, for the fellowship of believers has grown dim, and only a few clear voices ring out in the twilight. You and I can be the instruments of the opening of God's life. But it is heroic work, not work for the milder Quaker. The fires of God burn bright. In their light we are judged or consumed, in their light the world is condemned. In their light we may discover what so many have really lost, namely, God himself. And what is a greater discovery?   [60]

311

THE GATHERED MEETING

IN THE PRACTICE of group worship on the basis of silence come special times when the electric hush and solemnity and depth of power steals over the worshipers. A blanket of divine covering comes over the room, a stillness that can be felt is over all, and the worshipers are gathered into a unity and synthesis of life which is amazing indeed. A quickening Presence pervades us, breaking down some part of the special privacy and isolation of our individual lives and blending our spirits within a superindividual Life and Power. An objective, dynamic Presence enfolds us all, nourishes our souls, speaks glad, unutterable comfort within us, and quickens us in depths that had before been slumbering. The Burning Bush has been kindled in our midst, and we stand together on holy ground.

Such gathered meetings I take to be cases of group mysticism. . . . The gathered meeting I take to be of the same kind, still milder and more diffused, yet really of a piece with all mystical experience. For mystical times are capable of all gradings and shadings, from sublime heights to very mild moments of lift and very faint glimpses of glory. In the gathered meeting the sense is present that a new life and Power has entered our midst. And we know not only that we stand erect in the holy Presence, but also that others sitting with us are experiencing the same exaltation and access of power. We may not know these our neighbors in any outwardly intimate sense, but we now know them, as it were, from within, and they know us in the same way, as souls now alive in the same areas and as blended into the body of Christ, which is his church. Again and again this community of life and guidance from the Presence in the midst is made clear by the way the spoken words uttered in the meeting join on to one another and to our inward thoughts. This, I presume, has been a frequent experience for us all, as a common life and current sweeps through all. We are in communication with one another because we are being communciated to, and through, by the Divine Presence.

[75]

#   #

I believe that the group mysticism of the gathered meeting rests upon the Real Presence of God in our midst. Quakers generally hold to a belief in Real Presence, as firm and solid as the belief of Roman Catholics in the Real Presence in the host, the bread and the wine of the Mass. In the host the Roman Catholic is convinced that the literal, substantial Body of Christ is present. For him the Mass is not a mere symbol, a dramatizing of some figurative relationship of man to God. It rests upon the persuasion that an Existence, a Life, the Body of Christ, is really present and entering into the body of man. Here the Quaker is very near the Roman Catholic. For the Real Presence of the gathered meeting is an existential fact. To use philosophical language, it is an ontological matter, not merely a psychological matter. The bond of union in divine fellowship is existential and real, not figurative. It is the life of God himself, within whose life we live and move and have our being. And the gathered meeting is a special case of holy fellowship of the blessed community. [81]

#   #

One condition for such a group experience seems to be this: some individuals need already, upon entering the meeting, to be gathered deep in the spirit of worship. There must be some kindled hearts when the meeting begins. In them, and from them, begins the work of worship. The spiritual devotion of a few persons, silently deep in active adoration, is needed to kindle the rest, to help those others who enter the service with tangled, harried, distraught thoughts to be melted and quieted and released and made pliant, ready for the work of God and his Real Presence.

In power and labor one lifts the group, in inward prayer, high before the throne. With work of soul the kindled praying worshiper holds the group, his comrades and himself, high above the sordid and trivial, and prays in quiet, offering that Light may drive away the shadows of self-will. Where this inward work of upholding prayer is wholly absent, I am not sure that a gathered meeting is at all likely to follow. [82–83]

313

QUAKER SPIRITUALITY

# #

He who carries a Shekinah daily in his heart, and practices continual retirement within that Shekinah, *at the same time as he is carrying on his daily affairs,* has begun to prepare for worship, for he has never ceased worshiping. Such worship is no intermittent process, but a foundation layer of the life of the children of the kingdom. And such a special sense of bondedness and unity with others as is experienced in the gathered meeting is only a time of particular enhancement of the life of bondedness and fellowship in love among souls which is experienced daily, as we carry one another in inward upholding prayer.

A second condition concerns the spoken words of the meeting. Certainly the deepness of the covering of a meeting is not proportional to the number of words spoken. A gathered meeting may proceed entirely in silence, rolling on with increasing depth and intensity until the meeting breaks and tears are furtively brushed away. Such really powerful hours of unbroken silence frequently carry a genuine progression of spiritual change and experience.   [84]

# #

But I have more particularly in mind those hours of worship in which no one person, no one speech, stands out as the one that "made" the meeting, those hours wherein the personalities that take part verbally are not enhanced as individuals in the eyes of others, but are subdued and softened and lost sight of because in the language of Fox, "the Lord's power was over all." Brevity, earnestness, sincerity—and frequently a lack of polish—characterized the best Quaker speaking. The words should rise like a shaggy crag upthrust from the surface of silence, under the pressure of river power and yearning, contrition, and wonder. But on the other hand the words should not rise up like a shaggy crag. They should not break the silence, but continue it. For the Divine Life who is ministering through the medium of silence is the same Life as is now ministering through words. And when such words are truly spoken "in the Life," then when such words cease, the *uninterrupted* silence and worship continue, for silence and words have been of one texture, one piece. Second and third speakers only continue the enhancement of the moving Presence, until a climax is reached, and the discerning head of the meeting knows when to break it.   [85–86]

314

THOMAS R. KELLY

\# \#

But what if the meeting has not been a gathered meeting? Are those meetings failures that have not been hushed by a covering? Quite definitely they are not. *If we have been faithful,* we may go home content and nourished from any meeting.

Like the individual soul, the group must learn to endure spiritual weather without dismay. Some hours of worship are full of glow and life, but others lack the quality. The disciplined soul, and the disciplined group, have learned to cling to the reality of God's Presence, whether the feeling of Presence is great or faint. If only the group has been knit about the very springs of motivation, the fountain of the will, then real worship has taken place. [89]

\# \#

To you in this room who are seekers, to you, young and old who have toiled all night and caught nothing, but who want to launch out into deeps and let down your nets for a draught, I want to speak, as simply, as tenderly, as clearly as I can. For God *can* be found. There *is* a last Rock for your souls, a resting place of absolute peace and joy and power and radiance and security. There is a Divine Center into which your life can slip, a new and absolute orientation to God, a Center where you live with him, and out from which you see all of life, through new and radiant vision, tinged with new sorrows and pangs, new joys unspeakable and full of glory. [102]

315

BIBLIOGRAPHY

Barbour, Hugh. *The Quakers in Puritan England.* New Haven: Yale University Press, 1964.

———and Roberts, Arthur O. *Early Quaker Writings.* Grand Rapids: Eerdman, 1973.

Braithwaite, William C. The Rowntree Quaker History Series.

———. *Spiritual Guidance in Quaker Experience.* Swarthmore Lecture. London: Headley Bros.) 1909.

———. *The Beginnings of Quakerism.* London: Macmillan, 1912.

———. *The Second Period of Quakerism.* London: Macmillan, 1919.

Brayshaw, A. Neave. *The Quakers.* New York: Macmillan, 1938.

Brinton, Howard H. *Creative Worship.* Swarthmore Lecture. London: Allen Unwin, 1931.

———. *Divine-Human Society.* Wallingford, Pa.: Pendle Hill Pub., 1938.

———. *Guide to Quaker Practice.* Pendle Hill Pamphlet No. 20, 1943.

———. *The Quaker Doctrine of Inner Peace.* Pendle Hill Pamphlet no. 44, 1948.

———. *Friends for 300 Years.* New York: Harpers, 1952.

———. *Ethical Mysticism.* People Hill Pamphlet no. 156, 1967.

———. *The Religion of George Fox.* Pendle Hill Pamphlet no. 161, 1968.

———. *Quaker Journals.* Wallingford, Pa.: Pendle Hill Pub., 1972.

Castle, E. B. *The Undivided Mind.* Swarthmore Lecture. London, Allen Unwin, 1941.

Churchman, John. *An Account of Gospel Labors.* Philadelphia: Crukshank, 1779.

Comfort, William Wistar. *Stephen Grellett.* New York: Macmillan, 1942.

———. *Quakers in the Modern World.* New York: Macmillan, 1949.

Creasey, Maurice. *Bearings.* Swarthmore Lecture. London: Friends Home Service, Committee, 1969.

Doncaster, L. Hugh. *God in Every Man.* Swarthmore Lecture. London: Allen Unwin, 1963.

Edmundson, William. *Journal.* Dublin; Samuel Fairbrother, 1715.

BIBLIOGRAPHY

Elliott, Erroll. *Quakers on the American Frontier.* Richmond, Ind.: Friends United Meeting Press, 1969.

Fairn, Duncan. *A Faith for Ordinary Men.* Swarthmore Lecture. London: Allen Unwin, 1951.

Forbush, Bliss. *Elias Hicks.* New York: Columbia University Press, 1958.

Graham, John W. *The Faith of a Quaker.* Cambridge: Cambridge University Press, 1951.

Grubb, Edward. *The Historic and the Inward Christ.* Swarthmore Lecture. London: Headley Bros., 1914.

————. *Quaker Thought and History.* New York: Macmillan, 1925.

Harvey, T. Edmund. *The Rise of the Quakers.* London: Headly, 1905.

————. *Authority and Freedom in the Experience of Friends.* Selly Oak: Woodbrooke, 1935.

Hodgkin, L. Violet. *Silent Worship.* Swarthmore Lecture. London: 1919.

Jones, Mary Hoxie; *Rufus M. Jones.* Friends Home Service, London: 1955.

Jones, Rufus M. The Rowntree Quaker History Series.

————. *Studies in Mystical Religion.* London: Macmillan, 1909.

————. *Quakers in the American Colonies.* London: Macmillan, 1911.

————. *Spiritual Reformers in the 16th and 17th Centuries.* London: Macmillan, 1914.

————. *The Later Periods of Quakerism.* 2 vols. London: Macmillan, 1921.

————. *Quakerism as a Spiritual Movement.* Philadelphia: Philadelphia Yearly Meeting, 1963. Contains Rufus M. Jones's Prefaces to each of the Rowntree Quaker History Series.

————. *Faith and Practice of the Quakers.* London: Methuen, 1928. Reprint. Richmond, Ind.: Friends United Mtg. Press, 1980.

————. *Mysticism and Democracy in the English Commonwealth.* Cambridge, Mass.: Harvard University Press, 1932.

Kelly, Thomas R. *Testament of Devotion.* New York: Harpers, 1941.

————. *The Eternal Promise.* New York: Harpers, 1966.

Kenworthy, Leonard S. *Quakerism.* Dublin, Ind.: Prinit Press, 1981.

Loukes, Harold. *The Discovery of Quakerism.* London: Harrap, 1960.

————. *The Quaker Contribution.* London: SCM, 1965.

Christian Faith and Practice. London: Friends Book Center, 1959.

Moore, John M., ed. *Friends in the Delaware Valley.* Haverford, Pa.: Friends Historical Association, 1981.

Newman, Daisy. *A Procession of Friends.* New York: Doubleday, 1972.

Nuttall, Geoffrey. *The Holy Spirit in Puritan Faith and Practice.* Oxford: Blackwell, 1946.

Peare, Catherine Owens. *William Penn.* Philadelphia: Lippincott, 1957.

Penington, Isaac. *Works.* 4 vols. New York: Sherwoods, 1863.

Penn, William. *No Cross, No Crown.* London: B. Clark, 1682.

————. *Fruits of Solitude.* London: Ben. Johnson, 1794.

BIBLIOGRAPHY

Scott, Job. *Journal.* New York: Isaac Collins, 1797.

Steere, Douglas V. *Where Words Come From.* Swarthmore Lecture. London: Allen Unwin, 1955; New York: Harpers, 1955 (under title *On Listening to Another*).

———. *On Being Present Where You Are.* Pendle Hill Pamphlet no. 151.

———. *Mutual Irradiation.* Pendle Hill Pamphlet no. 175.

———. *On Speaking Out of the Silence.* Pendle Hill Pamphlet no. 182.

Tolles, Fredrick. *Meeting House and Counting House.* Chapel Hill, N.C.: University of North Carolina Press, 1948.

Trueblood, D. Elton. *The People Called Quakers.* New York: Harpers, 1966.

———. *Robert Barclay.* New York: Harpers, 1967.

Vining, Elizabeth G. *Friend of Life: Rufus M. Jones.* Philadelphia: Lippincott, 1958.

———. *William Penn: Mystic.* Wallingford, Penn.; Pendle Hill Pamphlet no. 167, 1969.

———. *Mr. Whittier.* New York: Viking, 1974.

Webb, Marie. *The Penns and Peningtons of the 17th Century.* London: Kitto, 1867.

Whitney, Janet P. *Elizabeth Fry.* Boston: Little Brown, 1936.

———. *John Woolman, Quaker.* London: Harrap, 1943.

INDEX TO INTRODUCTION

Acts, the Book of, 5, 13, 42
Agassiz's View of Creation, 34
Apology (Barclay), 19
Apostolic Age, the, 5–6
Augustine, St., 4

Babcock, Maltie, 45
Backman, Herman, 41
Baker, Augustine, 25
Barclay, Robert, 15, 19, 25, 33
Bible, the. *See* Scriptures, the
Boehme, Jacob, 25
Braithwaite, William C., 35
Britain, 6
Bryn Mawr College, 33
Butler, Bishop, 20

Cedegren, Elsa, 41
Centuries of Meditation
    (Traherne), 15
Chantal, Madame de, 5
Charles II, King, 48, 49
Charlton, Robert, 43–44
Christian Faith and Practice, 19
Christ Jesus, 7, 8, 11, 15, 16
Churchman, John, 32
Claudel, Paul, 27
Coffin, Levi, 51

"Commonest he," the, 6, 12, 14,
    17
Court, Donald, 28
Crimean War, the, 43–45
Cromwell, Oliver, 6, 48

Darwin's Theory of Evolution,
    34
De Chantal, Madame, 5
De Sales, Francis, 30
De Vigny, Alfred, 42
Dewsbury, William, 32

Earlham College, 33
Eastern Orthodox, the, 28
Edmundson, William, 24
Ellwood, Thomas, 19
Enthusiasm (Knox), 20
Erie Canal, the, 33
Eucharist, the, 18

Fell, Judge Thomas, 10
Fell, Margaret, 10–11
Fenelon, 24
Fifth Monarchy, the, 20–21
Fireflies (Tagore), 47
Fox, George: and the Bible, 21;
    and Christ within, 7, 8,

INDEX

11–12; and the clergy, 32;
and the "commonest he,"
12, 17; and corporate
worship, 8; and God, 8; and
the Holy Spirit, 7, 29;
hostility against, 12–13, 18;
his *Journal*, 7, 10; his leather
breeches, 12; and Margaret
Fell, 10; and notionism, 19;
and the Quaker movement,
6–8; and silence, 8–9; and
the Valiant Sixty, 11, 13;
mentioned, 24, 26
Friends University at Wichita,
33
Friends World Committee for
Consultation, the, 4
Fry, Elizabeth, 51

George Fox College, 33
God, 8, 11
Gould, Anne, 24
Guilford College, 33
Gustaf V, King, 41
Guyon, Madame, 25

Harris, Rendel, 34
Haverford College, 33
Heard, Gerald, 4
Heiler, Friedrich, 17
"Holy Experiment," the, 49
Holy Spirit, the, 5, 6, 11, 15, 18,
28
Holy Wisdom (Baker), 25
Hosea, the Book of, 17
Howgill, Francis, 9

Imitation of Christ, The, 25
Israel, 3

James II, King, 48
John of the Cross, St., 16
Johnston, William, 17
Jones, Rufus, 34

Kendal Fund, the, 11
Knox, Robert, 20, 21

Letters (Fenelon), 24
Locke, John, 49
London Yearly Meeting, the, 19
Loucks, Harold, 47

Meeting for Sufferings, the, 13
*Meetinghouse and
Countinghouse* (Tolles), 51
Meetings for business, the, 14
Meetings for worship, the, 15

Nayler, James, 20
Nicholas I, Czar, 43
Noble, Emma, 45
No Cross, No Crown (Penn), 21
Nonconformists, the, 35, 47, 49
Norlind, Emelia Fogelklou, 14,
41
Notionism, 19
Nuttall, Geoffrey, 8, 10

Pacific College, 33
Palmerston, Prime Minister, 44
Paquet, Alfons, 39–40
Parker, Alexander, 26
Paulist Press, 3
Pease, Henry, 43
Pendle Hill, 10
Penington, Isaac, 11, 19, 24, 28,
29, 31, 34
Penn, Gulielma, 23

INDEX

Penn, William, 19, 21, 23, 27, 48–49
Penn-Meade case, the, 48
Pennsylvania, 49
Penrose, J. Doyle, 27
Perrot position, the, 36
Philadelphia, 50
Poland, 16
Prayer (Heiler), 17

Quakers, the: and the Bible, 21–22, 34; and business dealings, 50–51; the children of, 25–26; and Christ within, 18, 19; and the committee of clearness, 43–46; and corporate worship, 5, 13–14; and group decision-making, 36–39, 41–43, 46–47; and higher education, 33–34; the individualism of, 3; and intuition and reason, 34; and inward communion, 18; and marriage, 52; the Meeting for Sufferings of, 13; meetings of, 36–39, 41–43; the meetings for business of, 14; the meetings for worship of, 15; and the mystical, 16–17; and obedience, 5, 26, 29; and outward sacraments, 18; and the priesthood of all believers, 13–14; and the prophetic, 17; and revelation, 5–6; and silence, 5, 15, 26, 29; and the Spirit, 18, 28; the spirituality of, 3–5

Queries, 22
Quietism, 33, 50

Ranterism, 20
Religious Society of Friends, the. *See* Quakers, the
Restoration, the, 21, 36
Rowntree, John Wilhelm, 34
Ruffini, Cardinal, 5–6

Sales, Francis de, 30
Schweitzer, Albert, 19, 46
Scott, Job, 24
Scriptures, the, 5, 21–22, 34
Speyr, Adrienne von, 30
Stokeley, Anna May, 30
Sturge, Joseph, 43–45
Suenens, Cardinal, 5–6
Sullivan, Dr. William, 7
Sundberg, Gunnar, 41
Sundberg, Per, 40–41
Swarthmoor College, 33
Swarthmoor Hall, 10
Sydney, Algernon, 49

Tagore, 47
Tatman, Laurie, 51
Tolles, Fred, 51
Traherne, Thomas, 15–16
Training for the Life of the Spirit (Heard), 4
Truman, President Harry, 3
Tuke, William, 51

Valiant Sixty, the, 11, 13
Vatican Council II, 4, 5
Viggbyholm School, 40
Vigny, Alfred de, 42
Von Speyr, Adrienne, 30

INDEX

Water baptism, 18
Weizmann, Chaim, 3
Wesley, John, 20
Whitehead, Professor, 25
Whittier, John G., 37
Whittier College, 33
Wilkinson-Story separation, the, 36
William and Mary (the rule of), 47

William Penn College, 33
Williams, Charles, 22
Wilmington College, 33
Woolman, John, 24, 33, 48, 50, 51
Word of Remembrance and Caution to the Rich, A (Woolman), 51
World War, the First, 16

INDEX TO TEXTS

Abraham, 280
Adam, 68, 120, 282
Adler, Alfred, 307
Aldham, Thomas, 89
Allison, William J., 229
"American Christianity," 306
Amor mundi, 295
Anabaptists, the, 281
Andrews, Isaac, 171
Appleby, England, 84
Ardonia, N.Y., 274
Argonauts, the, 264
Armageddon, 275
Armscote, England, 121
Atherstone, England, 71
Atley, Bridget, 143, 144
Audland, John, 81, 86
Aylesbury Gaol, 141

Baldock, Mr., 93
Banbury, England, 230
Barbados, 118, 220–21
Barclay, Robert, 247
Barton, Colonel, 75
Beard, Nicholas, 91, 105
Beeson, Henry, 283
Benezet, Anthony, 222
Bennett, Justice, 73

Benson, Colonel, 84
Bible, the. *See* Scriptures, the
Birmingham, England, 231, 274
Bishoprick, England, 123
Boston, Mass., 109, 118, 195
Boulding, Kenneth, 96n20
Bright, John, 286
Bristol, England, 86, 96, 103, 115
Broadmead, England, 96
Brother Lawrence, 289, 292
Buckingham, England, 193
Buckinghamshire, England, 101
Buffington, Benjamin, 179
Burlington County, N.J., 163,
    171, 179, 206, 221, 224
Burning Bush, the, 312
Burrough, Edward, 82, 86,
    108–09, 110–11

Cadbury, Henry J., 124
Cadwalader, John, 213
Calvin, 277
Cambridge, England, 91
Cambridge University, 65, 241
Cambridge University Press, 59
Camm, John, 81, 86
Camp Creek, 183
Carolina, 118, 171

INDEX

Caution and Warning to Great Britain and Her Colonies, A (Benezet), 222
Cedar Creek, 183
Center, the, 298, 303–05
Charles II, King, 102, 105, 108–09, 124
Chester River, 218
Children, 262, 268
Christ Jesus: died for slaves, 184; his experience of God, 30; Fox and, 65–66, 72, 129–30, 135; the inner, 310–11; as living access to God, 253; Penington on, 143, 144, 145; as Prince of Peace, 283; Quakers and, 278; as the Seed of God, 67, 71, 78, 103, 129–30, 145, 148, 247, 248; simplicity in, 221–22; the state of, 68; took away sin, 72; is the Word of God, 247; mentioned, 91, 106, 209, 241–42, 257, 276, 306
Churchman, John, 179, 191–92
Church of England, the, 243
Claypole, the Lady, 99
Cleveland, England, 77
Cobb, Sir Francis, 113
Cocken, England, 82
Coddington, William, 110
Columbus, Christopher, 264
Concerns, Quaker, 302–03
Concord, 218
Considerations on Keeping Negroes (Woolman), 201
Contemptus mundi, 295
Conventicle Acts, the, 117
Conway, Lady, 149
Coomaraswamy, Dr., 308

Copeland, James, 186
2 Corinthians, 222
Cornwall, England, 93–94
Coutant, Sarah, 273
Coventry, England, 71, 231
Cox, William, 180
Cranswick, England, 76
Craven, Robert, 89
Cromwell, Elizabeth, 99*n*21
Cromwell, Oliver: the death of, 101; and Fox, 87–90, 94, 97, 98, 102; and the Oath of Abjuration, 92; mentioned, 104, 123
Cromwell, Richard, 101, 104, 123
Crook, John, 98
Crosfield, George, 234
Crosfield, Jane, 235
Cumberland, England, 84, 123
Curtis, John, 211

Darby, Pa., 226
David, 264
Derbyshire, England, 65, 123
Derby's House of Correction, England, 72–76, 281
Detachment, 295
Dewsbury, William, 95
Divine Presence, the, 243, 299–300
Doomsdale prison, England, 94
Drayton-in-the-Clay, England, 63
Drury, Captain, 87–90
Dry, the widow, 117

Earlham College, 289
Eastburn, Samuel, 193, 194
Eckhart, Meister, 290, 296
Eliot, Charles William, 161

INDEX

Ellis, Sarah, 173
Ellwood, Thomas, 59, 141
Emlen, Samuel, Jr., 224, 225, 226
Endicott, Governor John,
109–10
Ephesians, the Book of, 221
Erasmus, 281
Eternal, the, 298–300, 303, 307
Eternal Now, the, 300–01
Eve, 120
Exeter, England, 94, 96
Exodus, the Book of, 180
Ezekiel, the Book of, 222–23
Ezekiel, the prophet, 168

Fall, the, 293
Farnsworth, Richard, 80
Fell, Henry, 105
Fell, Judge Thomas, 79, 80,
82–83, 84
Fell, Margaret: and Fox, 79–81,
115–16, 120; imprisoned,
116; and the King, 105, 107;
on trial, 111–12; mentioned,
59, 95
Fell, Rachel, 120
Fell, Sarah, 80, 116, 120
Fell, Yeamans, 115
Fifth-Monarchy, the, 104
Fines, Francis, 144
Five Foot Book Shelf, The, 161
Fort Allen, 206
Fort Creek, 183
Foster, Hannah, 195
Foulke, Samuel, 205, 206, 213
Fox, Christopher, 63
Fox, George: biography of, 59;
the birth of, 63; on business
dealings, 130–31, 134; and
Christ, 65–67, 72, 129–30,

135; and Oliver Cromwell,
87–90, 94, 97, 98, 102; the
death of, 125; on being a
doer of the Word, 129; on
experience, 81; and
Margaret Fell, 79–81,
115–16, 120; on the Holy
Spirit (or Spirit of God),
131, 133; hostility against,
69–72, 108, 135; illness of,
117–18; on Indians
(American), 119, 135; on
marriage, 120, 136; marries,
115; on meetings of
Quakers, 129, 131; as a
mystic, 248; and the Oath of
Abjuration, 92, 111; and
James Nayler, 80, 82, 93,
94–96, 98; Penn on, 60–62;
on persecution, 135–36; on
the power of God, 132–33,
135; and prayer, 61; in
prison, 69–70, 72–76, 111–13,
121–22; on the Scriptures,
65, 130, 247; and silence,
250; on sin, 72; and slavery,
119; on the voice of the
Lord, 126; and Waltham
School, 114; against war,
106–07, 281–82; the youth
of, 63; mentioned, 140, 146,
241–42, 247, 256, 266, 276,
278, 293, 296, 297, 314
Franco-Prussian War, the, 286
Freetown, 195
Friends' Review, The, 229

Gainsborough, England, 78
Galatians, the Book of, 235
Gee, George, 63*n*2

327

INDEX

God: communion with, 244, 246, 250, 251, 252, 254, 255; everlasting strength from, 186; the finger of, 248; the Life of, 303; living access to, 253; the presence of, 299–300, 307–08, 312–15; is no respecter of persons, 184; the Seed of, 67, 71, 78, 103, 129–30, 145, 148, 247, 248; and slaves, 184, 189; the spirit of, 83; worship of, 248
Golden Fleece, the, 264
Goldsmith, Ralph, 109
Green, Theopholis, 91n18
Grellet, Stephen, 247
Grimsden, Abraham, 149
Grou, Jean-Nicholas, 297
Gunpowder, 218

Habakkuk, the Book of, 195
Hacker, Colonel Francis, 87–88, 92, 101
Haddonfield, 171, 201, 218
Haines, Reuben, 237
Hale, Lord Chief Justice, 122–23
Harris, Rowland, 121
Harvard, 161
Harvey, Charles, 89, 91n18, 101
Haverford College, 261, 273, 289
Head, John, 224
Hemmings, Widow, 147
Hiorns, M., 155
Hodgkin, Thomas, 241
Holme, Thomas, 86
"Holy Experiment," the, 124, 276, 283
Holy Ghost, the. See Holy Spirit, the

Holy of Holies, the, 309
Holy Spirit, the, 177, 193, 199, 212, 221, 280
Hooten, Elizabeth, 65
Horne, William, 226
Hotham, Justice, 76
House of Assembly, the (Newport), 195–96
Howgill, Francis, 81–82, 85, 86
Hubbersty, Miles, 82
Hubbersty, Stephen, 82
Hubberthorne, Richard, 82, 86, 110
Hunt, William, 236
Hyde Park (England), 97

Incarnation, the, 275
India, 308
Indians (the American), 119, 204–13, 216, 283–84
Inner life, the, 294
Inner Light, the, 246–47, 290–92, 295
Invading Love, the, 299, 301, 308
Inward Guide, the, 161
Iowa, 264
Ireland, 98, 100, 115, 123
Isaiah, the Book of, 218, 234

Jacob, 280, 297
Jamaica, 118
James, the Apostle, 74
James, William, 296
James Park (England), 97
James River, the, 183
Jehovah. See God
Jenkins, Walter, 92
Jeremiah, the Book of, 178
Jesus Christ. See Christ Jesus

INDEX

Jones, Lowell, 273–74
Jones, Rufus M.: biography of, 261–66; and children, 262, 265; and God's presence, 263–64; and itinerant ministers, 267–68; and Scriptures, 264, 266; and silence, 263; and truth, 266
Joseph, 264

Kellet, England, 80
Kelly, Richard, 289
Kelly, Thomas R., 289
Kendal, England, 235
Kingston, England, 101
Kirby, Colonel, 112
Klingsor, 309

Lago, Mary, 63
Laiton, Dulcibella, 147
Lamb, Charles, 161
Lampitt, the priest, 79
Lancashire, England, 123
Lancaster, England, 82–83, 84, 86
Lawrence, Brother, 289, 292
Leicestershire, England, 63, 64, 65, 71, 86, 123
Light, the Inner, 246–47, 290–92, 295
Lightfoot, William, 206
Liverpool, England, 274
London, England, 113, 123, 229, 231
Long Island, N.Y., 172, 184
Long Parliament, the, 84, 100–01, 123
Lower, Mary, 116

Lower, Thomas, 59, 116, 120, 121–22
Luther, Martin, 277–78
Luxury, 256, 280

Maine, 267, 272
Makefield, England, 193
Mancetter, England, 63n2, 64
Mannock, John, 150
Mansfield, England, 67, 70
Mansfield-Woodhouse, England, 70
Marriage, 120, 269–70
Marshall, the priest, 83
Mary and Elizabeth, the ship, 224
Maryland, 171, 180, 217
Mass, the, 313
Matthew, the Gospel of, 222
Middletown, 218
Milner, James, 84
Monongahela River, the, 283
Moore, Thomas, 107
Moravian brother, the, 208–11
Moses, 301
Moulton, Phillip, 161
Mount Holly, N.J., 166, 187
Mudd, Thomas and Ann, 146
Myers, Richard, 84
Mysticism: children and, 262; group, 312–13; Quakerism and, 248; and social responsibility, 306; mentioned, 242

Nantucket, 198
Narragansett, 194
Nayler, James (known by Fox), 80, 82, 93, 94–96, 98, 226–27

INDEX

Nayler, James (known by Woolman), 226–27
Newbegun Creek, 185
Newcastle, England, 236
New London, Conn., 194
Newport, 194, 195–97, 202
Nonconformists, the, 253
Northampton, England, 230
Northampton, N.J., 163
Notionists, the, 76
Nottingham, England, 70, 179, 231
Nottinghamshire, England, 65, 67, 123
Nova Scotia, 268

Oath of Abjuration, the, 92, 111
Obedience, 296–98
Ogburn, John, 166
Ohio, 264, 267
Overseers of the Press, the, 201–02
Owen, Dr. John, 97
Oxford, 65
Oxfordshire, England, 231

Papunehang, 212
Paradise, 120
Parker, Alexander, 114
Parker, Henry, 121
Parliament, 76, 100–01, 286
Parliament, the Long, 84, 100–01, 123
Parsifal, 309
Parvin, Benjamin, 206, 213
Pascal, 296
Patapsco, 181
Patience, Cosmic, 304, 307
Patuxent River, the, 181
Paul, St., 278

Pearson, Anthony, 84
Pemberton, Israel, 206
Pemberton, John, 206
Pendle Hill, 78
Penington, Isaac: biography of, 139–42; on Christ as the foundation, 143; on Christ as the Seed, 145, 148, 156; on coolness of spirit, 156; on disputes, 152; on family prayer, 151; met Fox, 140; on the inward life, 145; on the Lord as teacher, 146, 154; on meetings, 154–55; on new creation in Christ, 148; on parenting, 151–52; on prayer, 151, 154; in prison, 141; on the righteousness of Christ, 144; on the Scriptures, 145; on true conviction, 152; on trust in God, 143; on waiting upon God, 146, 147, 149–50, 153, 154, 155, 156–57; mentioned, 101, 247
Penington, Mary (Springett), 139, 141
Penn, Admiral, 124
Penn, Gulielma, 139
Penn, William, 59, 60, 120, 124, 139–40, 276, 282–83
Pennsylvania, 124, 171, 283
Philadelphia, Pa., 179, 187–88, 190, 204–05, 214, 218, 220–21, 224–25, 232, 276
Philippines, the, 264
Pikeland, 206
Pittsburgh, Pa., 205
Plato, 300
Pordage, Catharine, 146, 154

Port Royal, 181
Potomac River, the, 181
Prayer: Fox on, 61; Kelly on, 290–98, 307, 313; Penington on, 151, 154; Stephen on, 252
Presence, the Divine, 243, 299–300
Preston Patrick, England, 233
Price, Peter, 92
Priestman, Robert, 237
Priestman, Thomas, 236, 237n33
Proverbs, the Book of, 164
Providence, divine, 177
Providence, R.I., 218
Psalms, the Book of, 181, 188, 293, 296, 297
Puritans, the, 277
Pursloe, Captain, 76
Pyott, Edward, 96, 97, 103

Quakers, the: and aids to devotion, 251; and the autonomy of the soul, 277; and the Bible, 247, 252, 258; and Christ, 278; and civil power, 256; and communion with God, 244, 246–47, 276; and "concerns," 302–03; and the covenant of peace, 281–86; and doctrines, 277–78; the elders of, 245; and evangelical fervor, 275; the faith and practice of, 275–86; and family meetings, 252; as humanists, 278; and individualism, 255, 277; and liberation of ministers, 270; as a living organ of the Spirit, 275; and luxury, 256, 280; and marriage, 269–70; and the ministry, 245, 253, 255, 257; and the ministry of women, 250; and mysticism, 248, 269; and the name "Quakers," 73, 276; and oaths, 92, 257; the organization of, 244–52; persecuted, 105–06, 108–09, 118, 124–25, 253, 255; and prayer, 61, 151, 154, 252, 290–98, 307, 313; and public meetings for worship, 244–51; Queries of, 245; and religious experience, 275; and religious rites, 246, 253–54, 277–79; and "saying grace," 252; and the Scriptures, 252, 258; and silence, 244, 246, 249–50, 251–52; and the simple life, 279–80; and testimony, 255; and tithes, 246, 257; and war, 106–07, 245, 256, 281–82, 283–85
Quaker Summer School, the, 274

Ranters, the, 77, 91
Rappahannock River, the, 181
Reformation, the, 277, 281
Religion, 272, 308, 310
"Religious retirement," 252
Revelation, the Book of, 163
Revolutionary War, the, 283
Rhode Island, 110
Richland, 205, 213
Richmond, England, 236
Roberts, Gerald, 120
Roman Catholics, 313

INDEX

Romans, the Book of, 310
Rous, John, 120
Rowntree, John Wilhelm, 299
Royalists, the, 74
Rush, John, 93
Rushworth, England, 231

Salem, 192
Samuel, 264
Sandys, Captain, 80
Satan, 67
Saunders, Mary, 91n18, 97
Sawrey, Justice John, 79, 80, 82, 83
Scotland, 90, 123
Scriptures, the: Fox and, 65, 130, 247; Jones and, 264, 266; Penington on, 145; Quakers and, 252, 258; the Spirit and, 69, 83; mentioned, 90
Self-indulgence, 249
Selly Oak, England, 274
Sermon on the Mount, the, 254
Settle, England, 231
Severn, 181
Sewel, 227
Shacklewell, England, 114
Shane, Lettice, 91n18
Shattuck, Samuel, 109
Sheffield, England, 231
Shekinah, 314
Sherrington, England, 230
Shipley, Elizabeth, 195
Shipston, England, 230
Shrewsbury, Pa., 201
Silence: children and, 268; Fox and, 250; healing through, 249; Jones and, 263; at Quaker meetings, 244, 246, 249–50; and true worship, 250, 251–52

Simple life, the, 176–77, 232–33, 302
Simplicity, 233, 251, 303
Sin, 72
Slavery: and conduct toward slaves, 183–84, 218; Fox and, 119; Quakers and, 184–85, 187–97, 201, 215, 218–19, Woolman and, 162, 168–69, 171–72, 173–76, 180–84, 187–96, 201–03, 215, 217, 218–21, 227, 232, 235, 236
Sleeper, John, 217
Smith, John, 214
Social responsibility, 302–03, 306–07
Sparks, James, 224
Spence Manuscript, the, 59
Springett, Gulielma, 139
Springett, Lady Mary, 139
Squan, 201
Squankum, 201
Stagecoach travel, 232
Stanley, James, 183
Stanley, William, 183
Stanton, Daniel, 191
Stephen, Caroline, 241
Stephen, Sir James, 241
Stephen, Sir Leslie, 241
Stoddard, Captain Amor, 92
Stonar, Nathaniel, 145
Storer, John, 195, 197
Sturge, Joseph, 286
Suffering, 309–11
Susquehanna River, the, 180, 204, 217
Swansea, 195
Swarthmoor, England, 79, 80, 81, 84, 86, 111

Swarthmoor Hall, 84, 124
Sykes, John, 191

Tauler, 280
Taunton, 195
Taylor, Christopher, 81
Taylor, Thomas, 81
Terry, E., 152
Tertullian, Carthaginian, 277
Thames River, the, 228
Thompson, Justice, 82–83
Tickhill, England, 78
Tredington parish, England, 121
Truth, 178, 179, 188, 198, 209
Tuke, Esther, 237
Tuke, William, 237
Tunkhannock River, the, 212
Twycross, England, 71

Ulverston, England, 79
Underbarrow, England, 80

Virginia, 118, 171, 202

Waldenses, the, 281
Walmsley, Thomas, 143
Walney Island, England, 82
Waltham, England, 114
Warwick, England, 231
Warwickshire, England, 64, 123
Wennington, Miles, 84
West, Colonel, 83
West Indies, the, 219, 220–23
Westmoreland County, England, 234
Westmorland, England, 123, 235
West River, 218
Whetstone, England, 86
Whisper, the holy, 304

White, Joseph, 193, 226
Whitehall, England, 97
Whitehead, George, 86, 121
Whitehead, John, 113
Whittier, John Greenleaf, 161, 229, 279, 286
Widder, Robert, 80
Wilmington, Ohio
Wisdom, 147–48, 216
Women, the ministry of, 250
Woodbrooke Settlement, the, 274
Woolf, Virginia, 241
Woolman, Anne, 174
Woolman, Elizabeth, 174
Woolman, Elizabeth, Jr., 172
Woolman, John: and American Indians, 204–13, 216; his *Considerations on Keeping Negroes*, 201; on credit and debt, 177; and the Cross, 165, 166, 167, 176; the death of, 237; on fear of man, 178; the garments of, 203–04; 237; in Great Britain, 224–30; housing soldiers, 187; illnesses of, 203, 234; on the inward life, 165–66; his *Journal*, 161–62; on luxury and superfluities, 176–77, 232–33, 284–85; and merchandising, 170, 176; and the Moravian brother, 208–11; on oppression, 225, 232–33, 235, 236; on outward affairs, 166–68, 177; on receiving gifts, 180; on simplicity, 233; on slavery, 162, 168–69, 171–72, 173–76, 180–84, 187–96, 201–03, 215,

INDEX

217, 218–21, 227, 232, 235, 236; on speaking at meetings, 167; as a tailor, 170, 171, 176; traveling in steerage, 226–28; begins travels, 171; on trusting in God, 165–68; on Truth, 178, 179, 209; and understanding, 167; and war, 185–86, 209; on his own wickedness (weakness, temptation), 163–65, 166–67; on wisdom, 178; mentioned, 241, 247, 284

Woolman, Samuel, 173
Worcester, England, 75, 121–23
Wordsworth, 262
Worship, 250–52, 309, 312–15
Wright, Joseph, 150
Wyalusing, 205, 208–13
Wyoming, 206, 209, 210

York, England, 241
Yorkshire, England, 86, 123, 224

Other Volumes in this Series

Julian of Norwich • SHOWINGS

Jacob Boehme • THE WAY TO CHRIST

Nahman of Bratslav • THE TALES

Gregory of Nyssa • THE LIFE OF MOSES

Bonaventure • THE SOUL'S JOURNEY INTO GOD, THE TREE OF LIFE, and THE LIFE OF ST. FRANCIS

William Law • A SERIOUS CALL TO DEVOUT AND HOLY LIFE, and THE SPIRIT OF LOVE

Abraham Isaac Kook • THE LIGHTS OF PENITENCE, LIGHTS OF HOLINESS, THE MORAL PRINCIPLES, ESSAYS, and POEMS

Ibn 'Ata' Illah • THE BOOK OF WISDOM and Kwaja Abdullah Ansari • INTIMATE CONVERSATIONS

Johann Arndt • TRUE CHRISTIANITY

Richard of St. Victor • THE TWELVE PATRIARCHS, THE MYSTICAL ARK, and BOOK THREE OF THE TRINITY

Origen • AN EXHORTATION TO MARTYRDOM, PRAYER AND SELECTED WORKS

Catherine of Genoa • PURGATION AND PURGATORY, THE SPIRITUAL DIALOGUE

Native North American Spirituality of the Eastern Woodlands • SACRED MYTHS, DREAMS, VISIONS, SPEECHES, HEALING FORMULAS, RITUALS AND CEREMONIALS

Teresa of Avila • THE INTERIOR CASTLE

Apocalyptic Spirituality • TREATISES AND LETTERS OF LACTANTIUS, ADSO OF MONTIER-EN-DER, JOACHIM OF FIORE, THE FRANCISCAN SPIRITUALS, SAVONAROLA

Athanasius • THE LIFE OF ANTONY, A LETTER TO MARCELLINUS

Catherine of Siena • THE DIALOGUE

Sharafuddin Maneri • THE HUNDRED LETTERS

Martin Luther • THEOLOGIA GERMANICA

Native Mesoamerican Spirituality • ANCIENT MYTHS, DISCOURSES, STORIES, DOCTRINES, HYMNS, POEMS FROM THE AZTEC, YUCATEC, QUICHE-MAYA AND OTHER SACRED TRADITIONS

Symeon the New Theologian • THE DISCOURSES

Ibn Al'-Arabī • THE BEZELS OF WISDOM

Hadewijch • THE COMPLETE WORKS

Philo of Alexandria • THE CONTEMPLATIVE LIFE, THE GIANTS, AND SELECTIONS

George Herbert • THE COUNTRY PARSON, THE TEMPLE

Unknown • THE CLOUD OF UNKNOWING

John and Charles Wesley • SELECTED WRITINGS AND HYMNS

Meister Eckhart • THE ESSENTIAL SERMONS, COMMENTARIES, TREATISES AND DEFENSE

Francisco de Osuna • THE THIRD SPIRITUAL ALPHABET

Jacopone da Todi • THE LAUDS

Fakhruddin 'Iraqi • DIVINE FLASHES

Menahem Nahum of Chernobyl • THE LIGHT OF THE EYES

Early Dominicans • SELECTED WRITINGS

John Climacus • THE LADDER OF DIVINE ASCENT

Francis and Clare • THE COMPLETE WORKS

Gregory Palamas • THE TRIADS

Pietists • SELECTED WRITINGS

The Shakers • TWO CENTURIES OF SPIRITUAL REFLECTION

Zohar • THE BOOK OF ENLIGHTENMENT

Luis de León • THE NAMES OF CHRIST